A Roosevelt in the World of

Diplomacy and Journalism

A Roosevelt in the World of Diplomacy and Journalism

Nicholas Roosevelt and American Domestic and Foreign Policy in the First Half of the Twentieth Century

Zoltán Peterecz

Helena History Press

Copyright© by Zoltán Peterecz, 2025

All rights reserved
Published in the United States by:

Helena History Press LLC
A division of KKL Publications LLC, Reno, NV USA
www.helenahistorypress.com

Publishing scholarship about and from Central and East Europe

ISBN: 978-1-943596-45-4 (Paperback Edition)

Order from Ingram Spark, any on-line bookseller or your local bookstore

Photos Courtesy of: Photographs courtesy of Getty Images, AP Photos

Book Jacket Cover: Nicholas Roosevelt, retiring U.S. Minister to Hungary, is shown on his arrival in New York, June 1, 1933, aboard the liner Washington. He said the commercial future of Central Europe, "depended upon the agreements to be reached at the World Economic Conference." Present conditions in that area are improving, he said, "but it will be a black picture if the London Economic Conference fails". (AP Photo)

Copy Editors: Jill Hannum, József Litkei

Graphic Designer: Zsolt Gembela

Printed by: Könyvpont Nyomda: Budapest

Contents

Chapter 1
The Political Initiation of a Young Man 7

Chapter 2
The First Taste of Europe 21

Chapter 3
The Making of a Journalist and Author 51

Chapter 4
The American Minister to Hungary 73

Chapter 5
Nicholas Roosevelt in the New Deal and World War II 109

Chapter 6
Retirement and Reminiscing 147
    Conclusions 161

APPENDIX 163
1. *Account of the Republican National Convention at Chicago, June 1912, compiled from notes taken on the spot by Nicholas Roosevelt.* Typescript, after 1912. MS Am 2915. Houghton Library, Harvard University, Cambridge, Mass. 163
2. *A History of a Few Weeks. Being an Account of Experience in Austria and Hungary during the Armistice.* by Nicholas Roosevelt, Captain, 322d Infantry, Member of the Austrian Field Party, American Commission to Negotiate Peace, 1919 171
    Chapter VIII. Austrian Politics 171
    Chapter XV. Budapest for the First Time 177
    Chapter XIX. Bucharest 184
    Chapter XXX. Going Before the Commissioners 193
3. Nicholas Roosevelt, *The Philippines. A Treasure and a Problem*, New York: J. H. Sears & Company, Inc., 1926. 197
    Chapter XV. Bearing A Thankless Burden 197

4. Box 59 Dispatches from Hungary 1930–1933, Nicholas Roosevelt Papers 205
5. Nicholas Roosevelt, "Franklin Delano Roosevelt," *The American Mercury* 39, no. 155 (November 1936): 329–331 214
6. Nicholas Roosevelt, "Partners for Peace," November 27, 1941, Folder: Lectures—Mills College 1941, Box 59, Nicholas Roosevelt Papers. 217

Bibliography 233

Index 247

Chapter 1

The Political Initiation of a Young Man

Nicholas Roosevelt (1893–1982), similarly to most of his extended family members since the middle of the seventeenth century, has always stood and will stand in the shadows of the two outstanding Roosevelt success stories in American history: Theodore Roosevelt (1858–1919) and Franklin Delano Roosevelt (1882–1945), the 26th and 32nd presidents of the United States, respectively. Despite the social standing and various talents of the Roosevelt clan over hundreds of years, nothing can compete with reaching the highest office of the land, being transformative executives and larger than life. Still, Nicholas Roosevelt was a relatively prominent American in the twentieth century—an author, journalist, conservationist, and, for a short time, a diplomat, who liked to believe that he had such a wide array of knowledge and sharp insight that his voice carried the truth. It is without doubt that Nicholas Roosevelt was a well-educated man who, most of the time, really did see events in the right light if historical hindsight is an indication, and therefore his various writings were of interest and bore a degree of educational value. On the other hand, he was an unapologetic judge of the personalities he came across. Since he was also a product of his times and upbringing, many of his attitudes would be clearly declared to be politically incorrect in the present century. However, exactly this approach opens a window onto the past and allows a glimpse into the thinking of the upper-class American of the early twentieth century. His political and other activities were strongest in the first half of the twentieth century, and the entirety of his career provides a history lesson—through Nicholas Roosevelt's prism—on the outstanding issues of American domestic and foreign policy between Theodore Roosevelt's presidency and the end of World War II, which was basically the end of Franklin D. Roosevelt's presidency as well. Nicholas Roosevelt was an ardent student of his uncle and mentor Teddy Roosevelt, and he absorbed both the progressive and conservative traits typical of that president. However, he became a fervent critic of his distant cousin FDR and of what he saw as a populist presidency and a failed economic approach in the form of the New Deal, although he respected FDR in the domain of foreign affairs. Thus, sandwiched between the presidencies of two other Roosevelts, Nicholas Roosevelt's thoughts and writings offer a unique glimpse into that period of American history.

NR[1] was never as important a figure as the presidents with whom he shared a patronym, but despite, or because of his family name, and thanks to his diligence and often keen powers of perception, he provided penetrating analyses of many historical events, and his insights were often borne out later. Also, he had a finger in many pies, which ensured his exposure to the worlds of diplomacy, economics, war, domestic and foreign policy, and the dynamic American journalism of the era. His connections to many leading personalities of the first five decades of the twentieth century, both in the United States and Europe, his positions inside and outside the U.S. government (held regardless of party affiliation in the executive branch) provide a unique and often insightful a perspective on a cross section of American and European history.

The Roosevelts first arrived in New Amsterdam, present-day New York, around the mid-seventeenth century. Claes Martenszen van Rosenvelt (1626–1660), and his wife, Jannetje Samuel-Thomas (1629–1660), produced six children, one of them called Nicholaes. The family members were all admitted to the Reformed Dutch Church of New York, which became their family denomination. The first Nicholas Roosevelt was born in 1687, one of his three children receiving the same first name. Throughout the eighteenth century, the family got more extended and wealthier, therefore more influential in business and politics. A relatively famous Nicholas Roosevelt was born in 1767, who became an inventor whose main contribution was the vertical steamboat paddle wheel. In the course of the eighteenth and nineteenth centuries, the extended family took up two different locations. Johannes Roosevelt (1689–1750) founded the Oyster Bay branch of the large clan on Long Island. Theodore Roosevelt's grandfather, the banker Cornelius Van Schaaick, made the Oyster branch rich through real estate deals after the Panic of 1837. The Hyde Park branch of upstate New York was established mainly by Isaac Roosevelt (1726–1794). Among the Roosevelts one can find merchants, bankers, economists, lawyers, and doctors among other professions. As the most recent biographer of the

---

[1] I will use this format throughout the text in order to avoid overusing his full name.

Roosevelt family wrote, until the two Roosevelt presidents in the twentieth century, "the Roosevelts were a prosaic, self-satisfied lot, generally free from genius, public service, or almost any creative spark."[2] NR's maternal grandmother was Laura Wolcott Gibbs, whose father was Colonel George Gibbs of Rhode Island, while her mother was Laura Wolcott, daughter of Oliver Wolcott, Jr. NR's father was James West Roosevelt (1858–1896), first cousin and close friend of Theodore Roosevelt's. He was a well-known doctor, hospital director, and a member of many medical societies. He married Laura Henrietta d'Oremieulx (1858–1945) in 1884. The couple had five children, two of whom died while in childhood. The youngest child was Nicholas Roosevelt, born in 1893, and three years later he found himself without a father who prematurely died of pneumonia.[3]

NR thus was born under socially favorable circumstances on June 12, 1893, in New York. City. After losing his father so early, of whom he could not have direct memories, he had only one parent left. His mother had French ancestors on the paternal branch, "studied music in Europe, and who had the French fondness for conversation and amusement, sometimes found life with her in-laws constricting."[4] She was active in musical circles and vice president of the New York Philharmonic Society for many years.[5] On the maternal side of the family such prominent ancestors can be found as Oliver Wolcott, Sr. (1726–1797), one of the signers of the Declaration of Independence in 1776, while his son, Oliver Wolcott, Jr. (1760–1833), held the post of secretary of state under George Washington and John Adams, between 1795 and 1800.

In lieu of a biological father, NR was in many ways brought up in the Theodore Roosevelt household, which led an indelible mark on his worldview and eventful life. Nicholas received his bachelor's degree from Harvard in 1914. He served as an attaché at the American Embassy in Paris for the next two years, and as secretary to the American mission to Spain in 1916–1917. At the time of the armistice, he served in the rank of captain, and joined the Coolidge Mission as such in the last

---

[2] Stephen Hess, *America's Political Dynasties* (New Brunswick and London: Transaction Publishers, 1997), 170.
[3] For the bibliographical data on the extended Roosevelt clan, see, Charles B. Whittelsey, *The Roosevelt Genealogy, 1649–1902* (Hartford, CT: J. B. Burr & Company, 1902); *New York Tribune*, April 11, 1896, 7; Nicholas Roosevelt, *A Front Row Seat* (Norman, OK: University of Oklahoma Press), 1953, 3–28; Allen Churchill, *The Roosevelts: American Aristocrats* (New York: Harper & Row, 1965), 1–23; Kenneth S. Davis, *FDR: The Beckoning of Destiny, 1882–1928* (New York: History Book Club, 1972), 17–44; Nathan Miller, *The Roosevelt Chronicles* (New York: Doubleday & Company, 1979), 3–152; Hess, *America's Political Dynasties*, 167–216.
[4] Nicholas Roosevelt, *A Front Row Seat*, 28.
[5] *New York Times*, March 24, 1945.

days of 1918. After the Peace Conference, he worked as a foreign correspondent and editorial writer for the *New York Times* (1921–1923), then for the *New York Herald Tribune* as an editorial writer (1923–1930, 1933–1942); from 1944 he went back to the *New York Times* as assistant editor. Occasionally he also contributed pieces to other newspapers such as the *Christian Science Monitor*, and since he was a member of the Council on Foreign Relations, he wrote for its journal, *Foreign Affairs* as well. In 1926, Roosevelt wrote and published a book, *The Philippines, A Treasure and a Problem*, in which he argued against the United States granting the Philippines premature independence on the grounds that Filipinos were incapable of governing their own affairs. In 1930, President Herbert Hoover appointed Roosevelt to serve as Vice-Governor to the Philippines, but he was released from the post after only a few months due to nation-wide protests by Filipinos, who were upset about Roosevelt's depiction of their country and people. Shortly after this debacle in the Philippines he was named minister to Hungary. This appointment was the pinnacle of his career, and he stayed in Budapest two and a half years (1930–1933) during the worst years of the Great Depression, and he only resigned because Franklin Delano Roosevelt, a Democrat, had won the presidency. After the diplomatic stint in Europe, NR returned to journalism as an editorial writer for the *New York Herald Tribune*. He was a life-long Republican and often criticized FDR's New Deal and big-government policies. He served in the Office of War Information during World War II, where he was responsible for propaganda activities. After the war he soon resigned from journalism and resided at Big Sur, California, with his wife, Tirzah Maris Gates (1906–1961), but the couple had no children. NR was a prolific author outside the newspaper world, and wrote twelve books altogether, including his autobiography, *A Front Row Seat*, which was published in 1953. In his later life he devoted much time and energy to cooking and conservationism, on which topics he published books. Nicholas Roosevelt died in 1982.[6]

All his life NR felt that he was important, or wished himself to be seen in such a role. A smart and educated man, he was utterly self-confident in his judgment, seldom thought that his opinion was not the right one, and his many written texts carried the voice of omniscience. This mindset often broke through in his personal letters and diaries as well. In his memoirs, he denoted his profession as "author," which suggests that he was the proudest of his books and not of his short diplomatic

---

[6] "Biographical History," Syracuse University, https://library.syr.edu/digital/guides/r/roosevelt_n.htm#d2e101, accessed June 18, 2022; Wolfgang Saxon, "Nicholas Roosevelt is Dead; Writer and Diplomat Was 88," *New York Times*, February 17, 1982; *Time*, June 15, 1936; Nicholas Roosevelt, *A Front Row Seat*, 1953.

Chapter 1 – The Political Initiation of a Young Man

Edward S. Curtis helps the sons and cousin of Theodore Roosevelt bury a dog in sand at Sagamore Hill. Left to right: Quentin Roosevelt, Archie Roosevelt, Edward S. Curtis and Nicholas Roosevelt. January 01, 1904 (Photo by Edward S. Curtis/Library of Congress/Corbis/VCG via Getty Images)

career or governmental service, and not even of his long years in journalism. But no matter which occupation one looks at, the omniscient nature of his authorship always comes to the fore: he rarely wrote on a subject about which he did not formulate a definite opinion, believing that was the right one and should be automatically understood and shared by others.

NR's childhood years were dominated by "Cousin Theodore." He remembered the popular hero and future president as "an example of fearlessness, fairness, and fineness," who possessed "brains, brawn, charm, energy, courage, and a positive passion for what was right and decent, all rolled into one."[7] The president was always the dominant figure among the boys (his own sons and Nicholas) and tried to instill in them such characteristics as overcoming fear, finishing a commenced job, loyalty, and truthfulness.[8] It is little wonder that NR looked up to TR all his life, and actually

---

[7] Nicholas Roosevelt, *A Front Row Seat*, 21.
[8] Ibid., 24.

got a taste of practical life, especially in politics, by the side of this giant. Following TR's footsteps, NR enrolled in Harvard and expected a bright future ahead of him.

The first big political adventure for the Harvard student was Theodore Roosevelt's bid for the 1912 presidency. The election of 1912 was a watershed moment in American history. Rarely had there been four major aspirants for the presidency, or such an exciting politician as Theodore Roosevelt. Of course, the former president's decision to run again divided the Republican Party. But TR was dissatisfied with William Howard Taft's presidency, especially as he had handpicked Taft as his successor. The reform-minded Roosevelt believed that only he could lead the reform forces in the country and threw his hat in the ring again. After he failed to gain the Republican Party's nomination, because the party machinery worked against him, he founded a new political party, the Progressive Party, or Bull Moose Party as it was called popularly, and therefore he divided the Republican forces. Actually, all four major candidates were professing to bring reform to a nation suffering from many social ailments. But all of them needed to walk a tightrope not to alienate any major voting block that could deliver the votes to occupy the White House. After the rift in the Republican Party, it was perhaps inevitable that the Democrats' time had come to recapture the presidency after twenty years.[9]

The major issues leading up to and during the 1912 elections were the following. First, there was the question of protective tariff—the sacred cow of the more conservative wing of the Republican Party. Partly because of this question, Republicans had a disunited party where so-called "insurgents," or progressive elements, wanted to see large-scale social and economic reforms. Race was also important, that is, it was an open question whether any of the competing forces would be ready to open the doors for the oppressed African American minority to take a bigger slice of the American Dream. The question of immigration, immigrants' votes and restriction thereof also created tangible tension. Many wanted the people of a given state to have a referendum for concerning judicial review. They believed that the ability of the electorate to reverse a judicial decision if it went against popular sentiment was a path to more direct democracy. (TR was a leading advocate of this.) In the

---

[9] The latest major studies of the election of 1912 are Brett Flehinger, *The 1912 Election and the Power of Progressivism: A Brief History with Documents* (Boston: Bedford/St. Martin's, 2003); James Chace, *1912: Wilson, Roosevelt, Taft and Debs—The Election that Changed the Country* (New York: Simon & Schuster, 2004); Lewis L. Gould, *Four Hats in the Ring: The 1912 Election and the Birth of Modern American Politics* (Lawrence, KS: University Press of Kansas, 2008); and Edmund Morris, *Colonel Roosevelt* (New York: Random House, 2010), 144–252. Also is of interest Nicholas Roosevelt own account of his experience in the 1912 campaign: Nicholas Roosevelt, *A Front Row Seat*, 46–56; and *Theodore Roosevelt: The Man As I Knew Him* (New York: Dodd, Mead & Company, 1967), 75–101.

same spirit, the direct election of senators featured prominently as an election issue, which was supposed to clean up the corrupt method by which senators had been chosen since the early days of the Republic. Women's suffrage had been a long and ongoing struggle, and by 1911 five states had allowed women to take part in presidential elections (TR favored giving women the franchise, which was achieved in 1920 in the form of the Nineteenth Amendment). Another issue going back many years was the temperance movement, which achieved its goal in 1919 in the form of the (later repealed) Eighteenth Amendment). Other significant issues were the role of and relation to big business, the environment, and, of course, the scandals.[10]

And, inevitably, there was the third-term issue. In 1904 TR unequivocally ruled out running again for the highest office of the land. At that point such an announcement was politically the wise thing to do, but it tied TR's hands in 1908 and played a huge role in why he did not seek another term and basically handed over the presidency to Taft. But the years of the Taft presidency convinced him that the Republican Party was going in a direction that he could not deem wise or useful. After much thought, the ever-energetic TR decided that he needed to recapture the White House in order to be able to steer the country back to what he considered the right path. He wanted to run because of his immense desire for political leadership through which he could push through certain reform agendas. He formally announced his candidacy on February 26, 1912, which ensured that a clash was inevitable with the Republican Party's conservative core and influential machinery.

The presidential election of 1912 was one of a kind. It was characterized by infighting within the Republican Party, and as a result, it saw the birth of a new political party: the Progressive Party. It was one of the rare occasions when other serious challengers took center stage in the traditional American two-party system—there were four major political groups vying for dominance: the Republican Party, the Democratic Party, the Progressive Party, and the Socialist Party (all of which faced their own internal divisions). In a sense, this was a repetition of what took place four years earlier; but with opposing forces within the Republican Party creating a split and stirring up the competition, much more drama was in store. To complicate things further, the progressive movement that had been going strong (but not strong enough to win in a presidential election) for the last twenty years or so had its last desperate chance to capture the White House. However, the progressive forces were roughly evenly divided between Democrats and those who supported Theodore Roosevelt's nascent Progressive Party.

---

[10] A good summary of such issues can be found in Gould, *Four Hats in the Ring*, 22–30.

The most famous and dramatic aspect of the campaign of 1912 was clearly Theodore Roosevelt's entry. After leaving the White House, TR went off to hunt and travel around the world. The seeming lack of progress during Taft's presidency (as TR saw it), the obviously growing influence of big business (compared to during TR's years in Washington), and the reactionary wing of the Republican Party taking over policy making all pointed to the failed state of Taft's leadership in TR's eyes. Roosevelt loved power but also believed that more progressive policies were needed, which mainly he could provide. Once he announced his plan to run on the Republican Party ticket, the political machine of that party frantically started to work against him. As an innovative and more democratic measure, primary elections were introduced in several states, which would have tipped the scale in TR's favor. However, there were only twelve such primaries for the Republican Party in 1912, nine of which were won by Roosevelt, while the rest were divided between the incumbent Taft and reformer Republican Robert M. La Follette of Wisconsin. The number of votes Roosevelt received in the primaries was, however, twice as high as those of the other two contenders.[11] This direct show of voter popularity was insignificant in comparison to the member states where the Republican party bosses could—through corrupt machinations, bribery, and threats—organize to send their own delegates to the convention held in Chicago in the summer.

In the end, only 42 percent of the attending delegates were selected through primaries, which basically made the outcome of the convention a foregone conclusion. This June gathering of the Republican Party was where, after being denied the candidacy, Roosevelt founded the Progressive Party and irrevocably threw his hat into the ring. It is important to note that just in May 1912, the Seventeenth Amendment to the Constitution was approved by Congress and was ratified the next year, which declared that Senators would be directly elected by the people. It came too late, and in 1912 it could not help Roosevelt. Four years later, the majority of the member states held primaries: 25 out of the 48 states chose this method, which constellation might have been enough to secure a Roosevelt victory four years earlier.

In the end, in the four-way election Woodrow Wilson and the Democratic Party triumphed. This victory was, however, only thanks to the split among the Republican ranks. The combined vote for the Republican Party and TR's Progressive Parties was 50.5 percent, as opposed to Wilson's 42 percent, and Wilson garnered about 115,000 fewer votes than did William Jennings Bryan for the Democrats four years

---

[11] Chace, *1912*, 113.

earlier. It also must be mentioned that the socialist, Eugene V. Debs, managed to get 6 percent of the popular vote, some 900,000 out of a total of 15 million, therefore the election of 1912 "marked the apogee of the Socialist movement in America."[12] It is naturally only idle speculation as to where the votes cast for Debs would have gone had there been only three parties vying for victory, but in all likelihood the results would not have changed tremendously. The presidential election of 1912 was the last political hurray for Theodore Roosevelt.

As for Nicholas Roosevelt, this campaign season was a rite of passage into American politics. In 1912 he was a sophomore at Harvard, which TR had also attended a generation earlier. The young intellectual was obviously very biased toward his uncle and surrogate father. He looked up to the former president as if he were a demigod, and he did not question that TR's cause was righteous, while it was equally clear to him that the Republican Party stood for reaction and "stand-patting." Thinking of himself as a man of letters thrown into the maelstrom of history, NR made a thorough personal account of the Republican National Convention in Chicago. Indeed, his account of what transpired was often sourced in the major historical volumes concerning Theodore Roosevelt's political comeback and the Republican convention of 1912. Since this piece of writing was in many ways a launching pad for NR to establish himself as a writer-to-be, it merits a close look.

By 1912, NR's approach and technique for crafting a more momentous story already exhibited the mature and established form that was to characterize his style for the remainder of his life, especially when it came to authoring books. His account was based on his memories, observations, and diary excerpts. Almost every day he jotted down his impressions and the major events of the day, sometimes in the early hours of the next day so they could be as fresh as possible. Later he worked these passages into the final form of the narrative. Therefore the text is interesting for its relatively faithful account of the convention—through the prism of the author—of the rarely seen political machinations of such an event, and his own small errands for the Roosevelt camp. It also records his impressions about the atmosphere and unfolding events, and allows the reader a glimpse into his worldview as well.

From the outset NR reached an emotional peak, as his diary accounts testify. The Roosevelt entourage's arrival in Chicago and how enthusiastically people welcomed TR was a spectacle he tried to describe faithfully:

---

[12] Ibid., 239.

> We finally drew in, and under instructions to keep tight with the old man, he led the way and we followed him. The crowd had broken through the police lines, and were packed on the platform, yelling and cheering and surging around. With Teddy Douglas taking one arm, and Frank Harper taking the other, and George and I behind, we managed to wedge through this shrieking mob, out into the street which was a sea of cheering people. With much difficulty we forced our way into one of the special flag decorated autos, and then followed what was the most absolutely thrilling and remarkable event of my life. People packed the windows and lined the roofs and the elevated tracks and were so thick in the streets we could hardly move in the procession. [...] Everyone cheered. Everyone screamed. Everyone was hurled along in the irresistible force of the delighted mob. [...] I have never before seen or felt such a thing. It was absolutely beyond description. [...] Such terrific excitement, such overwhelming emotion, I have never felt. Everywhere as far as I could see were people crazy with delight and mad with enthusiasm.[13]

Such thunderous jubilation at the sight of the former president was in sharp contrast with what the young Harvardian experienced at the incumbent president's rallies. He witnessed, for example, the rally speech of William Barnes Jr. of Albany, an important Republican from New York. Barnes, as NR remembered,

> spoke, without fervor, to a listless, sedate and very polite audience. It was made all the more preposterous by the fact that a very ancient colored gentleman stood back of Barnes, and whenever Barnes paused, would point to the crowd and feebly begin clapping his hands. They would then slowly and very politely take up the applause, in every case waiting for his signal. It was almost pathetic.[14]

NR made a point of returning to the opposing camp's rallies, but "never found it even one tenth full, I never saw any enthusiasm. It was kept like a ladies' parlor. [...] However ridiculous this may sound, it is perfectly true that there was no quieter place within a mile. No one spoke above a whisper, and there was not a sound to

---

[13] Nicholas Roosevelt, *Account of the Republican National Convention at Chicago, June 1912, compiled from notes taken on the spot by Nicholas Roosevelt*, Typescript, after 1912. MS Am 2915, Houghton Library, Harvard University, Cambridge, MA, 7.

[14] Nicholas Roosevelt, *Account of the Republican National Convention at Chicago*, 12.

disturb."[15] He obviously enjoyed using a sharp tongue in describing others who were not so much to his liking, whether for political reasons or otherwise. For instance, after he visited a women's suffrage meeting at the convention, he wrote: "A whole lot of women spoke, in rather silly ways, and I came away without a deep-seated conviction that the only way to save the country was to give the women the vote [...] a more thoroughly dilapidated, tired, and altogether flabby looking set of people I have scarcely ever seen. It was an excellent opportunity for a cartoonist."[16]

On the opening day of the convention, Theodore Roosevelt said to NR at the hotel where they had their headquarters, "It's a bully fight, and we're going to win!"[17] At this point the former president may still have believed he was going to be nominated, but the chairman of the convention, Elihu Root, with "extreme cold-bloodedness" made sure that the Taft forces would dominate.[18]

NR's account of the convention also expresses one aspect of his worldview that remained a constant for the next thirty years, and probably beyond: his anti-Semitism. On the first day of the Republican Convention he characterized the presiding chairman of the Republican National Committee, Victor Rosewater, as "a low mean weak little jew [sic]."[19] This is not surprising. Since colonial times, but especially after the mass migration of Jews from Eastern Europe toward the end of the nineteenth and the beginning of the twentieth centuries, Americans had expressed a tangible adversity toward this group of immigrants. This was manifest in several aspects of social distancing and was most prevalent among the American upper and upper-middle classes. It was not necessarily a malign thought on the part of these people; rather, it was much more part of a worldview. NR's innate dislike of Jews was not the exception but rather the rule in the circles he came from.[20]

---

[15] Ibid., 17.
[16] Nicholas Roosevelt, *Account of the Republican National Convention at Chicago*, 14.
[17] Ibid., 24.
[18] Ibid., 29.
[19] Ibid., 25.
[20] For more detail about the history of anti-Semitism in the United States, and especially in the first half of the twentieth century, see, Nathaniel Weyl, *The Jew in American Politics* (New Rochelle, NY.: Arlington House), 1968, 77–109, 232–47; Leo P. Ribuffo, "Henry Ford and 'The International Jew,'" *American Jewish History* 69, no. 4 (June 1980): 437–77; David A. Gerber, *Anti-Semitism in American History* (Urbana, IL: University of Illinois Press), 1986; Leonard Dinnerstein, *Anti-Semitism in America* (New York, Oxford: Oxford University Press, 1994); Neil Baldwin, *Henry Ford and the Jews: The Mass Production of Hate* (New York: Public Affairs, 2001); Robert Michael, *A Concise History of American Antisemitism* (Lanham, MD: Rowman and Littlefield Publishers, 2005). Works with special emphasis on the anti-Semitism at Ivy League colleges, like Harvard, where Nicholas Roosevelt also graduated, include Oliver B. Pollak, "Antisemitism, the Harvard Plan, and the Roots of Reverse Discrimination," *Jewish Social Studies* 45, no. 2 (Spring, 1983): 113–22; Tamar Buchsbaum, "A Note on Antisemitism in Admissions at Dartmouth," *Jewish Social Studies* 49, no. 1 (Winter, 1987): 79–84; Jerome Karabel, *The Chosen: The Hidden History of Admission and*

In his final assessment of what had unfolded at the convention, NR expressed mixed feelings. On the one hand he believed that the Republican Party was finished, but that did not mean that Theodore Roosevelt automatically was a winner either. On the last day, June 22, he wrote that he felt "terribly sorry about it all, and I hate to see Cousin Theodore in a such a position."[21] Perhaps already thinking of the November election, his realism seeped into the analysis, because with the Republican Party split, the road to the White House was wide open for the Democratic Party. "The Republican Party died hard, and I hated to see it go," he wrote. "For some unknown reason, it caused numerous pangs. I had to wait till the next day before I could really feel cheerful about it."[22] Cheerful he may have been, and, naturally, on the spur of the moment that was understandable, but calling a spade a spade was important to him. Even Theodore Roosevelt had doubts of winning. Three weeks after the Progressive Party unanimously chose TR as its candidate, he wrote to his son, "Of course I do not for a moment believe that we shall win."[23]

A sign that NR was a burgeoning writing talent is evident in a letter written to NR's mother by George Haven Putnam, the well-known publisher. A few years after the convention NR's mother sent Putnam her son's account of it in typed form, as if to test whether there was a chance to publish it. Although the material did not see publication (probably it was too short for a book, and while World War I and the impending American participation commanded people's attention the campaign of 1912 was almost forgotten), Putnam praised NR's effort: "Your son has the writer's touch. He knows how to present a scene."[24] When NR revisited the topic in his book on Theodore Roosevelt more than half a century later, he was still convinced that "I was an alert observer."[25] Despite the fact that this was true, one can conclude that modesty was never Nicholas Roosevelt's strong suit.

The Republican National Convention, the bolt, and the foundation of the new political party were a watershed event both in American politics and in NR's life, and he confidently predicted in a letter sent home from the Windy City: "Never

---

Exclusion at Harvard, Yale, and Princeton, Boston: Houghton Mifflin Company, 2005. Anti-Semitism often was a part of anti-foreignism in the United States and thrived in the interwar period. See Tibor Frank, *Double Exile: Migrations of Jewish-Hungarian Professionals through Germany to the United States, 1919–1945* (Oxford: Peter Lang, 2009), 279–86.

[21] Nicholas Roosevelt, *Account of the Republican National Convention at Chicago*, 51.
[22] Ibid., 52.
[23] Theodore Roosevelt to Kermit Roosevelt, July 13, 1912, quoted in Morris, *Colonel Roosevelt*, 230.
[24] G. Haven Putnam to Mrs. J. West Roosevelt, March 5, 1917. This letter was included in the final form of the manuscript as a covering letter before the text.
[25] Nicholas Roosevelt, *Theodore Roosevelt*, 76.

again will I experience such a thing."[26] Probably this was the high point of his life as far as domestic events went, and he could not have known that he was later to witness historical moments in Europe to equal the importance or significance of the 1912 campaign.

In the fall of 1912 NR returned to Harvard and graduated in 1914, just before World War I started in August that year. The young man did not think that he would soon be close to that conflagration, or that in the span of the next five years he would become a veteran diplomat of European affairs.

---

[26] Nicholas Roosevelt, *Account of the Republican National Convention at Chicago*, 8.

Chapter 2

The First Taste of Europe

Nicholas Roosevelt soon found himself in the whirlpool of international diplomacy. Starting in 1914 and for the next five years he was a participant, in various capacities, in the American diplomatic establishment. The background and necessity for such an adventure was provided by World War I and its immediate aftermath in Central Europe.

After receiving his BA degree at Harvard, he started working on his MA at the same institution, where he was an assistant in the department of American history to Edward Channing. A classmate enquired whether he would consider going to Europe as a secretary in the entourage of the newly appointed American ambassador to France, William Graves Sharp. NR asked for guidance from A. Lawrence Lowell, president of Harvard, and Professor Archibald Coolidge, head of the European History Department of the same institution. Both advised him to go, since they thought the experience he might gain there would surpass anything Harvard could offer.[27] He stopped in London before arriving in Paris, and in both capitals he met a score of important and famous or would-be-famous people like Walter Hines Page, Henry James, Colonel Edward M. House, Edith Wharton, or George Clemenceau, not to mention lesser diplomats, politicians, and artists.[28]

The United States was initially no party to the carnage of the fighting in Europe. Considering the traditionally prevailing isolationist view in the United States, as far as Europe was concerned, it is hardly surprising that the American government chose to stay away from what was seen as a European war, and, accordingly, President

---

[27] Nicholas Roosevelt, *A Front Row Seat*, 66.
[28] Ibid., 67–79.

Woodrow Wilson was quick to reinforce traditional neutrality. For the next two and a half years, this was the official stance of the United States, while economically the war proved to be a source of great profit. American loans and material poured mainly into Great Britain and its allies, which led to a collective debt by Europeans to America in the neighborhood of $10 billion by the end of the war. With respect to diplomacy, however, when NR served in France in the first half of the war, he represented a country that was only distantly interested in the ongoing war.

In France, NR was responsible to prepare official correspondence for his immediate chief, John W. Garrett, special agent to the American ambassador at Paris. From September 1914 until the end of the year, together with the French government, the Americans moved to Bordeaux, fearing a possible German occupation of the capital. With time, NR's main job was "looking after the interests of German and Austro-Hungarian prisoners of war and civil internees. This involved inspecting the prison and internment camps throughout France," Corsica included.[29] Also, the American diplomatic corps, using the help of a lot of civilians, represented the interests of other countries in addition to the United States: Great Britain, Japan, Serbia, Guatemala, Nicaragua, and from November the Turkish Empire as well.[30]

NR was on a few days' leave in London when the *Lusitania* was torpedoed, with 128 American casualties. The incident had a profound effect on him, which he conveyed to his mother: "This thing hit me as, I believe nothing in my whole life ever has. It has knocked the bottom out of me."[31] Despite this clear and brazen atrocity on the part of Germany, Wilson did everything in his power to avoid being drawn into the war at this juncture. This was a point on which Theodore Roosevelt constantly attacked the incumbent president. And NR remembered that the *Lusitania* incident, "this barbarous and inhumane act," immediately turned him, together with his colleagues at the American Embassy, "into bitter anti-Germans." It made him decide to join the army.[32]

NR resigned from the foreign service in March 1916, partly because he knew he could no longer afford it, and in the summer he joined a reserve officers' military

---

[29] Ibid., 76–77.
[30] On the work and life of the American Embassy at Paris in the years of the war when NR served there, see Lindsay Sarah Krasnoff, *Views From the Embassy: The Role of the U.S. Diplomatic Community in France, 1914*, Preview Edition, September 15, 2014, (Washington, D. C.: U.S. Department of State: Office of the Historian), https://static.history.state.gov/wwi/views-from-embassy-paris/Views%20from%20Embassy%20Paris%20WWI.pdf, accessed April 18, 2022.
[31] Nicholas Roosevelt, *Theodore Roosevelt*, 169. Even fifty years after its publication, the best book on the *Lusitania* is Colin Simpson, *Lusitania* (London: Longman, 1972).
[32] Ibid., 170.

training camp in Plattsburg, New York.³³ (In those days diplomatic service, even at a lower rank, was mostly a matter of modest or greater wealth.) After his return to the United States, NR had many occasions to speak about the international situation with TR, and he favored the United States joining the war. Actually, he drove TR to the polling place on election day.³⁴ The winter of 1916/1917 found NR in Spain representing the American International Company and trying to create a steadily increasing demand for American goods. He participated in a good deal of diplomatic life in Madrid, and accompanied the American ambassador on his visit to Alfonso XIII, the Spanish king.³⁵

Despite the effort on the American side to remain neutral, various issues worked against it: the rights of neutral countries being ignored by Germany, the principle of free trade, increasing American casualties as a result of more and more reckless German submarine warfare on the high seas, the Zimmermann telegram that brought national security questions to the table,³⁶ the financial commitment in the form of the various loans, and, last but not least, the desire on Wilson's part to shape the postwar world. All these led to the American war declaration on April 6, 1917. Shortly thereafter, although he understood that he "was not cut out to be a soldier," he nevertheless volunteered as an infantry captain on August 15, 1917, and he remained in that capacity throughout the war.³⁷ According to this military service card, he served in Europe from July 31, 1918, to June 18, 1919, with honorable discharge

Nicholas Roosevelt – World War I – July 1917 (Image by Severance, Public Domain via Wikimedia Commons)

---

33   Nicholas Roosevelt, *A Front Row Seat*, 81.
34   Nicholas Roosevelt, *Theodore Roosevelt*, 108.
35   Nicholas Roosevelt, *A Front Row Seat*, 82–88.
36   The January 1917 Zimmermann telegram was a secret German message that proposed an alliance with Mexico—and through Mexico, with Japan—against the United States if the U.S. entered the war. As a reward, Mexico would regain most of its territories lost in the Mexican–American war, 1846–48. The telegram was captured and decoded by the British and handed over to the U.S. government in February. President Wilson decided that it should appear in the press, and this played a part in the U.S. entering the war in April.
37   Ibid., 81.

Nicholas Roosevelt – World War I – July 1917
(Image by Severance, Public Domain via Wikimedia Commons)

six days later.[38] Despite his training and commission as a captain, he did not see action because he contracted pneumonia and was taken to hospital before his unit was sent to the battlefield. By the time he recovered, the armistice ending the war had been signed.[39]

NR may not have seen much action on the Western Front, but after the armistice he got into the thick of things, and almost in spite of himself became witness to history in the making. He arrived in Paris in early December 1918. At the U.S. headquarters at the Hotel Crillon he found confusion, and "into this chaos I found myself thrust."[40] His first station was the Paris Peace Conference, where he was assigned to the Military Section of the American Peace Commission as of December 11, 1918.[41] His earlier experience in war diplomacy and his knowledge of German and French made him a valuable asset for the upcoming months. His first job was to be an aide to preparing for Woodrow Wilson's arrival in mid-December,

---

[38] "World War I military service abstract for Nicholas Roosevelt, Army Officer," https://digitalcollections.archives.nysed.gov/index.php/Detail/objects/40266, accessed April 21, 2022.
[39] Henry Kittredge Norton, "Minister to the Magyars," *Washington Star*, November 9, 1930, 2.
[40] Nicholas Roosevelt, *A History of a Few Weeks*, (unpublished manuscript), Box 61, Nicholas Roosevelt Papers, Syracuse University Libraries, United States, 2.
[41] Special Orders, no. 340, December 17, 1918, Orders, Box 1, Nicholas Roosevelt Papers.

but he had no personal contact or dealings with the president. He was rather one foot soldier in the large American contingent in the French capital trying to "save the world for democracy" at the diplomatic table.

The goal had already been declared in Wilson's Fourteen Points and was straightforward, at least from Washington's perspective: in order to provide sovereignty and self-determination to countries to the east of the Elba, the whole of Europe should embrace basic American values such as free trade and other international rights, while an organization ought to be called into being to provide collective security, the League of Nations. Hundreds of Americans worked at Paris to reach a peace treaty that would ensure the above-mentioned idealistic aims. This meant an immense organizational effort. The main task fell to Joe Grew, whom NR characterized as one "schooled in the mysteries of precedent and protocol" who "found that he has the task of organizing the American Commission to Negotiate Peace, creating order out of chaos."[42] Although NR did not experience much activity, let alone important work at the Seine, he was soon thrown into the whirlpool of postwar diplomacy and action.

At the end of December, he was relieved of his then-current position and attached to the Coolidge Mission, one of the American field missions in Europe in the immediate aftermath of the war. Archibald Cary Coolidge was one of many intellectuals travelling with the American Commission to Negotiate Peace. As an expert on Central European and Eastern European history, his expertise was called upon to give advice concerning the successor states of the Austro-Hungarian Monarchy. Although for a long time Wilson did not wish to see the empire dismembered, by the spring of 1918 he had changed course and now wished to see new and independent democratic states in place of the Monarchy. When the Paris Peace Conference opened on January 18, 1919, the Coolidge Mission was already working in Vienna.

The Coolidge Mission was a motley crew of military officers, university and college professors, and lawyers sent to Vienna to set up a headquarters and then travel to all the countries in the greater region: Hungary, Czechoslovakia, the future Yugoslavia, Romania, and Poland, as well as within Austria. The goal of the various one- or two-person missions was to collect as much information as possible in the confusing aftershock of the war and the ongoing Peace Conference at Paris. The mission's only task was to gather valuable information concerning the present political and economic position and outlook of the countries visited and

---

[42] Nicholas Roosevelt, *A History of a Few Weeks*, 1.

relay the useful data to Paris to help the American Peace Delegation in making decisions. Archibald Coolidge sent the various mission members to the aforementioned countries and tried to keep the flow of information to Paris at a sustainable and satisfactory pace.[43] Not everybody in the group was necessarily a zealous Wilsonian, and those individuals displayed a somewhat sardonic approach, especially toward the concerns of the populations of the successor states and the outlook for healthy democracies to emerge in the area. NR belonged to the skeptical wing of the Coolidge Mission.

As mentioned, NR had had personal knowledge of Coolidge at Harvard, and this may have played a role in his being chosen to go along. In all likelihood, Coolidge must have believed that NR had gathered enough experience and was practical and clearheaded enough to be a valuable member of the group. Thanks to the young man's habit of being an avid diary keeper, we have first-hand knowledge of his experiences and thoughts during his months with the Coolidge Mission. His diary entries, offer a look into contemporaneous Vienna, Budapest, and Bucharest. Although his time spent in the Hungarian capital was much shorter than his months in Vienna, it proved to be more significant from history's point of view, because NR was present when the Hungarian Soviet Republic was established in March 1919.

A few words are necessary regarding the historiographical importance of diaries in general, because that was the main recording device for NR as well. Diaries are, by their very nature, a personal mirror on history. Although reflected and retained through this personal lens, and therefore distortions are natural, history presented from the first person singular perspective enriches one's knowledge about a certain event or period. The diary as a form of and mirror on history has been around for centuries, but the first detailed diary entries came into being during the Renaissance, which era produced a previously unknown measure of self-consciousness and, in the wake of it, a greater need for self-reflection.[44] The almost universal practice of putting down observations in a diary, however, really came into vogue in the mid-nineteenth century. Most typically, persons belonging to the upper classes in general grabbed

---

[43] For the history of the Coolidge Mission, see, Harold Jefferson Coolidge and Robert Howard Lord, *Archibald Cary Coolidge: Life and Letters* (Boston and New York: Houghton Mifflin, 1932), 192–216, Foreign Relations of the United States, The Paris Peace Conference, 1919, Vol. XII (Washington: Government Printing Office, 1947), 240–527; Peter Pastor, *Hungary between Wilson and Lenin: The Hungarian Revolution of 1918–1919 and the Big Three* (Boulder, CO: East European Quarterly Distributed by New York: Columbia University Press, 1976), 100–104.

[44] David L. Ransel, "The Diary of a Merchant: Insights into Eighteenth Century Plebeian Life," *The Russian Review* 63, no. 4 (Oct. 2004): 596.

their pens, but diplomats and politicians in particular were active in this field. Today, this form of preserving the present moment seems to be on the wane, largely due to the digital and globalized world, where the visual image is taking its place.

The diary entry is a living imprint of history, since those persons scribbling down events into their diaries reflect fresh experience and observation, and they do it immediately, or shortly, after the event takes place, so the usually distorting feature of many years and distant memory do not play a role in being historically correct. On the other hand, the diary entry can also be seen as a form of literature, even if the notes, sometimes in short form, are not representatives of fine literature. That is why it has an "unsure status," because the diary is "an uncertain genre uneasily balanced between literary and historical writing, between spontaneity of reportage and the reflectiveness of the crafted text, between selfhood and events, between subjectivity and objectivity, between the private and the public."[45]

Obviously, one always has to be on guard when faced with a diary entry, because, if nothing else, unavoidable subjectivity will play a part. Still, these entries usually reflect history well. This does not mean that we should look at diaries as irrefutable historical artifacts, since these texts are personal "images" only.[46] Coloring, magnifying, and distorting facts, as well as errors are all characteristic of diaries, but that also holds true for professional history writing. Although there are naturally plenty of counter-examples, in most cases the author of a diary entry does not purposefully distort the story he or she writes down. The author's primary goal is clearly to preserve the present and not to lie about history.[47] The author either wishes on rereading the entries to be able to reproduce events and feelings ten, twenty, thirty, or more years later, irrespective of their nature—whether family, politics, or war; or they wish to leave an intellectual inheritance to their family. Therefore, while a historian mainly analyzes the past, a diary entry mainly preserves it. This preservation may show signs of idiosyncrasies, also signs of the analytical mind of the observer, but it presents history as it was for that individual. Also, diary entries made during a crucial time period, the period of the Paris Peace Conference in this case, may contain information that is missing from diplomatic messages and other official reports. The latter contain information regarding as "strictly business," that is, what is connected to the job and position of the author. That is the reason why the personal

---

[45] Rachael Langford and Russell West, eds., *Marginal Voices, Marginal Forms: Diaries in European Literature and History* (Amsterdam: Rodopi, 1999), 8.
[46] Gábor Gyáni, "A napló mint társadalomtörténeti forrás" [The diary as source for social history], Szabolcs-szatmár-beregi levéltári évkönyv, 1997, vol. 12, 25.
[47] Pál Pritz, "Napló és történelem" [Diary and history], *Múltunk* 62, no. 1 (2017): 4–6.

dimension of the diary is suitable to record private impressions that clearly nuance our understanding of the events and personalities of a given time.

Depending on time and place, the level of "freedom" of the diary entries may also differ. If someone lives in a society and jots down events when they do not need to worry about the material getting into the wrong hands, the opinion will be a more open one, the author will be committed to a more "honest" style. On the contrary, in the atmosphere of an oppressive regime, a diary keeper will choose circumventing wording and style, even inventing a code perhaps, driven by the fear of what might happen if the authorities find the entries, read them, and, as a consequence, punish the author and/or their family. Seen from this point of view, NR could write as freely as he wished, even if some of his entries were written down in foreign countries. Naturally, only when looking back a hundred years later can we appreciate the historical significance of some of his entries.

NR was a man of the written word. He had kept a diary from early on to record his observations and feelings. His chance to immerse himself in postwar diplomacy provided another perfect platform to express his opinion on persons and events that he met, saw, and experienced. In times when he had no official outlet to contribute to, he often preserved his thoughts in a diary. He likely did this so that, under more settled circumstances, he could make use of those entries. NR's writing technique was similar to that he had already put to test in the case of the Republican National Convention in 1912: based upon his diary entries, he created a narrative with a continuous flow.

There have been diary writers who knew that the public would read what they wrote, so they composed diaries through this prism.[48] In the case of NR this cannot be detected. Despite his obvious ambitions and a very strong ego, in 1919 he was too young to really believe that posterity would want to read his entries as a point of reference. Still, since he did hope to see his diary entries in print one day, it might be surmised that he wanted to show himself in a more favorable light than reality called for. And his final manuscript, which he based upon his diary, is edited so that narration connects the entries. But the language in that compilation is often critical—of almost everybody and everything—and aside from a touch of too much assumed wisdom on the author's part, it is hard to believe that he left out important sections. Most probably, he thought that the narration would make the entries easier to understand and thus promote the chances of publication.

---

[48] One of the best examples is: George F. Kennan. *The Kennan Diaries*, ed. Frank Costigliola (New York: W. W. Norton, 2014).

When one reads NR's diary entries, which can be taken as authentic, one is struck by certain features. These features speak not only about NR's personality, but they well represent and reflect the mood and thinking of a wide layer of American society in the immediate postwar period. Therefore, it is worth taking a look at these entries to detect some interesting facts about the author's thinking which certainly does not mirror but to a considerable degree echoes the larger American worldview at the time.

NR's diary reveals two important things. First, it conveys the Coolidge Mission's—and presumably those of other American missions—rhythm of work, daily tasks and challenges, and the general mood that surrounded it. The reader gets to know the hardships of travelling through postwar Europe, also the difficulty of finding accommodation and securing provisions, and the intrigue involved in information gathering. Second, based upon our knowledge about the period and locations, the diary gives a fair picture of the historical and political background of the three major locations it deals with: Vienna, Budapest, and Bucharest. This gives credence to the entries as a trustworthy reflection of history. There are not many such diaries that we know of reflecting this time and place, but the diaries of two other members of the Coolidge Mission confirm many of NR's observations.

Walter Goodwin Davis (1885–1966) was born in Portland, Maine. He attended Exeter and later Yale, in 1908. After completing his law studies at Harvard in 1911, he joined the firm of Shearman and Sterling in New York. Subsequently he pursued a business and banking career in his hometown. Following the American declaration of war against Germany in April 1917, Davis likewise attended the Officers Training Camp at Plattsburg, New York, and received a commission as infantry captain in early 1918. He was assigned to the Military Intelligence Service, and served as Assistant Military Attaché at Berne, Switzerland. After the November armistice he was attached to the American Commission to Negotiate Peace in Paris, subsequently being transferred to Vienna as a member of the Coolidge Mission, where he remained until March 1919.[49]

Charles M. Storey (1889–1980) came from a rather prominent New England family. His father, Moorfield Storey, was a well-known lawyer in Boston, Massachusetts, with a long practice and various titles in associations. He was a liberal in his political and legal outlook.[50] His son, Charles Moorfield Storey, was a Harvard graduate,

---

[49] The information was gleaned from Guide to the Walter G. Davis Papers MS 469, Manuscripts and Archives, Yale University Library, U.S.A, compiled by N. X. Rizopolous with the assistance of Anne Willard, March 1973, New Haven, CT.

[50] Eugene Wambaugh, "Moorfield Storey (1845–1929)," *Proceedings of the American Academy of Arts and Sciences* 71, no. 10 (Mar. 1937): 552–56.

who, after getting his law degree, worked in the Justice Department until the end of World War I. After the war he became a member of a law firm, where he stayed for the remainder of his life. He held the position of president or trustee in various organizations of which he was a member, that of Harvard overseer for five years was the one that made him proudest.[51] Storey was also a member of the Coolidge Mission. As it will be shown, the diaries of these two mission members corroborate most of what NR put down in his diary.

After his arrival in Austria, NR spent the first weeks in Vienna, where the mission took up residency at the New Bristol Hotel while office space was found at the American Consulate. In the following months he met scores of Austrians of various professions and shades of political outlook. "My particular duty," he remembered, "was to follow the newspapers, gathering news of all sorts, paying special attention to the internal political situation. As a side interest I was given Roumania [sic]."[52] Within a few days, many members of the mission travelled to their respective territory of interest: Prague, Belgrade, or Budapest. Meanwhile in Vienna, Coolidge had so many visitors that he had to put an advertisement in the newspapers making it clear that he would not be able to meet every caller and that the mission's duty was to gather information and did not have any official role.[53]

The mission kept contact with the representatives of other countries but mainly with Austrians: people in government, especially those of the Austrian Foreign Office, politicians, journalists, priests, and soldiers. For example, NR managed to have frequent talks with the editors of the *Neue Freie Presse*, the *Arbeiter Zeitung*, or the *Reichspost*—Ernst Martin Benedikt, Friedrich Austerlitz, and Friedrich Funder, respectively. The principal themes regarding Austria were its economic situation (mainly the food situation in Vienna—food being "the one great and invincible political weapon"[54]), the question of the Anschluss, that is, the union of Germany and Austria, and the extent to which the Bolshevik movement presented a danger to order and the traditional way of life.

These areas of interest did not reflect unfounded fears. Secretary of State Robert Lansing, for example, famously connected the food question and the fear of Bolshevism: "Food is the real problem. Empty stomachs mean Bolshevik. Full

---

[51] Theodore Chase, "Charles Moorfield Storey," *Proceedings of the Massachusetts Historical Society*, Third Series 92 (1980): 151–56.
[52] Nicholas Roosevelt, *A History of a Few Weeks*, 57. The spelling "Roumania" was current practice at the time this was written. In subsequent quotations, it will be retained as written, without appending [sic].
[53] Ibid., 63.
[54] Ibid., 136.

stomachs mean no Bolsheviks. The feeding of Europe must take place as rapidly as possible to defeat chaos which threatens society."[55] Hugh Gibson, another American diplomat on the rise, remarked in his dairy just a few days before the armistice that "there is a good deal of fear that Austria might break out in Bolshevism and steps are being taken to avert it."[56] The American Relief Administration under Herbert Hoover under the cover of providing food for the devastated Eastern European countries, was working for broader American interests, most typically creating stability and working against Bolshevism and any other revolutionary ideas.[57]

These were the circumstances under which NR began his work for the Coolidge Mission in Vienna. His chronicle of the next few months is both important and interesting because it tried to record history as he watched it unfold. He also wrote entertaining vignettes featuring various people and his conversations with or situations involving them, which makes the material more valuable.

NR's basic view coincided with the overall wish of the Paris Peace Conference, namely, to create a buffer zone of smaller states between the defeated but revenge-minded Germans and the unpredictable and dangerous Bolshevik Russians. NR believed that imposing harsh peace terms on Germany might be the solution: "Absolutely I am convinced that the only solution is to squeeze Germany like a lemon." This conviction sprang from the fear that inevitably Germany would be strong again:

> 1st that the German speaking peoples sooner or later will unite, regardless of what may temporarily be decided by a Peace Conference; 2nd that the old-time "Deutschland uber alles" forces will do everything possible to worm their way back into power under the cloak of the Republic. They will have the force of Germany's past glory back of them, and of riches for the nation

---

[55] Robert Lansing, memorandum of October 28, 1918, quoted in John M. Thompson, *Russia, Bolshevism, and the Versailles Peace* (Princeton, NJ: Princeton University Press, 1967), 15–16. On the food situation and American policy concerning Central Europe after the armistice, see, Franz Adlgasser, "The Roots of Communist Containment: American Food Aid in Austria and Hungary after World War I," *Austria in the Nineteen Fifties, Contemporary Austrian Studies* 3 (1995): 171–88.

[56] Diary entry, November 2, 1918, quoted in Adlgasser, "The Roots of Communist Containment," 173.

[57] On the politically motivated role of the ARA see Frank Costigliola, *Awkward Dominion: American Political, Economic, and Cultural Relations with Europe, 1919–1933* (Ithaca, NY: Cornell University Press, 1984), 39–54. In more detail about the ARA's work in Hungary, see Tibor Glant, "Herbert Hoover and Hungary, 1918–1923," *Hungarian Journal of English and American Studies* 8, no. 2 (2002): 95–109. On the general Central and Eastern European relief work, which in the greatest part was provided by American sources, see Herbert Clark Hoover, *The Memoirs of Herbert Hoover*. vol. 1–3. (New York: The Macmillan Company, 1951–1952), vol. 1, 282–430.

to hold out as a bait, and in a few decades Germany will be back again, the same as ever. [...] Our only guarantee is to see that the last drop of blood is wrung out of them.[58]

At the same time, however, NR believed this should not be done blindly to other factors, and in order to lessen the blow, extra punishment ought not to be used against the Germans. That is why he was "opposed to taking territory. The principle of dishonesty is the dominant note of the day. That is, boundaries must be determined according to race. What Germany has that doesn't belong to her must be amputated; but there is no need to cut off a leg where a foot only should go. In fact to exceed this is criminal."[59]

His talks with various Austrians of different professional and political shades were interesting enough, but he was still dissatisfied. He drew up reports of his conversations with these and other persons for Coolidge's use. NR respected Coolidge immensely as the ideal man for the job, given his knowledge of the Monarchy, but as a mission head he left a lot to be desired in the young man's eyes. It was mainly Coolidge's indecisiveness regarding accepting reports and forwarding them to Paris that caused this ill-feeling, and it "was therefore almost impossible for us to know whether we were doing what would be of use to him or merely wasting our own time, his time, and the time of the Government."[60] Indeed, at the end of February he asked Coolidge to relieve him of duty and send him back to Paris so that he could join his regiment and sail home, but his boss instead sent him to Romania for a field trip.

Another member of the Mission, Storey, had visited the mainly Hungarian-populated Transylvania already, and Coolidge wanted to hear about the Romanian point of view as well. On his way to Romania, NR first spent a few short days in Budapest, where he managed to meet such notable personalities as Dénes Berinkey, the prime minister, Oszkár Jászi, former minister and a radical in his views, Albert Apponyi, the grand old man of Hungarian politics, Pál Teleki, the politician and renowned geographer, and the president of the newly established Hungarian Republic, Mihály Károlyi, with whom he had two long talks—mainly on Hungarian foreign policy. Apponyi struck NR as being impossible. The two had met fifteen years earlier, when Apponyi visited Theodore Roosevelt at Oyster Bay. For NR, TR's earlier friend embodied "a pan-German of the extreme type and in a way the

---

[58] Diary entry of January 27, 1919, Nicholas Roosevelt, *A History of a Few Weeks*, 104–5.
[59] Ibid., 105.
[60] Nicholas Roosevelt, *A History of a Few Weeks*, 192.

Hungarian counter part of Tirpitz," or "the Ludendorff or Bethmann Holwig of Hungary. D----d old scoundrel!"⁶¹ The Apponyi of the present basically gave a presentation on how Hungary would seek revenge if it were mutilated by having millions of Hungarians left outside the mother country. Worse, the count implied that in case of dismemberment, the Hungarians living in the United States, together with the Germans there, would make a united effort against Wilson and the Democratic Party. NR was, of course, a Republican, but such a brazen threat against American democracy left him irate. No wonder that his assessment of Apponyi was mixed at best. He admitted Apponyi's wide knowledge of Europe and beyond, but altogether he saw the old conservative as "an interesting old scoundrel—very intelligent, perfectly unrepentant, and a thorough Chauvinist."⁶²

On the other hand, President Károlyi impressed NR favorably:

He is a remarkable man. He is wall-eyed, has a harelip, and a cleft palate—and after five minutes' talk I had forgotten all three! One can't help admiring a man who has three such handicaps and yet can rise to the position of leading politician in his country. He speaks beautiful English—is distinctly a man of the upper classes—and my guess is that he has discovered a new and fascinating game. I think he is sincere in that he really believes in advanced ideas. By tradition and all else, however, he belongs to the old school.⁶³

NR's characterization of Károlyi was full of praise and exhibited a mild enchantment. He called him "a sincere patriot," who "through his patriotism [...] took the helm, only to be faced by impossible problems, attacked from within and without, with nowhere to turn."⁶⁴

Other Americans also met and held conversations with Károlyi at that time. The Hungarian leader struck Storey "as being sincere, honest, a man prone to think better of the world that it deserved, an idealist [...] an extremely human person, capable of exciting a blind affection, based as much on his weakness as on his strength."⁶⁵ In his view, Károlyi was "an idealist, something of a dreamer, scrupulously honest, considered by some a poor judge of men and subject to the influence of stronger characters. Personally he is extremely attractive, a good talker and has made on all

---

61 Ibid., 198–99, 208.
62 Diary entry of February 28, 1919, ibid., 202.
63 Nicholas Roosevelt, *A History of a Few Weeks*, 217.
64 Diary entry of March 20, 1919, ibid., 279.
65 Dairy entry, January 15, 1919, C. M. Storey Journal 1918–1919, Massachusetts Historical Society, U.S.A.

of us a deep impression." He added that there was "no doubt as to the depth and sincerity of his conviction and to his force. To my mind he is an extremely forceful personality, and has displayed considerable political instinct."⁶⁶ NR's positive image of Károlyi was not an isolated perspective among Americans of the day.

Pál Teleki also made a very good impression on NR, partly because the latter gathered a lot of information from the renowned geographer, cartographer, and future prime minister of Hungary. Teleki came through as "the most intelligent and in his line the ablest" among all the Hungarians NR had met.⁶⁷ As he noted in his diary, Teleki "gave me a mass of information that filled up many gaps in my scant knowledge of Hungarian affairs. [...] I got almost everything I wanted to know."⁶⁸ Naturally, Teleki was feeding the American careful propaganda regarding the large Hungarian ethnic blocs in the successor countries, just as almost everybody in those countries saw any American as a possible conduit to the highest decision makers at Paris. NR's observations about these prominent Hungarians in his diary add nuance to the accepted historical picture. Albeit the diary does not alter the accepted history, it still amply colors our perceptions about individuals and events.

Walter Davis, another member of the Coolidge Mission, wrote his own impressions of Hungarian nobles based upon his contact with them at Vienna. His opinion was not flattering. "These Hungarian aristocrats are absolutely impossible to converse with," he wrote in his diary. "Their ideas are hopelessly sixteenth century, and with every breath they prove against themselves those accusations of feudal mentality made by Mr. Seton-Watson."⁶⁹ He went on, "Countess Hadik told me as a proof of the uselessness of all Slovaques [*sic*], that the peasants on her husband's estates would never have learned even to speak Magyar if he had not built schools and compelled them to go to them! A frank admission of the forcible magyarization of this nationality which is willing to suffer martyrdom rather than give up its own language."⁷⁰

Storey wrote a quick study of the other end of the spectrum—the Transylvanian Hungarians. The Szekler people struck him as crude but honest folks: "I must say that the Szeklers made us feel very much at home. To my mind they resembled

---

⁶⁶ Charles Moorfield Storey to Allen Dulles, February 3, 1919, Storey, Charles M. 1919, Box 53 Folder 19, Allen W. Dulles Papers; Public Policy Papers, Department of Rare Books and Special Collections, Princeton University Library.
⁶⁷ Diary entry of April 16, 1919, Nicholas Roosevelt, *A History of a Few Weeks*, 418.
⁶⁸ Diary entry of February 28, 1919, ibid., 203.
⁶⁹ Robert William Seton-Watson was a British historian who played a role in bringing on the breakup of the Austro-Hungarian Monarchy after World War I. He was a fervent anti-Hungarian.
⁷⁰ Diary entry, February 13, 1919, Walter G. Davis Diary, Box 1, Folder 16, Walter Goodwin Davis Papers, Manuscripts and Archives, Yale University Library, U.S.A.

our New Englanders, with a certain simplicity, sturdiness, and an independence amounting to obstinacy in many cases."[71] But from a political aspect his verdict was harsh, especially after conducting a handful of interviews in Kolozsvár:

> In the first place all these people were so irreconcilable, so pigheaded, so narrow. In the second place they were utterly out of joint with the new tunes; and were being buoyed up with hopes for the return of the old royal order. Lastly they were not thinking; which were the saddest of all. The most that could be said was that they were brooding over present wrongs and idealizing a dull and long moribund past.[72]

In any event, Coolidge sent NR to Romania to study the situation on the ground and report "on the relations between the Rumanians[73] and the Hungarians in the newly occupied districts."[74] This was crucial mainly because of Transylvania. The old land of Hungarians, or Szeklers, was somewhat distant from the clearly Hungarian-populated areas to the west, and on the territory between the two regions Romanians formed a majority. The decision over this territory was one of the many headaches for the Paris Peace Conference.

Arriving from Budapest after a long train ride, NR's first diary entry on his first day in Bucharest, Romania, was, "God save us, what a Country!"[75] He had a very low opinion of the place and the people: "To outward appearances it is a mixture of Albuquerque, New Mexico, and Ellis Island. Of course the strange costumes are interesting—brigands in sheepskin coats and fur hats; highly embroidered vests and clothes; barefooted women; oxen-drawn carts; carriages with Russian garbed drivers, and Western American tinsel. But the rest ------!!"[76] While there, he met the French military leader, General Henri Berthelot, and, naturally, many Romanian military and civilian officials. At times he became weary of some Romanians trying to convince him of their right to the new territories, and in exasperation called them "D----d Oriental Scoundrels! Apparently honesty is not the best policy here."[77]

---

[71] Dairy entry, February 15, 1919, C. M. Storey Journal.
[72] Dairy entry, February 19, 1919, ibid.
[73] The spelling of the country's name as "Rumania" was current practice at the time this was written. In subsequent quotations, it will be retained as written, without appending [sic].
[74] Archibald Cary Coolidge (Vienna) to Captain Roosevelt, February 26, 1919, Orders, Box 2, Nicholas Roosevelt Papers. Nicholas Roosevelt's official reports can be read in FRUS., The Paris Peace Conference, 1919, Vol. XII, 404–10.
[75] Nicholas Roosevelt, *A History of a Few Weeks*, 239.
[76] Ibid., 251–52.
[77] Ibid., 240.

In sizing up the controversial Transylvanian question, he could not back either side in the debate. It was not only that both the Hungarians and Romanians put forward data to prove their historic right to the territory, but the aftermath of whatever decision was reached had to be taken into account as well. On his way to Romania, in Budapest had overheard avowals such that "if Hungary was dismembered she would never cease to make herself a thorn of irritation to her neighbors, and that in consequence the peace of Europe would be constantly endangered."[78] This was a clear threat to the hoped-for peace and, in NR's opinion, the "only apparent solution is the complete democratization of Hungary and the putting out of power once and for all of the Pan-Hungarians."[79] As for the Romanian attitude, NR described it as "extravagant."[80] NR thought that in the end it was essential to redraw the map in a fashion that would leave the fewest possible minorities in foreign countries, which minorities would be granted the guarantee of local autonomy, especially in education, religion, and the press. Knowing the countries involved, however, he was convinced that Americans should be involved in drawing up the future boundaries, and an international policing power should be used to maintain the peace, otherwise it would be a failure. In his concluding assessment he wrote that "the question of Transylvania centers about the proposition that if it belongs to Hungary there will be a Rumania irredenta, and if it belongs to Rumania there will be a Hungary irredenta."[81] In his cover letter to Paris, Coolidge said NR's reports were interesting, but the opinions therein were too sweeping, in his judgment.[82]

No sooner had he returned to Vienna than NR was one more time sent to Hungary, after trying to resign, again in vain, and this time he was thrown into the maelstrom. He was to be the head of the local American mission of three men (up until that point Philip L. Goodwin had been in charge, but he left for Vienna), and since Budapest was rife with revolutionary stirrings, it was expected that things might come to a head. On March 20, NR once again paid a visit to Mihály Károlyi. He found the president under great duress: Károlyi seemed "very tired—tired physically and mentally. He looked gray, and his face was drawn, and he spoke slowly and without much interest."[83] The information that NR gathered on March 19 and 20

---

[78] Nicholas Roosevelt to Archibald Cary Coolidge, March 12, 1919, *FRU.S.*, The Paris Peace Conference, 1919, Vol. XII, 405.
[79] Ibid.
[80] Ibid.
[81] Ibid., 407.
[82] Archibald Cary Coolidge to the Commission to Negotiate Peace, March 13, 1919, *FRU.S.*, The Paris Peace Conference, 1919, Vol. XII, 404.
[83] Nicholas Roosevelt, *A History of a Few Weeks*, 278.

portended the Bolshevik danger, but he believed that it was the common fear of the ultra conservatives, which he had already seen a fair share of in Vienna. He found a parallel with the conservative stand-patter Republicans of the 1912 campaign and the representatives of the ancient regime in Central Europe, so it is understandable he accepted with reservations what they had to say. But as some had prophesized, Hungary was indeed to be the locus of a revolution.

NR was present when the so-called Vix Note was handed to Károlyi.[84] Presented to him by the Allies, the Vix Note informed the Hungarian government that it was to withdraw very deep into its former territory, and it basically foreshadowed the dismemberment of Hungary at the Peace Conference. According to Roosevelt, at the reading of the note Károlyi said that living up to such a declaration would mean revolution, as no government could last a day if it gave up such huge territories as the Note demanded. That afternoon NR wrote to his brother that "the kettle is boiling over," and he also informed Vienna that the next day there would be "pandemonium." He was right.[85] The following day Budapest experienced a communist takeover with pure chaos, and since news, sometimes contradictory, reached the Americans intermittently, there was no way of knowing how reliable their knowledge of the events was. Based upon what he had heard, NR theorized in his diary and in his reports that the revolution and a shift to Bolshevism came about in order to defend the territorial integrity of the country. He chose to leave Hungary the very next day with Lieutenant Haynes of the American Food Mission on a special train that was carrying the cash payment for a held-up food train for Hungary in the Kingdom of Serbs, Croats and Slovenes. Then he proceeded to Paris to report to the American leaders in person about the events he had just experienced in Budapest. After he left Budapest, Professor Philip Marshall Brown remained to represent the United States and send reports to Vienna.[86]

NR's account on March 20 of the handing over the Allied Nix note to Károlyi well records the nervousness of the Hungarian government in the face of demands

---

[84] Fernand Vix (1876–1941), French military officer, the leader of the Inter-Allied Military Mission in Budapest in 1919. He handed over the allied note to President Mihály Károlyi on March 20, 1919, which the latter and his government could not accept and resigned instead, opening the way for a communist takeover.

[85] Nicholas Roosevelt, *A History of a Few Weeks*, 310, 314.

[86] On the Károlyi era and the reasons and events leading up to the Bolshevik takeover in March 1919, see, Pastor, *Hungary between Wilson and Lenin*; for an English language summary on the events in Hungary in the spring and summer of 1919, see, Tibor Hajdú, *The Hungarian Soviet Republic* (Budapest: Akadémiai Kiadó), 1979; Károlyi's memoirs do not mention the American members of the Coolidge Mission. For his summary of the fateful ultimatum handed over by Vix and the communist takeover, see, Michael Karolyi, *The Memoirs of Karolyi: Faith without Illusion* (London: Jonathan Cape, 1956), 152–57.

that basically determined its fall. Since the Allied and Associated Powers ordered the Hungarians to withdraw well behind the ethnic lines that they regarded as fair, it was obvious that the Hungarians were to be punished beyond what they conceived possible, and the note was the harbinger of the ruin to come in the form of the Treaty of Trianon the following year. The Allied note is well documented in history books, but NR's text vividly portrays the personal atmosphere of that morning, and this opens a somewhat new dimension to the resignation of Károlyi and his government and the communist takeover on March 21. The Bolshevik takeover not only gave the Peace Conference a headache as to how to deal with the new political formation in Central Europe, which many saw as a spreading ideological disease from Russia, it also sealed the fate of Hungary as to the outcome of the peace terms. Hungary could not have escaped the peace talks without serious territorial and population loss, but had there been no communist regime fighting the will of Paris, the outcome might have been less severe.

NR's first telegram to Paris after leaving Budapest reiterated his conviction that the Bolshevik movement was substantially of a nationalist nature: "nationalists have resorted to Bolshevism in hopes of being able to preserve integrity of country. Public opinion apparently favors armed aggression towards neighbors."[87] Partly based upon his reports, Lansing's advice to Wilson was to do everything to contain the revolution in Hungary and make sure it could not spread to neighboring countries.[88] A few days later, both NR and his longer and deeper analysis reached Paris.[89] In this he revisited his thesis that the Bolshevik revolution in Hungary was nationalist in origin rather than fueled by ideology, and it served as a unifying force in order to avoid the dismemberment of the country and preserve its territorial integrity.[90] In the conclusion to the report NR stated: "Unless immediate and vigorous action is taken the Allies will be met with a disastrous state of affairs in Central Europe which it may take years to straighten out. Hungary has defied the Peace Conference and allied herself with the Bolsheviki. It is Germany's turn next."[91]

He also stressed these points in person in front of the three American commissioners, Henry White, Tasker Howard Bliss, and Secretary of State Robert Lansing.

---

[87] Nicholas Roosevelt to Royall Tyler, March 23, 1919, Enclosure II, in Robert Lansing to Woodrow Wilson, Paris, March 24, 1919, Arthur S. Link, ed., *The Papers of Woodrow Wilson*. vols. 1–69. (Princeton, NJ: Princeton University Press), 1987. vol. 56, 241.
[88] Robert Lansing to Woodrow Wilson, Paris, March 24, 1919, ibid., 240.
[89] Enclosure, "The Hungarian Revolution," in Robert Lansing to Woodrow Wilson, Paris, March 27, 1919, ibid., 331–34.
[90] Ibid., 331.
[91] Ibid., 334.

He was asked to provide the American commissioners with a solution the situation in Hungary, which suggestion NR found preposterous, because in his eyes all he was supposed to do was to report the conditions as he had witnessed them. It should be the commissioners' job to decide on any possible action. NR, however, did not blink, and before the commissioners, with Coolidge also present, he once again advocated quick action to stem the tide of Bolshevism in Europe lest it should reach Germany. In light of the commissioners' puzzlement, it is little wonder NR had an acerbic commentary on the leaders of the American Peace Delegation. Lansing, echoing Henry Adams' characterization to NR, was "a first class clerk;" Bliss was "ancient, and living in the America of the [18]70's;" White was somewhat praised, because he "at least has heard of Europe."[92] Lansing, Bliss, and White were "dummies—figureheads—and also fatheads."[93] Woodrow Wilson scored no better. NR found the president "obstinate, self-willed, provincial and hardheaded to an appalling degree;" he was also "often ignorant of conditions and refused to avail himself of the information placed at his disposal."[94] NR thought the Big Four (Wilson, Georges Clemenceau, George Lloyd, and Vittorio Orlando) only "met and haggled and talked, while Europe toppled on the edge of Revolution. Action alone could save the day. But Mr. Wilson preferred words."[95] Nonetheless, he submitted his report (as quoted above, ending with "Germany's turn next."), concerning which he was in close contact with Allen Dulles, a future giant of American foreign affairs.

If there was one American NR truly appreciated in Paris, it was Herbert Hoover, then head of the American Relief Administration and future U.S. president. He found the food czar "someone who wasn't afraid to act, and who wasn't afraid to express a clear-cut, forceful opinion. Hoover was rather larger and heavier than I had expected, and has a massive jowl. I was admirably impressed by the man."[96] This observation and connection were important in light of what unfolded ten years later regarding NR's diplomatic career. NR's positive observations regarding Hoover were not the exception—many people expressed similar feelings. John Maynard Keynes, for example, also thought Hoover was "the only man who emerged from the ordeal of Paris with an enhanced reputation."[97]

---

[92] Nicholas Roosevelt, *A History of a Few Weeks*, 380.
[93] Ibid., 381.
[94] Diary entry of April 5, 1919, ibid., 379, 361.
[95] Ibid., 361.
[96] Nicholas Roosevelt, *A History of a Few Weeks*, 388.
[97] Quoted in Liaquat Ahamed, *Lords of Finance: The Bankers Who Broke the World* (New York: Penguin Books, 2009), 275.

After his Paris debriefing, NR returned to Vienna to continue his Coolidge Mission days. There the next two months passed in relative calm, although Bolshevism in Hungary was casting long shadows over the Austrian capital. Still, the workload started to decrease, the weather became nicer, and the overall situation in Vienna brighter. The members of the mission took long walks, sometimes hiking not far from Vienna. They played tennis and spent the evenings with other Allied members or with Austrians of various backgrounds, sometimes at the opera.

In Vienna NR experienced an attitude very similar to that of the Hungarians and those elsewhere: the Austrians, too, looked to the Americans in general, and to the Coolidge Mission in particular, as their salvation. Therefore, he urged that the mission leave Vienna, and he poured his heart out to Allen Dulles. His complaint is worth quoting at length because it bears upon the large issue of how the United States was seen in this corner of the world.

> It is my firm conviction that the same moment has been reached for Austria. Our remaining here in the false position in which we are placed—for it is a false position—is going to merely raise the odium of the United States to an ever greater degree when the crash comes. In spite of ourselves these people look to us as their greatest friend, and look on us as the one country with which they wish to be on good terms. They believe in us, and in our strength, our honesty and our disinterestedness. For this reason they persist in thinking, despite frequent denials, that this commission is more than a commission merely to get information. They refuse to realize that it is spineless—that it has not the slightest vestige of power—that it has the strength of a eunuch. And for this reason they still hope that we can or will do something more than merely study. And the greater their faith in us, the greater will be their disillusion when they discover that we have stayed long, listened sympathetically, studied much and done nothing.[98]

Shortly after he returned to the United States in the summer, NR put together the material from his time in Europe. The language of NR's diary entries and overall narrative provides easy reading, at places they are decidedly entertaining, but they also contain passages that today are deemed politically incorrect. He, for example, called General Pershing's maid and valet "a large, fat, jovial nigger wench, dressed

---

[98] Nicholas Roosevelt (Vienna) to Allen W. Dulles, April 20, 1919, Folder 13, Roosevelt, Nicholas, 1919, Box 49, Series 1: Correspondence, 1891–1969, Allen W. Dulles Papers, 1845–1971, Seeley G. Mudd Manuscript Library, Princeton, NJ, U.S.A.

up to make a killing, and beside her a big, portly, round-faced negro, both smiling and grinning as they had never smiled or grinned before."[99] One of the recurring elements is his anti-Semitism. In the first part of the twentieth century, this typical perspective of the American upper class, had racial underpinnings, since the Jews coming from Europe represented neither Anglo Saxon nor Protestant ways. Arriving from Central and Eastern Europe, they tried to keep their own culture, language, and, mainly, religion. This caused dislike among Americans who wanted to see immigrants melt into American society as quickly as possible and feared what might become of American values if Jews and other immigrant groups retained their own culture. In NR's diary the words "Jew" or "Jewish" appear 72 times, and a large percentage of these are in a negative context. Although in quite a few instances he recognized Jews' intellectual ability, most of these references were condescending in nature. NR met a great number of people in Central and Eastern Europe who were different from the American stock and style and whom he labeled without thinking according to their racial origin. For example, after his first meeting with the editor-in-chief of the *Neue Freie Presse*, Ernst Martin Benedikt, he offers the following characterization: "A most interesting Jew, large, fat, square-headed, but with the nose and mouth of the race."[100] Since NR belonged to the American aristocracy, perhaps it is not shocking that, despite his many liberal views, he carried his anti-Semitism quite far—at least in his own diaries. Fellow soldiers, service personnel, even the acting Romanian prime minister (Alexandru C. Constantinescu "looked like a fat Jew pig, with a fat, flabby snout."[101]) were all tarred with the same brush.

In the safe haven of his dairy, NR's unbridled style reflects the attitude of many of his peers in other ways as well. The text is saturated with a feeling of American superiority concerning Europeans in general and Southern and Eastern Europeans in particular. As he put it, "there is nothing in the world like the great blonde race of the North, out of which we have grown. It is greater than any Latin race, and greater than any Slav."[102] This was a complicated view that advertised that mainly the Anglo Saxon peoples, and related northern stock, were capable of establishing democratic government and achieving civilization par excellence. In sharp contrast, "the people living (or having their origin) south of the 51st parallel and east of the 16th, are incapable of steady, stable, just Government."[103] Therefore, the South and

---

[99] Nicholas Roosevelt, *A History of a Few Weeks*, 13.
[100] Diary entry of January 22, 1919, ibid., 79.
[101] Diary entry of March 12, 1919, ibid., 392, 238, 240.
[102] Diary entry without date, but it is from January 1919, Nicholas Roosevelt, *A History of a Few Weeks*, 77.
[103] Diary entry of January 27, 1919, ibid., 102–3.

the East meant backwardness, lower rungs of civilization, and ultimately danger, especially in the form of Bolshevism. The fear of what such "uncivilized" people might do, as happened at the end of the Roman Empire, was clearly on NR's and other Americans' mind. "The Barbarians are still coming out of the East," he wrote, "and the great menace of the coming generations is the Slav peril."[104]

The self-confident young American looked at European customs and thought of them with distaste—especially those in Central and Eastern Europe. In the aftermath of the terrible carnage of the war, he magnified the errors of the newly established independent nations and compared them with the prosperous and secure American homeland—a comparison which could only be negative for the Europeans. If someone came from this region, and the person was also a Jew, NR regarded them with distaste and suspicion. There was one thing that could make such a combination even worse: the communist ideology.

In the wake of the Russian Bolshevik Revolution, the fear of social upheaval was palpable in the Western world. Clearly, one of the most defining issues in the immediate postwar worldview in the West in general, and in the United States in particular, was the fear of bolshevism and the panic that it might spread there from the East. The antagonism between the two nations was not new. In 1837, for instance, a German-born American journalist wrote: "Russia is the evil genius of history; while America is its guardian angel. The power of Russia is opposed to the interests of humanity; that of the United States is based on wisdom and justice. [...] The power of Russia rests on bayonets; that of America on the superiority of mind over brute force. They are to each other as darkness to light. [...] The day of battle must come; the war of principles must ensue."[105] Toward the end of the nineteenth century this example saw print: "At heart the Russian is still more Asiatic than European. We call him Christian; but his religion is a mingling of superstition and fanaticism less attractive, and certainly less conducive to morality, than the religion of the Bedouins."[106]

So, when the Bolshevik revolution took place and started to show increasing antagonism toward western and, especially, American thinking, not much was needed for a crusade-like atmosphere to gather that was an amalgam of righteousness and fear. As Hoover put it, after the war was over:

---

[104] Diary entry of January 29, 1919, ibid., 109–10.
[105] Francis J. Grund, *The Americans, in Their Moral, Social, and Political Relations* (Boston: Marsh, Capen & Lyon, 1837), 392–93, quoted in C. Vann Woodward, *The Old World's New World*, New York: Oxford University Press, 1991, 88.
[106] William R. Thayer, "The Armed Truce of the Powers." *The Forum* 12 (Nov. 1891): 322.

There began to loom up a greater fear from a more potent enemy of freedom than anarchy, which after all is an unorganized force. Communism, which had captured Russia, was a new form of organized destruction of Liberty. And it was vengeance itself. The Communists had captured the Czarist gold reserves. Their agents spread over Europe, subsidizing a new revolution. Soon we began to realize that its infectious poison was spreading alarmingly among all starving peoples. Here loomed up a defeat of all we had fought for—to establish liberty.[107]

To Robert Lansing, the American secretary of state, bolshevism was "the most hideous and monstrous thing the human mind has ever conceived."[108] Many agreed with the conclusion of a U.S. Senate subcommittee's paper that declared: "The activities of the Bolsheviki constitute a complete repudiation of modern civilization."[109]

Since during the war quite a few Jewish-born immigrants, who were also revolutionary, protested against the war, and wanted the United States to withdraw from it, their actions only strengthened the anti-immigrant, anti-Semitic, and anti-Bolshevist sentiments already widespread in the United States—and NR was no exception. He opined:

Bolshevism as such, and communism in particular thrive first among the most ignorant and historically oppressed nations. Next, it benefits only those who have nothing, and ruins those who have even a little bit. And finally it works against the interests of all small shop-keepers and all farmers. It is so unsound economically that it cannot possibly live. Some good will come of it, I am sure. For there are much needed social reform. But much harm will come through this terrible destructive powers.[110]

The events unfolding in Russia proved to the American elite and a large portion of the citizens that Bolshevism was a twisted ideology where a minority tyrannically ruled over the majority, therefore they were anti-democratic, they wanted to do away with private property, pushed back religion, and had a vision of a revolutionary wave engulfing the globe—basically denying everything the United States stood

---

[107] Hoover, *The Memoirs of Herbert Hoover*, vol. 1, 283.
[108] Quoted in Michael H. Hunt, *Ideology and U.S. Foreign Policy* (New Haven and London, Yale University Press, 1987), 115.
[109] Ibid.
[110] Diary entry of April 25, 1919, Nicholas Roosevelt, *A History of a Few Weeks*, 431.

for. When he came face to face with revolutionary stirrings in Central Europe, NR declared,

> It isn't Bolshevism—these people aren't Bolshevists—it is merely the work of a few unscrupulous Hungarian and Russian Jews, working with a few scoundrelly [sic] Austrian Jews, and playing on the feelings of a hungry mob to ride into power themselves. The more I have seen of this movement, the wider I have gotten against the Jews. For clever as they are, it is they who are at the basis of this revolutionary movement throughout Europe.[111]

It has to be emphasized that, stemming from his liberal worldview, NR also recognized and conceded that some sort of social changes must take place, which would not necessarily be harmful. But he clearly could not overcome his prejudices. When he spent two days in Budapest before the Bolshevik seizure of power, a city where the communist takeover had been expected by some, Walter Davis of the Coolidge Mission commented wryly: "Today proved a disappointment. There was no Bolshevik revolution, no massacre of Christians."[112]

NR sometimes gave a detailed account of his talks with various newspaper editors in Vienna. The future journalist sought out these contacts for information as to the Austrian and more particularly the Viennese situation as these persons saw it. What he gleaned from Friedrich Austerlitz, Ernst Martin Benedikt, or Friedrich Funder, for example, was put down in the diary entries, and the questions and answers he included gave a nice summary of the difficulties that the new republic faced in the first few months of 1919. In addition to their predictions concerning the upcoming parliamentary elections, the leftist Austerlitz, for example, also said to NR that there was no Bolshevik danger in Austria, but the food shortage might lead to violent scenes. Benedikt, for his part, predicted the future Anschluss, and declared that only a Germany strengthened by the United States could stem the Bolshevik tide coming from the east. And from the Christian Socialist, Funder, NR learned that in the Austrian's view a new Austro-Hungarian Monarchy or a similar constellation might be created in the postwar era.

NR more often than not saw situations from a perspective that has been vindicated by history, and he appreciated some elements that others may have ignored. He and other members of the Coolidge Mission agreed that the various countries of

---

[111] Diary entry of April 21, 1919, ibid., 423.
[112] Dairy entry, February 2, 1919, Walter G. Davis Diary, Box 1, Folder 16, Walter Goodwin Davis Papers.

war-torn Europe looked to the United States as the possible redeemer, whether the issue was economic, financial, or political in nature. Storey, for instance, wrote that almost all of the European continent was "looking to America as a composite savior, guardian angel, boundary commission, and food supply."[113] In the defeated capitals of Central Europe, Americans were even more welcome. As Davis noted upon the Mission's arrival in Austria, "Everyone to whom we have talked says emphatically that American officers are a welcome sight. They would be better pleased if we were accompanied by occupying troops."[114] NR also perceived accurately that all countries and nations in the region were expecting help from the United States. "Everyone," he wrote, "no matter of what former persuasion or nationality, looks to America—Huns as well as Czechs; Slovaks as well as Slovenes; Austrians as well as Serbo-Croates; Roumanians [sic] as well as Ukrainians. America is apparently the referee in this big game, from their point of view."[115]

NR found it astounding, but had to accept the fact that since the United State could affect the outcome of the Paris Peace Conference, people saw political capital in Americans even if they served in minor ranks and only did information gathering in Central Europe. As in Vienna, in Budapest, too, "no amount of persuasion could convince the Hungarians that our mission was not political and did not carry great weight in Paris."[116] Given his analysis that the Hungarian Soviet Republic was basically a national unity for self-preservation that tolerated even Bolshevist leadership in order to keep the country intact, which also reflected well on what had taken place, NR noted accordingly: "The Hungarians are united in their conviction that Hungary must not be dismembered, have made use of Bolshevism as a last desperate resort to preserve the integrity of their country, and have openly defied the Allies, and set a precedent for Germany to follow."[117]

At the same time, NR soberly sized up the relationship among the various ethnic groups in the region, and what the American decision makers in the realm of diplomacy thought about it in the larger sense: "The violence of racial jealousy among the Eastern European peoples, is inconceivable to the more staid Anglo-Saxon mind. And the very strength of this feeling is a factor which our theorists on League of Nations ignore or deny. Yet it is a fact, an ever present fact; and failure to recognize

---

[113] Diary entry, November 26, 1918, Charles Moorfield Storey Journal.
[114] Diary entry, January 5, 1919, Davis Diary.
[115] Diary entry of April 21, 1919, Nicholas Roosevelt, *A History of a Few Weeks*, 152.
[116] Ibid., 229.
[117] "The Hungarian Revolution," Nicholas Roosevelt's report to the American Delegation at the Paris Peace Conference, March 26, 1919, in ibid., 367.

it shows a deplorable ignorance."[118] But in order to achieve a more just and lasting peace, NR believed the United States ought to have pursued a more active and courageous path. Well before the German peace treaty was in its final form, he clearly saw that it would end in failure, which would be connected to American amateurishness and indolence. If, he wrote, "we continue our inglorious meddling with international affairs, looked up to as The Hope of the Nations that are down, and as the ideal of disinterested and efficient action; whereas by our inaction we shall soon disappoint everyone and receive the just odium for the disaster to which we have so largely contributed."[119] From this opinion, it was a logical step to criticism of Woodrow Wilson, and this stemmed not only from party and political differences.

The author of the Fourteen Points loomed large on everybody's mind in those months, and victors and defeated parties alike hoped for salvation from their own interpretation of Wilson's peace agenda. This was a major problem: different countries understood in different lights what Wilson chose to say; their interpretation naturally favored their own cause. The Fourteen Points were so universal and so idealistic that they were unavoidably to create controversy and clearly could not satisfy all sides. The hub of the Fourteen Points was national self-determination, the lofty ideals of which were impossible to live up to, and consequently achieving justice among the existing ethnic conditions in Central Europe was unmanageable. Secretary of State Lansing was convinced "of the danger of putting such ideas into the minds of certain races. It is bound to be the basis of impossible demands on the Peace Congress and create trouble in many lands."[120] He found the phrase self-determination to be "loaded with dynamite" that would only raise hopes in vain and finally would be "discredited, to be called the dream of an idealist who failed to realize the danger until too late to check those who attempt to put the principle in force."[121] For his part, Storey only referred to the infeasibility of the principle while he was in Transylvania, where one purely Romanian village was followed by an adjacent, similarly pure Hungarian settlement, but he nonetheless criticized Wilson for his veneer of idealism that tried to conceal hard truths. The president, he said, "comes to the Conference, unprepared, and undismayed—Sir Galahad from the West with a wooden sword to carve the casques of some of the hardest-headed individuals in Europe today."[122]

---

[118] Nicholas Roosevelt, *A History of a Few Weeks*, 271.
[119] Diary entry of April 7, 1919, ibid., 410.
[120] Diary entry, December 30, 1918, In Robert Lansing, *The Peace Negotiations: A Personal Narrative* (New York: Houghton Mifflin, 1921), 97.
[121] Ibid., 97–98.
[122] Dairy entry, December 14, 1918, Storey Journal.

NR was once again more sharp-tongued than his fellow members on the Mission when it came to condemning Wilson. He was convinced that Wilson chose to use rhetorical sorcery where gaping wounds needed surgery, causing far more lasting damage in the long run. He accused the president of undue and exorbitant optimism, saying that he opted for "a well-worded, moralistic rhetorical sentence" instead of practical foreign policy. From NR's perspective, such rhetoric, and he mainly had Wilson's Fourteen Points in mind, would give the false impression that "this verbal patent medicine will purge Europe of her ills overnight, and introduce the reign of brotherly love."[123]

A further feature in the diary entries is NR's humor. It was the inheritance of his Anglo-Saxon tradition, that is, in the satirical vein of making especially witty comments to the detriment of others, which was typical of aristocrats and the elite throughout the nineteenth century.[124] He shunned diplomatic language and used wry, sometimes acrimonious humor in his summaries of events. For example, he regularly made notes about the operas he attended. On one occasion he became quite irritated over the performance of Erik Schmedes, the leading tenor of the Vienna State Opera at that time. "Unfortunately, they had Schmedes, who, as usual, sang perfectly vilely and received great ovations because he was famous as a singer before Franz Joseph came to the throne, and had sung in operas directed personally by Mozart, Beethoven and Wagner."[125]

Regarding serious issues, NR saw his country as a hapless amateur at the international podium of diplomacy:

> We are children—mere children—and fifty years from now we may have learned. Our present heads love to swim in a sea of non-policy, which they variously camouflage under the titles 'Watchful Waiting, Peace without Victory,' etc., with the result that we are losing our position, and losing our prestige, and losing out opportunities to lead ... If only we would decide something, even though the decision be purely negative, it would be better.[126]

But he also realistically saw what the future held for the United States:

---

[123] Diary entry without date, but it is from late March 1919, Nicholas Roosevelt, *A History of a Few Weeks*, 383.

[124] Rod A. Martin and Thomas E. Ford, *The Psychology of Humor: An Integrative Approach*, 2nd edition. (Cambridge, MA.: Academic Press, 2018), 22.

[125] Diary entry of May 23, 1919, Nicholas Roosevelt, *A History of a Few Weeks*, 483.

[126] Nicholas Roosevelt, *A History of a Few Weeks*, 407–8.

That we are horribly in the wrong, I realize only too well; and that we have once more failed to seize the chance of centuries—this chance offered us for the second time—and have instead talked the world out of a victorious Peace into imminent anarchy, is only too apparent. And yet, in spite of this, and in spite of our bunglers, we have had thrust upon us the role that England has played these last few centuries. Despite the best efforts of our least capable men, with their pin-head vision and their capacity for doing the wrong thing, we shall emerge the greatest force the world, and shall probably continue the Anglo-Saxon tradition of bludering [sic] into good fortune, and acquiring glory by accident. [127] [...] As far as the French are concerned, I have never changed my original idea of years ago, that win or lose they are done for as being a real factor is concerned [128]

"Things are coming to an inglorious pass, and I am merely living for the day when I can clear out of my present connection forever," NR noted in his dairy toward the end of April as he grew more restless to get away from Vienna.[129] But he had to stay until the end, since Coolidge saw him as a deputy of sorts. And when he was honest with himself, he appreciated being in the whirlpool of history: "We are in all ways getting a living experience of history which will give us an insight in reading history such as few persons possess."[130]

On May 19, the telegram from Paris finally arrived declaring that the mission should be closed down and everybody should return to Paris soon. A few days later and after farewell rounds in Vienna, NR's route took him through Venice and Milan and on to the French capital, where he arrived on May 29. After cutting through the bureaucratic fog and receiving his dismissal papers, he sailed home for the United States with his own 322nd Regiment on June 2, 1919.[131] As the Coolidge Mission expired, a letter from Allen Dulles must have been reassuring and pleasing to NR's ego: "As one of the men on this end of the Austria-Hungary wire, I want personally to tell you how helpful your work was. You may be assured that it was fully understood and appreciated by all who had anything to do with the field which you were helping to cover."[132]

---

[127] Ibid., 409–10.
[128] Ibid., 408.
[129] Diary entry of April 21, 1919, Nicholas Roosevelt, *A History of a Few Weeks*, 422.
[130] Diary entry of May 4, 1919, Ibid., 443.
[131] Special Orders, no. 151, May 31, 1919, Orders, Box 1, Nicholas Roosevelt Papers.
[132] Allen W. Dulles to Nicholas Roosevelt, May 31, 1919, Folder 13, Roosevelt, Nicholas, 1919, Allen W. Dulles Papers.

In *A Front Row Seat*, his sanitized 1953 version of the original diaries, NR summarizes his 1919 material in about thirty pages, only 11–12 percent of the length of the original material. Also, the 1953 version is outstandingly diplomatic in its language. This change must have been due to NR himself, who, together with the world around him, had changed in many respects in the intervening three decades. The original manuscript opens a private window on the events unfolding around the author in 1919; in the 1953 memoirs, however, a curtain rolls down on that private window, and the author wanted to highlight those Americans who were or had become famous: Archibald Coolidge, Allen Dulles, Herbert Hoover. In addition, he also felt that his conversation with Franz Lehár and the latter's younger brother would be of more interest to American readers than dialogues with Hungarian revolutionary or counterrevolutionary figures—probably he was right in this assessment. But precisely his meetings with Mihály Károlyi, Pál Teleki, or Albert Apponyi, and his diary entries about them are what make the original manuscript so valuable.

NR's chronicling of events and persons connected to the emerging new world order in defeated Central Europe adds to and nuances our knowledge about the period in general and the persons and events in Vienna and Budapest in particular. The diary bolsters the false image of the United States as the hope, the honest broker, and the possible savior of these peoples. In addition, the manuscript sheds light on the daily chores of the American fact-finding missions sent to the various postwar countries in Europe. Also, the diary notes offer a closer understanding (although filtered through only one individual) of the "American view" of the era: the importance of democracy, the perceived immaculate state of the United States as compared to Europe, but also the foreign policy inexperience that comes with that status, American cultural superiority, anti-Semitism, anti-Bolshevism, etc. It cannot be taken as an overall description of Americans' thinking and worldview in 1919, but aside from NR's idiosyncrasies, the text provides a fair understanding of a rather typical American approach to the postwar European chaos and the position of Central Europe in it.

There is no evidence to explain why the original manuscript did not appear in print. One plausible and apparent reason is that the narrative and diary entries of an infantry captain were not deemed all that interesting, especially when other works were coming out that dealt with the Peace Conference, and on account of the sometimes-well-known authors' names, those books were to enjoy greater interest and a larger readership.[133] At the same time, one cannot exclude the possibility

---

[133] In 1919 and 1920 various books were published reflecting on the Paris Peace Conference, which later were followed by others: Ray Stannard Baker, *What Wilson Did at Paris* (New York, 1919); Sisley Huddleston, *Peace-making at Paris* (London, 1919); John Maynard Keynes, *The Economic Consequences*

that since the manuscript was really a side-story to the dramatic events at Paris, publishers felt— and in all likelihood they were right—that the American reading public would not be interested in a complicated story of Central Europe, which was largely unknown territory to the average American. Another possibility is that NR changed his mind in the meantime, and this may have happened for various reasons as well. One of them is that the outcome of the Peace Conference and the spectacular American turnaround concerning Europe in its wake had a profound effect on NR, and he may have thought that the text was often too critical, at places clearly offending certain persons. This may also have been the very reason publishers refused the manuscript. Almost everybody mentioned in the material was still alive in 1953, many of them prominent figures; and aside from ethnicity and race, NR gave no quarter in his judgments—regardless of whether the person was American or European, a lower ranked man or a high-status official. Publishers may not have wanted to carry the burden and invite attacks if they printed the original text. In any event, the material was not published, and NR had to find a new occupation as the 1920s began.

---

of the Peace (London, 1919); Vernon Bartlett, *Behind the Scenes at the Peace Conference* (London, 1920); Bernard M. Baruch, *The Making of the Reparation and Economic Sections of the Treaty* (New York, 1920); Henry Wilson Harris, *Peace in the Making* (London, 1920); Charles Homer Haskins and Robert Howard Lord, *Some Problems of the Peace Conference* (Cambridge, MA, 1920); Charles T. Thompson, *The Peace Conference Day by Day* (New York, 1920).

Chapter 3
The Making of a Journalist and Author

After being away for the better part of five years, Nicholas Roosevelt returned to the United States. The diplomatic service was too expensive and had turned out to be fraught with disappointment, therefore he needed to find another outlet for his tangible ambition. He took an interim political detour as secretary and aide to General Leonard Wood in an unsuccessful campaign to win the Republican nomination for the 1920 elections. The experience was both "illuminating and disillusioning," and if anything, it steered NR out of everyday politics into the role of an observer and commentator instead.[134] Since he had a way with words and an opinion on almost everything, journalism was an obvious option for the still young man. This career started in earnest in 1921, although his first article had appeared in 1918 in the *New York Tribune*, and from 1921 he worked for this paper as an editorial writer. In addition, he was also a special correspondent to such European papers as the Vienna *Neue Presse*, *Le Temps* of Paris, or *De Haagse Post* of Holland.[135] His first serious assignment came when he was detailed to cover the Washington Naval Conference, 1921–22.[136]

This Naval Conference was a momentous post-World War I diplomatic affair. The world's preeminent naval powers gathered in the U.S. capitol in order to find a path to disarmament measures that could help to ease existing and possible future tensions, mainly in the Far East. The Conference was led by its host, Secretary of State Charles Evans Hughes, who had the delicate task to achieve an understanding that would ensure peace for at least the near future. The Conference, which lasted

---

[134] Nicholas Roosevelt, *A Front Row Seat*, 125.
[135] Biographical Sketch about Nicholas Roosevelt (without date), Box 64, Appointment as Minister to Hungary, Nicholas Roosevelt Papers; Nicholas Roosevelt, *A Front Row Seat*, 132–33.
[136] Nicholas Roosevelt, *A Front Row Seat*, 133–39.

almost three months, produced three treaties: the Five-Power Treaty, the Four-Power Treaty, and the Nine-Power Treaty. The first and most significant one set a ratio of warship tonnage among the signatories: 500,000 tons each for the United States and Great Britain, 300,000 tons for Japan, while France and Italy were allowed 175,000 tons each. Also, the five nations were to stop building capital warships and start scrapping older ones, thus reducing the size of their respective fleets. However, since other categories were not included in the limitation, a new competition began right away in other warship classes. The Four-Power Treaty declared that the United States, Great Britain, France, and Japan would consult each other before taking any action in case of a future crisis in the Far East. The Nine-Power Treaty made sure that the Open Door Policy acclaimed some twenty years earlier by Secretary of State John Hay would continue: all foreign countries would enjoy equal commercial opportunities, while the territorial integrity of China would be maintained.[137]

In retrospect it was easy to give low marks for American diplomacy at the time, and NR's observation made in the early 1950s well describes the general thinking in the wake of World War I: "Most American observers—myself included—failed to see that America's vital interests in Asia, *ipso facto*, gave it vital interests in Europe. We were thinking regionally instead of globally."[138] Indeed, the overall majority in American public discourse and even among the decision makers was in favor of keeping out of any possible trouble either in Europe or in the Pacific. The peace narrative that characterized the American political landscape in the 1920s and 1930s inevitably brought on short-term thinking and temporary goals in the field of diplomacy. Because the Washington Naval Conference left so many questions up in the air, first the Geneva Naval Conference in 1927, then the London Naval Conference in 1930 were convened. They, however, also failed to ensure a more peaceful world, and from 1931 on, starting with the Japanese invasion of Manchuria, it became a bitter fact that international treaties were really worth very little.

---

[137] For the Washington Naval Conference history see, Norman Gibbs, "The Naval Conferences of the Interwar Years: A study in Anglo-American Relations," *Naval War College Review* 30, no. 1 (Special issue, Summer 1977): 50–52; Erik Goldstein and John H. Maurer, eds., *The Washington Conference, 1921–22: Naval Rivalry, East Asian Stability and the Road to Pearl Harbor* (London and New York: Routledge, 1994); Richard W. Fanning, *Peace and Disarmament: Naval Rivalry & Arms Control, 1922–1933* (Lexington, KY: The University Press of Kentucky, 1995), 3–16; Phillips Payson O'Brien, *British and American Naval Power: Politics and Policy, 1900–1936*, Praeger Studies in Diplomacy and Strategic Thought (Westport, CT, London: Praeger, 1998), 149–78; Margot Louria, *Triumph and Downfall: America's Pursuit of Peace and Prosperity, 1921–1933* (Westport, CT, London: Greenwood Press, 2001), 37–63; Bruce A. Elleman, *International Competition in China, 1899–1991: The Rise, Fall, and Restoration of the Open Door Policy* (London and New York: Routledge, 2015), 73–86.

[138] Nicholas Roosevelt, *A Front Row Seat*, 138.

In any case, with the Washington Conference NR gained another glimpse into the big game of international diplomacy, which served him well later on. Thanks to his web of European connections, an impressive last name, and his budding talent as a journalist, his career picked up. In 1923 he switched to the *New York Times*, where his experience in the foreign field was put to use. In the winter of 1923 the *Times* sent him to Europe as a special editorial correspondent. His assignment was to study the economic conditions in Germany and its neighbors.

French and Belgian troops occupied the Ruhr Valley on January 11, 1923, the reason being Germany defaulting on its reparation payments, and this deteriorated an already precarious situation. This region was the industrial heart of Germany, therefore crucial to production and the capability to pay the heavy reparations under the Versailles Peace Treaty. The Germans in response began a long and passive resistance that led to the collapse of the Reichsmark, the German currency. The situation was not conducive to trade and cooperation, and therefore, as the financial centers of the world the American and the British governments pushed France hard to devise a workable scenario.[139]

As the *New York Times* foreign correspondent, NR travelled around Central Europe and sent a flurry of articles back to the United States at the very end of 1923 and the beginning of 1924. The tour itself lasted one and a half months, from November 20 until January 5, and he arrived back in New York on January 13. In order to facilitate his reporting, he carried with him in Europe letters of introduction from such prominent people as Adolph Ochs, owner of the *New York Times*, Senator Henry Cabot Lodge, Archibald C. Coolidge, and Secretary of Commerce Herbert Hoover, the latter asking the commercial attachés and trade commissioners in Europe to help Roosevelt. In addition, the local *New York Times* correspondents paved the way for him to meet with people who could provide information on the issues he wanted to write about. He visited France, the Netherlands, Germany, Czechoslovakia, Austria, Switzerland (where he could watch a League of Nations Council meeting in session), Belgium, and England. His first impression of Germany was that "outwardly all is quiet and natural. But one sees that politically they are shot to pieces, and that socially their troubles will increase on account of the impossible currency situation."[140]

---

[139] For a detailed discussion of the Ruhr occupation, see, Conan Fischer, *The Ruhr Crisis, 1923–1924* (Oxford: Oxford University Press, 2003).

[140] Nicholas Roosevelt to Ogden Mills Reid, November 26, 1923, Folder 7: Nicholas Roosevelt (1922–1933), Box 34, Adolph S. Ochs Papers, New York Times Company Records, New York, U.S.A.

During his travels he managed to talk to, among others, the American ambassadors and other Americans serving in these European cities (consuls, commercial and naval attachés), to people at the foreign offices and Ministries of Finance, such as Hjalmar Schacht in Berlin or Edvard Beneš in Prague, League officials in Vienna, foreign diplomats serving in these countries, people of various shades of political outlook, economists, bankers, and, naturally, editors of prestigious local newspapers in every city he visited. His opinion regarding this fresh experience was that despite what various Europeans coming to Washington might have said about America's responsibility to save Europe, "there was no Europe, but only a group of nations with utterly conflicting interests and policies. Europe as a matter of fact, did not exist."[141] This view only strengthened his already solid conviction that the United States must stay away from Europe, where in "each country which I visited at least one person pulled me aside to tell me of the horrible iniquities of the people of the neighboring countries. In fact, as far as I could see, they spent all their time damning their neighbors."[142] This meant only enmity and instability, not a Wilsonian utopia.

As the professional result of his tour, he had six articles published in fewer than three weeks. He wrote a summary of the year-old occupation of the Ruhr region, and he analyzed French intentions concerning primarily security. He clearly saw that the occupation of the Ruhr was to make the Germans understand that they had lost the war and must pay reparations to the French.[143] NR also dealt with Belgium's situation, a country in need of having German exports go through it and on to the larger world, but also of reparations coming from the Germans. It was also a country that was afraid of what Germany might do in the future. Therefore, Belgium tried to find the golden mean: trade and reparations—both in a limited amount but at least something tangible.[144]

As for Germany, NR concluded that they had not accepted defeat and tried to find the blame in others, mainly in Wilson and the French. But the "great tragedy in Germany" was "the annihilation of the middle classes," which had been the backbone of the spectacular development prior to the war.[145] The successful League-orchestrated financial reconstruction that had been launched in Austria in 1922 was, however, a good sign for Germany that there was a possible way out of its

---

[141] December 4, 1923, European trip 1923–1924, Box 21, Nicholas Roosevelt Papers.
[142] December 21, ibid.
[143] Nicholas Roosevelt, "Fear of Germany Dominates France," *New York Times*, January 12, 1924.
[144] Nicholas Roosevelt, "Belgium Chooses a Middle Course," *New York Times*, January 14, 1924.
[145] Nicholas Roosevelt, "Germany Pleads Injured Innocence," *New York Times*, January 13, 1924.

calamity, and this became reality in the form of the Dawes Plan.¹⁴⁶ NR also studied the other small neighboring nations and what they thought about the Ruhr occupation. He found that the Dutch were not happy with the occupation because it hurt their economy, and they were also afraid of a possible French hegemony in the area. The Swiss likewise looked askance at the Ruhr occupation. The Czechs, like the Belgians, wanted Germany to pay, but, at the same time, they wanted to make sure Germany could pose no menace to Europe in the future. Again, some middle way had to be found between money and security.¹⁴⁷ Later on, NR summarized his experience with the Ruhr occupation in an article for *Foreign Affairs*, in which he gave a succinct description of the history of the occupation and concluded that the occupation largely worked as a diplomatic weapon.¹⁴⁸

His reporting appeared in other outlets as well during these years. One such occasion was the launch of the Dawes Plan in the fall of 1924. This was to resolve the German reparation question, reach a settlement, and smooth ruffled feathers, especially between the French and the Germans. Although the American government did not take part officially in drawing up the plan, and therefore in the German reconstruction, American experts still played a crucial role. The plan was named after Charles Gates Dawes, one of the two American members on the committee (the other was Owen D. Young). The plan also built on the previously-launched Austrian and Hungarian reconstruction schemes orchestrated by the League of Nations. While in these latter undertakings the United States played an unexceptional role, this time the stakes were much higher.

Americans judged Europe simply through the prism of Germany. To the east, it was essential to have stable governments so the Bolshevik ideology could not spread westward and fester within the new states; to the west, the task was to ensure that Germany would be able to climb back to join the community of strong and prosperous states. If Germany were made safe and stable, so would the rest of Europe be, argued Americans; and President Calvin Coolidge admitted that much: "I trust that private American capital will be willing to participate in advancing this loan. […] We have determined to maintain, and can maintain, our own political independence, but our economic independence will be strengthened and increased when the economic stability of Europe is restored."¹⁴⁹ Secretary of State Hughes echoed

---

146 Nicholas Roosevelt, "Austria's Recovery Spurs German Hope," *New York Times*, January 15, 1924.
147 Nicholas Roosevelt, "How Small Nations View the Situation," *New York Times*, January 16, 1924.
148 Nicholas Roosevelt, "The Ruhr Occupation," *Foreign Affairs* 4, no. 1 (Oct. 1925): 112–22.
149 Speech delivered by Coolidge on April 22, 1924, at the Annual Luncheon of the Associated Press in New York, in Hughes to Herrick, April 23, 1924, *FRU.S.*: 1924, vol. 2, 14.

this sentiment in the summer: "You may count upon our interest and assistance in the necessary measures to assure the economic rehabilitation of Europe. It does not matter that this aid is not given by the government [...] we believe that the Dawes plan opens up the path of confidence and prosperity. For that reason, we are deeply interested in its prompt execution."[150] Therefore, the lines were blurry as to the U.S. government's role and that of private Americans taking part in the rehabilitation of Germany and Europe—this was the basic American foreign policy recipe in the 1920s.

France balked first, so it was blackmailed into accepting the Dawes Plan.[151] J. P. Morgan bank's partners used scathing rhetoric when they put the question to France whether they wanted "a rehabilitated Germany" together with American money, or "a broken Germany and what has been called 'security.'"[152] In addition to the financial aspect, soon politically sensitive breakthroughs were achieved. For example, in 1925 England, France, Italy, and Germany signed the Treaties of Locarno, which finally established the permanent western borders of Germany and began the withdrawal of occupation forces along the Rhine. Although a success on the surface, what basically happened was that during the Dawes Plan American capital was pumped into Germany, which was used to pay for reparations. On the other hand, mainly American loans were typically used for non-productive purposes, and this foreshadowed what would happen if the capital stopped coming, which happened toward the end of the decade, and the German payments indeed ceased. At the launch of the Dawes Plan, NR wrote in *The Outlook* a somewhat philosophical argument about war and peace, and why there was not really peace in Europe. He blamed Germany mainly, which was evading most of the penalties in order to remedy them later. He astutely predicted that Germany would "use every opportunity to undermine the Versailles Treaty."[153]

---

[150] Hughes' speech at the Pilgrims' Dinner in London, July 21, 1924, quoted in Hughes, *The Pathway of Peace*, 108.

[151] In more detail, see, Stephen V. O. Clarke, *Central Bank Cooperation: 1924–1931* (New York: Federal Reserve Bank of New York, 1967), 68; Edward M. Lamont, *The Ambassador from Wall Street: The Story of Thomas W. Lamont, J. P. Morgan's Chief Executive* (Lanham, MD: Madison Books, 1994), 203; Sally Marks, "The Myths of Reparations," *Central European History* 11, no. 3 (Sep. 1978): 248–49.

[152] Quoted in Costigliola, *Awkward Dominion*, 122. For more detail on the Dawes Plan, see, Harold G. Moulton, *The Reparation Plan* (New York: McGraw-Hill Book Company, 1924); Stephen A. Schuker, *The End of French Predominance in Europe: The Financial Crisis of 1924 and the Adoption of the Dawes Plan* (Chapel Hill, NC: University of North Carolina Press, 1976), 171–382; Ahamed, *Lords of Finance*, 197–216.

[153] Nicholas Roosevelt, "When There Is No Peace," *The Outlook*, November 5, 1924, 370.

When NR analyzed the relationship of the United States government and the League of Nations, he concluded that in the next few years Washington would lead a policy of "co-operation without commitments, of independence without isolation."[154] He argued that the term "isolation" could be applied only if possible American membership were investigated, otherwise America would look after only its interests in Europe and would be active if needed. Indeed, the United States very much wanted to remain on the sidelines regarding Europe, and the government continuously made clear that it would have no official relationship with the League of Nations. However, in the financial sphere, starting with the Dawes Plan, the private banks became notably active until the end of the decade. The emphasis is on the unofficial nature, because Washington closely watched whatever unfolded among the ranks of the League at Geneva. As proof, an unofficial American representative was appointed to the League's Reparations Commission accompanied by a small delegation so that the American government would be informed about everything related to the thorny issue of reparations. Secretary of State Hughes defined the status of the various Americans delegated to the League of Nations as "official representatives acting in an unofficial capacity."[155] The American ambassador to Switzerland was also entrusted with the task of collecting material on and about the League and maintaining the best possible relations with other countries' League representatives, but he was to carry out such a task in the most concealed way.[156]

The United States was also implicated in the issues of the Far East, to which the Washington Naval Conference bore witness. Here the main issues were possible Japanese moves on the one hand and American interests in the Philippines and China on the other. After the Spanish American War of 1898, the United States took control of the Philippines (after a bloody war against the native insurgents), which archipelago was seen as a stepping stone to China. In China, Secretary of State John Hay's famous letters in 1899 and 1900 launched the Open Door Policy, which declared that equal commercial opportunity should be provided for the powers present and the territorial integrity of China must be preserved. Therefore, for the next half century these two countries meant the pivot of the United States' Asian policy. While China stood in the constant shadow of Japanese aggression, the more everyday concern for Washington was to transform the Philippines into

---

[154] Nicholas Roosevelt, "America and the League," *Review of Reviews*, March 14, 1925, 130.
[155] Clarence A. Berdahl, "The United States and the League of Nations," *Michigan Law Review* 27, no. 6 (April 1929): 629.
[156] Waldo H. Heinrichs, *American Ambassador: Joseph C. Grew and the Development of the United States Diplomatic Tradition* (Boston and Toronto: Little Brown and Company, 1966), 52–53.

a working democracy. The idea was that by introducing American-type democracy and investing in the archipelago's infrastructure, the locals would embrace American values and become "civilized," thereby adding to American security in the Far East. However, the slow and inadequate progress in addition to the fervent independence movement on the islands gave a constant headache to the American political leadership as to what to do with the Filipinos. This was an early example of faulty American foreign policy: Washington falsely believed that these distant peoples would be happy to be under "superior" American tutelage and concepts of civilization. Therefore, despite its obvious strategic importance to the United States, the Philippines proved to be more of a liability than an asset.

The *New York Times* sent NR to this geographical area in 1925 and 1926, which opened new avenues for him. The months-long journey included China, the Dutch East Indies, Japan, and, naturally, the most important stop, the Philippines. His work was largely augmented by the fact that, in addition to his family name, which opened a lot of doors, General Leonard Wood was the Governor General of the archipelago. The very man for whom, in 1920, NR had acted as a secretary and aide when the General attempted in vain to secure the Republican Party nomination for president. They had remained on good terms.[157]

The Philippines had always been a thorny problem for Washington. After securing military victory over the Filipino freedom fighters in 1902, the Americans set up their own system with the backing of a narrow elite of island dwellers. In many ways it was an imperialist undertaking, but in the spirit of missionary zeal of uplifting lesser nations the U.S. government also wanted to help the native population to reach a higher standard of living and take on many American values. The American point of view was that with time independence should be given back to the Filipinos—but only when they had mastered the ways of self-government and democracy. When the Jones Act (Philippine Autonomy Act) was passed in 1916, the Filipinos started to enjoy various powers regarding their domestic affairs, and it was reiterated that as soon as they had a stable government, the United States would indeed withdraw its control and leave the Filipinos to their own devices. With the Republican ascendancy in the beginning of the 1920s, General Leonard Wood was named Governor General; he had a complicated relationship with the local leaders.

His visit to the islands led NR to another decades-long though intermittent phase in his life. He began writing books, and being an author was the profession that made him proudest. NR was convinced that he had gathered enough expertise

---

[157] On his Far East tour, see, Nicholas Roosevelt, *A Front Row Seat*, 140–60, 163–83.

on foreign policy while in Europe, and that he was a good enough writer to author a book. The situation in the Philippines and the enlarged perimeter that included the whole of the Far East were strategically important to the United States, so many people had dealt with the topic. NR's first book, *The Philippines: A Treasure and a Problem*, joined this debate. It appeared in the fall of 1926.

The sentiment of the whole book was one of American superiority. The text was condescending toward the Filipino people and saturated with a firm belief in Social Darwinism, that is, that among nations as in the animal kingdom the same laws prevail: the survival of the fittest. As a consequence, the conviction was that the most developed and advanced nations had an inherent right to meddle with weaker countries' internal affairs and spread their own culture and dominance in those places. Darwin himself laid down the premise when he wrote: "There is apparently much truth in the belief that the wonderful progress of the United States, as well as the character of the people, is the results of natural selection."[158] John W. Burgess, a prominent professor at the time, declared that the Teutonic nations must be seen "as the political nations par excellence, and [this will] authorize them, in the economy of the world to assume the leadership in the establishment and administration of states."[159] This aggressive belief about the superiority of the Anglo-Saxon nations met with the duty that it entailed: "Indifference on the part of Teutonic states to the political civilization of the rest of the world is, then, not only mistaken policy, but disregard of duty and mistaken policy because disregard of duty."[160] NR's book wished to give an analysis and proof of this thesis, and he used Rudyard Kipling's famous poem "The White Man's Burden" as a tool. At the beginning of every chapter, he quoted a few lines from the poem to introduce and underpin the chapter at hand.

On the one hand, he called the Filipinos "spoiled children" who were ungrateful for the many things given to them by the United States.[161] According to this paternalistic view, he thought that the islanders wasted money, lived in corruption, only made use of the American presence, and wanted to enjoy the umbrella of security provided by Washington while not living up to a higher standard of civilization on the archipelago. Their political traditions, NR felt, were not conducive to American-style democracy, since they tended toward a "despotic form

---

[158] Charles Darwin, *The Descent of Man, and Selection in Relation to Sex* (London: John Murray, 1882), 142.
[159] John W. Burgess, *Political Science and Comparative Constitutional Law* (Boston: Ginn & Company, 1890), 39.
[160] Ibid., 48.
[161] Nicholas Roosevelt, *The Philippines: A Treasure and a Problem* (New York: J. H. Sears & Company, Inc., 1926), 4.

of government," and their local political bosses' "methods make Tammany seem clumsy and unimaginative."[162] He believed that the "idea of fair play is as alien to the Filipino as to all other Orientals," and saw in them "the natural capacity for manipulation which is common to Eastern peoples."[163] In his view, "the Filipino peoples are neither ready for nor anxious to have applied democracy," which stemmed to a large degree from the fact that they were "primitive and addicted to strange customs and costumes."[164] Rarely can a more racist opinion be found in a book on another nation.

But on the other hand, NR also argued rather realistically that the American system was not the best for these people since they were not ready for such a governmental system for various reasons, especially because they were not familiar with democracy. "We transplanted our own system bodily," he wrote, "instead of building a new one for the needs of our pupils."[165] He found the root of the trouble in the American initiative in the first place: "The blame should rest on us for thinking that seventeen years of American rule was enough to prepare them for independence."[166] He further argued that the United States could not leave the Philippines, for the likely result would be revolution and chaos in the Far East, which would destroy the intricate balance of power in that part of Asia to the detriment of U.S. interests. In many ways, it was the same argument as was heard at the time of the Vietnam War, the Afghanistan War, or the Second Iraq War. This proves the point that this was a watershed moment in American foreign policy. Had the American leadership understood that America's culture and democratic system were not exportable to such "exotic" places as Cuba or the Philippines, the United States might have chosen a different path during the Cold War and beyond when it came to deciding between intervention and relying on diplomacy only. He concluded that America's "first quarter of a century in the Philippines has been an experiment in misapplied altruism," and he believed two more generations would pass before independence might come to the archipelago.[167]

In many of these thoughts, a great dose of Theodore Roosevelt can be discovered. Well before his presidency TR loudly praised spreading higher civilization to perceived primitive peoples on coveted or strategically crucial land. Regarding

---

[162] Ibid., 62, 64.
[163] Ibid., 76, 69.
[164] Ibid., 75, 80, 81.
[165] Nicholas Roosevelt, *The Philippines*, 17.
[166] Ibid., 66.
[167] Ibid., 276.

the Indian wars of the 1780s, he claimed, for example: "Whether the whites won the land by treaty, by armed conquest, or, as was actually the case, by a mixture of both, mattered comparatively little so long as the land was won. It was all-important that it should be won, for the benefit of civilization, and in the interests of mankind."[168] NR's venerated uncle injected most of his political philosophy, the above-mentioned included, into young Nicholas, who applied those learned tenets to his own experience and line of thinking. Similarly to the Indians, TR also saw the Filipinos as a group that needed to be civilized. When this particular civilizing mission bore no fast fruits and the domestic political landscape started to sour on the question of the Philippines, TR changed his mind and started to see the archipelago as a liability.[169] As the former president put it in his memoirs: "Either we should retain complete control of the islands, or absolve ourselves from all responsibility for them. Any half and half course would be both foolish and disastrous."[170] In many ways, NR was a latter-day TR in his views about the Philippines, and since civilizing the population had not yet been achieved, he thought that leaving the archipelago would be a terrible decision.

NR, it must be reemphasized, was a man of his times, and the feedback on his book echoed many of the arguments that he expounded in it. Thus, the mostly positive reviews. Willis Fletcher Johnson of the *New York Tribune*, for example, gave it high marks. He praised the clarity and the substance of the argument, and stated that the book "measures easily up to the standard of a masterpiece."[171] He also expressed his fervent wish that the book should become "the illuminator of the minds of the American people, and the inspiration and guide of the American Government."[172] History professor George Matthew Dutcher of Wesleyan University also praised NR's book, judging its observations "always frank, sometimes severe, usually just;" though he also believed the author somewhat distorted the record achieved there.[173] James Alexander Robertson, an expert on the Philippines who had written on its history and spent ten years there wrote that "few books on the Philippines have

---

[168] Theodore Roosevelt, *The Winning of the West* (New York: The Review of Reviews Company, 1910), vol. 3, 128.

[169] For more detail on Theodore Roosevelt's ideas concerning the Philippines, see, Stephen Wertheim, "Reluctant Liberator: Theodore Roosevelt's Philosophy of Self-Government and Preparation for Philippine Independence," *Presidential Studies Quarterly* 39, no. 3 (September 2009): 494–518.

[170] Theodore Roosevelt, *An Autobiography* (New York: The Macmillan Company, 1913), 544.

[171] Willis Fletcher Johnson, "The White Man's Burden," *The North American Review* 223, no. 833 (Dec. 1926–Feb. 1927): 713.

[172] Ibid., 716.

[173] George Matthew Dutcher, "*The Philippines, a Treasure and a Problem* by Nicholas Roosevelt," *Political Science Quarterly* 42, no. 4 (Dec. 1927): 625.

been written in so thoughtful a vein as this." However, with the experience he had gained first-hand on the archipelago, he predicted that without a doubt, "many Filipinos and some Americans will disagree fundamentally with the author."[174] The smaller-scale firestorm that brewed in the wake of the book is discussed below.

This activity of writing books remained with NR for the next decades, and he soon returned to the topic of the Far East. Basically, his new paths of being a journalist and a book author ran parallel to and were supportive of each other, and in the next few years he was active in both fields. His major pieces focused on foreign policy. Following his analysis of the Philippines, his next article concerned the British and Russians vis a vis China. He wrote that the British were trying to protect their commercial interests, while the Russians—using propaganda—were trying to undermine this and regain a foothold in northern China. Traditional anti-foreign sentiment was still strong there, however, which might delay any such plans. Even if "in no country is the venture of prophecy so hazardous as in China," NR still risked predicting that "Russia's role, therefore, is fundamentally an aggressive one. For Great Britain the great problem is to know how to hold what she already has."[175]

His book on the Philippines was soon followed by a new volume on the problems of the East. *The Restless Pacific* was another study on the challenges to the United States in the larger arena. It was basically a sensible foreign policy book, naturally concentrating on the Pacific region. The main thesis was that Americans had not seen the Pacific in realistic terms, and this led to chasing mirages: "We have complacently assumed that our fiat could remake the world, and that we had a mission to 'reform the heathen.' Our tasks remain and our ideals are unfulfilled. The problem which we face is how to make these ideals effective."[176] Although it seems like a repudiation of his views on social Darwinism and exporting American democracy to uncivilized people, rather it was a display of frustration that the United States had not done everything in its power to reach such a goal. His suggestion was that in order to make American idealism practical, "it must be supported by a consistent policy in which right will rest on fact rather than theory and, if challenged, will be supported by might."[177] Following from such a point of view the logical conclusion was that "the American Government must ever be ready to use such force as may be

---

[174] James Alexander Robertson, "The Philippines: A Treasure and a Problem," *The Hispanic American Historical Review* 7, no. 4 (Nov. 1927): 482, 483.
[175] Nicholas Roosevelt, "Russia and Great Britain in China," *Foreign Affairs* 5, no. 1 (Oct. 1926): 90.
[176] Nicholas Roosevelt, *The Restless Pacific* (New York, London: Charles Scribner's Sons, 1928), 11.
[177] Ibid., 205.

necessary."¹⁷⁸ This implied a much stronger navy in order to be able to project power to the Far East if American interests were attacked, an idea clearly echoing Alfred Thayer Mahan and Theodore Roosevelt.

In this book, he took into account one by one the powers interested in the Pacific (Japan, the Soviet Union, Great Britain, the Netherlands, and, of course, the United States), and in describing their Pacific politics, he displayed a wide range of knowledge. He in places also demonstrated remarkable prescience. Perhaps the most striking was his opinion and prediction about the foreign policy of the Soviet Union. He stated that just because the czar was gone, traditional imperialist Russian foreign policy would not disappear, only the technique would differ by being replaced by a more efficient Soviet one. And even if the Soviet regime collapsed, and "if a democratic or other government replaces the Soviets, its foreign policy will differ from that of its predecessors only in method, not in ultimate aims."¹⁷⁹ This resembles George Kennan's description of Soviet foreign policy in his famous Long Telegram and X-article written almost twenty years later.¹⁸⁰ NR also identified Manchuria as "one of the danger spots of the world," and events soon proved him right.¹⁸¹

Perhaps as a reaction to criticism that his first book was somewhat condescending, this book displayed much more cultural tolerance regarding the Philippines. Nonetheless, he described the Asian people in general in a negative light when it came to their perception of truth and morality. One of the discrepancies between westerners and Asians, he wrote, was in how they approached facts and truth. For the former, a fact was "compelling, definite, absolute," for the latter, however,

> a fact if inconvenient is a thing to be ignored, and to whom truthfulness is a relative ideal, to be adhered to or not according to expediency. The Easterner recognizes that falsehood has distinct value, and so does not regard lying with the same moral distaste as does the Occidental. A lie is reprehensible if it is rendered futile by discovery. It is a legitimate weapon in the battle of life.¹⁸²

The picture he painted was black and white without subtle nuances. This book, too, received favorable reviews for its clarity, timeliness, and lively presentation of

---

[178] Ibid., 282.
[179] Nicholas Roosevelt, *The Restless Pacific*, 123.
[180] George F. Kennan, "The Sources of Soviet Conduct," *Foreign Affairs* 25, no. 4 (July 1947): 566–78, 580–82.
[181] Nicholas Roosevelt, *The Restless Pacific*, 134.
[182] Nicholas Roosevelt, *The Restless Pacific*, 229.

problems of the Far East.[183] This reinforces the widespread acceptance of NR's views by both his profession and the greater public.

Soon, like the final volume of a trilogy, his third foreign policy book appeared. Published at the beginning of 1930, *America and England?* scrutinized the two countries and their roles in world affairs. This time his main focus was economic in nature. Possibly before or already while writing the manuscript, he wrote to Secretary of State Frank B. Kellogg that with the United States becoming the new center of the world, it might be "more and more obliged to follow England's footsteps."[184] The United States had indeed outgrown Britain and the rest of the world, but it was inexperienced and reluctant to play the predominant global role that such a position might have offered. Both the general population and the political elite were unaware of the great responsibilities such economic power entailed. The book must have been finished before the great crash of 1929, because there was no hint either of its coming or immediate effects. Thus, the book offered an interesting reading of the pre-Depression commercial era regarding Great Britain and the United States, but in many ways necessarily became at once outdated. Nonetheless, there were many sharp observations, especially concerning geopolitical questions, drawing mainly on the examples and lessons of World War I. Some of NR's points, however, were proved to be mistaken. Not surprisingly, another of TR's precepts surged forward at one point, where NR argued that the two Anglo-Saxon nations should better coordinate their foreign policies: "As part of this policy is the reservation that each, in its own spheres, has individual rights and duties of exercising police power for the suppression of disorder."[185] Such an approach might lead to an "enduring *pax Anglo-Americana*."[186] In light of his near-future diplomatic post, the following statement is interesting: "To make matters worse, the American foreign service is inadequately housed, underpaid, poorly trained and its members chosen

---

[183] William L. Langer, "Some Recent Books on International Relations," *Foreign Affairs* 6, no. 4 (July 1928): 693; Ray Lyman Wilbur, "*The Restless Pacific* by Nicholas Roosevelt," *Annals of the American Academy of Political and Social Science* 138, Some Aspects of the Present International Situation (July 1928): 182; J. W. Wheeler-Bennett, "*The Restless Pacific*. By Nicholas Roosevelt," *Journal of the Royal Institute of International Affairs* 7, no. 5, (September 1928): 345; F. C. S. "Roosevelt, Nicholas. *The Restless Pacific*," *Review of Current Military Writings*, no. 29, (April–June 1928): 448; Harley Farnsworth MacNair, "*The Far East: A Political and Diplomatic History* by Payson Jackson Treat; *The Restless Pacific* by Nicholas Roosevelt; *Within the Walls of Nanking* by Alice Tisdale Hobart," *The American Political Science Review* 23, no. 1 (Feb. 1929): 212–15.

[184] Nicholas Roosevelt to Frank B. Kellogg, December 10, 1928, Folder: Kellogg, Hon. Frank B., Box 8, Nicholas Roosevelt Papers.

[185] Nicholas Roosevelt, *America and England?* (London: Jonathan Cape, 1930), 226.

[186] Ibid., 231.

because they can pay their way rather than earn it. Despite the fact that matters of business now furnish the most important incidents in American diplomacy the average American 'career' secretary knows nothing of business."[187]

This book, too, was welcomed as providing a careful and convincingly written analysis of the issues.[188] Henry Louis Mencken, for instance, described it as "a singularly lucid and sensible work, done by a man with an unusual capacity for reducing complicated matters to simplicity," which was "free from every sort of chauvinistic fustian."[189] Another reviewer, however, found fault with the oft-found ambiguity and sometimes out-of-date treatment of the armament question.[190] It must have been a vindication to NR that Walter Lippmann, for one, also praised the book. Lippmann found it "both a sound and brilliant performance," written with "beautiful clarity and balance of the analysis," and he applauded "the healthiest tone for international discussion that I have seen in any book for a long time."[191] The U.S. minister to China, John Van Antwerp MacMurray, likewise praised the volume as "a careful and thoughtful book" and "an honest and broad-minded representation of things as they really are in this muddled Far East, rather than as they would be if all the people of this hemisphere were the same darling little replicas of our ideal American selves, that it flatters us to think them."[192] In light of the published reviews, NR's books on foreign policy matters were successful, although in all likelihood only a small group of intellectuals read them.

In parallel to writing his books, and to a certain extent on account of their content, he also edged closer to the Republican executive branch and could boast of such friendships as that of Henry L. Stimson, for example, who had been secretary of war under Taft, while President Calvin Coolidge appointed him Governor General to the Philippines in December 1927. After that appointment, NR was quick to praise Stimson for "the sterling intellectual qualities of this self-contained, quiet New Englander," who "understands the Latin and Oriental attitude towards

---

[187] Ibid., 192.
[188] See, for instance, W. L. H., "*America and England* by Nicholas Roosevelt; *America Conquers Britain* by Ludwell Denny," *Pacific Affairs* 3, No. 8 (Aug. 1930): 786–88.
[189] H. L. Mencken, "*America and England*," *Now and Then* (London), no 35 (Spring 1930), 11, 12.
[190] Benjamin H. Williams, "*America and England. by Nicholas Roosevelt*," *Political Science Quarterly*, 46, no. 1 (Mar. 1931): 118–20.
[191] Walter Lippmann to Nicholas Roosevelt, January 14, 1930, Box 29, Folder 1063, Roosevelt, Nicholas (1928–1930), Series I, Selected Correspondence, 1906–1930, Walter Lippmann Papers, MS 326 HM 257, Yale Archives.
[192] John Van Antwerp MacMurray to Nicholas Roosevelt, July 10, 1928, Folder 6, Roosevelt, Nicholas, 1928–1934, Box 60, Series 2, Correspondence and Papers, 1861–1960, John Van Antwerp MacMurray Papers, 1715–1988, Seeley G. Mudd Manuscript Library, Princeton, U.S.A.

life" and "recognizes that it is not for the Governor-General to deal with the question of independence or to mix into local politics."[193] He described anew the problem in the Philippines the way he saw it: "America undertook a task which she has not yet completed. She made promises which are still to be fulfilled," that is, to give independence to the Filipino people when they were ready for it.[194]

This was a sentiment that Stimson shared. In 1912 as outgoing secretary of war he wrote the following observation: "Until our work in the archipelago is completed, until the Filipinos are prepared not only to preserve but to continue it, abandonment of the Philippines, under whatever guise, would be an abandonment of our responsibility to the Filipino people and of the moral obligations which we have voluntarily assumed before the world."[195] His work in the Philippines was praised by the contemporary press for "the era of good feeling" he established, and the various authors writing on Stimson's career agreed, but they also mentioned his negative bias toward Latin Americans and Filipinos.[196]

When Herbert Hoover won the presidency in 1928, he chose Stimson as secretary of state, and that decision proved helpful to NR's career. Stimson and NR had corresponded over questions regarding Nicaragua and the Philippines at least since the fall of 1927. With Stimson's appointment as secretary of state, the matter of the post of general governor to the Philippines came to the fore. The former vice general governor, Eugene Allen Gilmore, became the acting G-G. On the same day that Stimson changed posts, NR wrote to him and advised that General Frank McCoy be named Stimson's successor.[197] Indeed, three weeks earlier he had written to President-elect Hoover in the same vein.[198] This plan did not bear fruit, and in the end Hoover appointed Dwight F. Davis to the post in July 1929.[199]

---

[193] Nicholas Roosevelt, "The New Governor-General of the Philippines," *The American Review of Reviews* 77, no. 2 (February 1928): 145.
[194] Ibid., 146.
[195] Henry L. Stimson, *On Active Service in Peace and War* (New York: Harper & Brothers, 1948), 120. On his fourteen-month Governorship in the Philippines, see, Ibid., 117–45.
[196] *New York Times*, February 17, 1929; Schmitz, *Henry L. Stimson*, 55; Elting E. Morison, *Turmoil and Tradition: A Study of the Life and Times of Henry L. Stimson* (Boston: Houghton Mifflin Company, 1960), 280–98; Godfrey Hodgson, *The Colonel: The Life and Wars of Henry Stimson, 1867–1950* (New York: Alfred A. Knopf, 1990), 133–41; David F. Schmitz, *Henry L. Stimson: The First Wise Man* (Washington, Delaware: A Scholarly Resources Inc., 2001), 61–69.
[197] Nicholas Roosevelt to Henry L. Stimson, February 23, 1929, Folder: Stimson, Henry L, Box 14, Nicholas Roosevelt Papers.
[198] Nicholas Roosevelt to Herbert Hoover, February 1, 1929, Folder: Hoover, Herbert, Box 7, Nicholas Roosevelt Papers.
[199] On Davis's job there, see, H. Ford Wilkins, "Dwight F. Davis: Governor General of the Philippines," *Current History* (1916–1940) 34, no. 3 (June 1931): 348–52. Davis was instrumental in launching the Davis Cup in 1900, the now highly prestigious international tennis competition among nations.

Always ambitious, NR soon started to campaign for his own appointment as vice general-governor. He wrote to Stimson about this idea. He even wrote the draft of a letter on how he saw the Philippines question, which Stimson sent, with some modifications, to the president for consideration.[200] In this ten-page draft NR put forward his by then oft-repeated idea that independence should not be granted to the Filipinos; if the United States wanted to leave, such a decision should be final and no further responsibilities should be undertaken by Washington.[201] The secretary of state, who in January 1930 traveled to Europe to the London Naval Conference, did not make a formal commitment but signaled that NR's name "should be most carefully considered and I should be inclined to favor it."[202] NR pondered the idea of a new opening for himself:

> If this new man [Dwight F. Davis] were to resign the Governorship in a couple of years and I were, in the interim, Vice-Governor, I should hope that my tenure of this office would not then mitigate against my being considered to replace him. In other words, I welcome an apprenticeship of a few years, but should not like to feel that this apprenticeship would bar me from ultimate consideration for the Governorship.[203]

NR clearly saw the post of vice general governor as a stepping stone to a prestigious government position. It was not that he sought fame necessarily; rather he genuinely believed that his views on the Philippines, which largely aligned with those of the Hoover administration, if put into practice, would be beneficial to both sides. Stimson pitched for NR, alongside with Walter Lippmann, and NR indeed received the nomination in July 1930 to the post of vice general governor of the Philippines.[204]

NR's acquaintance with President Hoover went back to the Paris Peace Conference, where the later president made a deep impression on the young NR. At

---

[200] Nicholas Roosevelt to Henry L. Stimson, December 25, 1929, and December 31, 1929, Henry L. Stimson to Nicholas Roosevelt, January 4, 1930, Folder: Stimson, Henry L., Box 14, Nicholas Roosevelt Papers.

[201] Nicholas Roosevelt to Henry L. Stimson, December 31, 1929, Ibid.

[202] Henry L. Stimson to Nicholas Roosevelt, March 11, 1930, Folder: Stimson, Henry L, Box 14, Nicholas Roosevelt Papers.

[203] Nicholas Roosevelt to Henry L. Stimson, March 25, 1930, Folder: Stimson, Henry L., Box 14, Nicholas Roosevelt Papers.

[204] Nicholas Roosevelt to Henry L. Stimson, July 31, 1930, Folder: Stimson, Henry L, Box 14, Nicholas Roosevelt Papers; Nicholas Roosevelt to Walter Lippmann, November 17, 1930, Folder 1063, Roosevelt, Nicholas, Box 29, (1928–1930), Series I, Selected Correspondence, 1906–1930, Walter Lippmann Papers, MS 326 HM 257, Yale Archives.

Nicholas Roosevelt, of New York, seen here in Washington D.C., was appointed Vice Governor of the Philippines by President Hoover, July 29, 1930. (AP Photo/Julian C. Wilson)

the time of his touring the Philippines, he wrote to Hoover, who at that time was secretary of commerce, reiterating "how utterly unprepared the Filipino people yet are for complete independence. The work which we began in those Islands is not yet finished and as far as I can see cannot be finished for many years to come."[205] In April 1930, NR, as the *New York Times*' expert on the topic, had lunch with the president in order to talk about the current situation in the Philippines.[206] So, with expertise and influential supporters, his name was put forward to the U.S. Congress.

In his Congressional hearing, he repeated his thesis that the United States must not withdraw since it would cause a serious disturbance in the balance of power in the Far East, likely to the detriment to America's interests.[207] After a successful performance before the House of Representatives, Hoover made a recess appointment of NR to the post, confident that the Senate, which had adjourned its special session without confirming the nomination, would do so in December when it reconvened.[208] In his news conference on July 29, Hoover declared that NR had "been so staunch in his support of the interests of the Philippine people in the United States and so sympathetic with them, so enthusiastic over their progress that I am sure any misunderstanding which has arisen in the Philippines as to his attitude will be quickly

---

[205] Nicholas Roosevelt to Herbert Hoover, January 24, 1926, Folder: Hoover, Herbert, Box 7, Nicholas Roosevelt Papers.
[206] George Akerson to Adolph S. Ochs, March 27, 1930, Folder 7: Nicholas Roosevelt (1922–1933), Box 34, Adolph S. Ochs Papers.
[207] "Senate Faction Gives Filipinos Powerful Veto," *Boston Transcript*, September 25, 1930.
[208] "Nicholas Roosevelt Gets Recess Appointment to the Philippines; Hoover Praises Him," *New York Times*, July 30, 1930; Norton, "Minister to the Magyars," 6.

cleared up."²⁰⁹ Privately, the president confirmed to the late Theodore Roosevelt's sister that sending NR to Manila "was a good appointment—because he comes from the proper stock."²¹⁰ NR wrote to the publisher of the *New York Times* that he hated to leave after seven years with the paper, especially since he had had so agreeable an environment to work in. Therefore, he approached the "new adventure with mixed feelings," but he saw this move as a step up and in the right direction.²¹¹

The appointment did not go down well in the Philippines. Back in 1926, the leaders of the Philippine independence movement had attacked NR and the book he had just published (*The Philippines: A Treasure and a Problem*). They magnified those passages that reeked of condescension. The Philippine Legislature unanimously protested against the appointment, and many high-ranking Filipino politicians threatened to resign *en masse* if the newly-appointed vice general-governor set foot in Manila, thereby making their legislative work impossible. They also let the U.S. Senate know their sentiments.²¹² There were public burnings of the book in the Philippines and copies were tossed in the sea. A local businessman even challenged Roosevelt to a duel.²¹³ In early August, in the midst of the controversy, NR gave an interview in which he put up a humorous front and admitted that in the Philippines "they consider me as an ogre or radical, set to throttle Philippine independence and eager to make changes in the order of things in the islands," while even in the U.S. press there was criticism of his "imperialist" views.²¹⁴ Even a decade later he remembered the incident with wry humor:

> I have often thought—and have boasted publicly—that I am probably the most provocative writer of books the world has ever known—not excepting Mr. Shakespeare and a few other lesser lights. I base this on the fact that my Philippine book not only was, on several occasions, burned publicly in Manila but that on one particular occasion, before being burned, a copy was

---

²⁰⁹ "The President's News Conference of July 29, 1930," in Herbert Hoover, *Containing the Public Messages Speeches and Statements of the President, January 1 to December 31, 1930, Public Papers of the Presidents of the United States* (Washington: United States Government Printing Office, 1976), 304.
²¹⁰ Herbert Hoover to Douglas Robinson [Corrine Roosevelt Robinson], August 21, 1930, Folder: Hoover, Herbert, Box 7, Nicholas Roosevelt Papers.
²¹¹ Nicholas Roosevelt to Arthur Hays Sulzberger, August 1, 1930, Folder 16: Roosevelt, Nicholas, 1926–1931, 1944–1962, Box 64, Arthur Hays Sulzberger Papers, New York Times Company Records, New York, U.S.A.
²¹² Norton, "Minister to the Magyars," 6; Congressional Record, 71st Congress, Special Session of the Senate, July 21, 1930, Washington: United States Government Printing Office, 1930, 380–81.
²¹³ Wilkins, "Dwight F. Davis," 351–52.
²¹⁴ James G. Wingo, "This Man Roosevelt," *Philippines Free Press*, September 13, 1930.

placed on an anvil and beaten with a sledgehammer. I maintain that this is the record in literary criticism and that any book that could produce such effects certainly must be pretty darn good.[215]

NR was more pragmatic than to let such a squabble hurt President Hoover and ruin his own still-ambitious future; and it is easily conceivable that the White House also advised him to find an elegant solution. Accordingly, on September 24, he resigned the post. In his letter of resignation Roosevelt pointed out that in his previous writings he had only looked at the Philippines with a beneficial and progressive eye, trying to find ways to help the population, only to be met by misinterpretation and misrepresentation of what he had written. In order not to ruffle Philippine–American relations, he found it the best to resign "believing that my services can be more useful elsewhere."[216]

On the very same day of his resignation, which the president accepted reluctantly, NR was appointed minister to Hungary by Hoover.[217] It seems safe to surmise that this was a deal worked out within the State Department in the interim political heat and with the president's knowledge and agreement. The Rogers Act of 1924 had aimed at reforming the diplomatic service of the United States, and it introduced, among other novelties, a system whereby the various diplomats were to rotate after three years' being stationed in one place.[218] This provided the basis for the solution. Leland B. Harrison, the minister to Uruguay, resigned from the Foreign Service, so Joshua Butler Wright, who was a key architect of the Rogers Act, and the present U.S. minister to Hungary, was sent to Uruguay. Since Wright had already spent more than three years at Budapest, the transfer could be justified as falling under the Rogers Act's requirements. Also, Montevideo, given its relative geographical proximity to Washington, was a more illustrious post than Budapest, so Wright had no reason to grumble. In addition, NR had already had experience

---

[215] Nicholas Roosevelt to Charles G. Moore, June 15, 1943, Box 15, Office of War Information 1943, Nicholas Roosevelt Papers.
[216] For the full text of the letter of resignation, see, Hoover, *Public Messages*, 379–80; Nicholas Roosevelt to Walter Lippmann, November 17, 1930, Folder 1063, Roosevelt, Nicholas, Box 29, Walter Lippmann Papers.
[217] Hoover, *Public Messages*, 379.
[218] On the Rogers Act, see, Heinrichs, *American Ambassador*, 95–106, 115–17; Robert D. Schulzinger, *The Making of the Diplomatic Mind: The Training, Outlook and Style of United States Foreign Service Officers, 1908–1931* (Middletown, CT: Wesleyan University Press, 1975); Richard Hume Werking, *The Master Architects Building the United States Foreign Service, 1890–1931* (Lexington, KY: University Press of Kentucky, 1977); Lawrence E. Gelfand, "Towards a Merit System for the American Diplomatic Service 1900–1930," *Irish Studies in International Affairs* 2, no. 4 (1988): 49–63.

in Hungary and Central Europe, so his "expertise" could be cited as a reason for his selection for the post.[219] Still, the scheme was clearly a face-saving maneuver.

Butler Wright left Budapest "with a deep feeling of regret," since he had spent an interesting three and a half years there. Hungarian domestic politics and the international controversies of Central Europe always gave a professional diplomat something to report and food for thought. He was also helpful in letters to NR that somewhat prepared the new minister for his future post. Wright recommended keeping the servants (cook, chauffeur, butler, and kitchen maid), but called attention to the possible wrangling NR might encounter with the owner of the house they had been renting. Wright added that the problem stemmed from the owner, Paul Strauss, being a Jew. He spoke in highly favorable terms of the legation staff, "a closely knit, efficient, congenial and most loyal group of men and women," and especially mentioned Somerville Pinkney "Kippy" Tuck, secretary of the legation, as the one to rely on. As a hint regarding the social life and entertainment awaiting NR, Butler Wright recommended that he "bring guns and a fishing rod, as well as golf clubs."[220] As for challenges, his predecessor mentioned that "political pitfalls are not many," and mostly "watchful waiting" would be NR's share as the economic situation would be the all-defining aspect for the near future. He highlighted agriculture as of the most significance in Hungary, and signaled that the Ministry of Agriculture was "pathetically weak."[221] This suited NR well, since he considered himself a semi-expert on economic issues in Europe.

NR traveled to Europe and on to Hungary to start a diplomatic stint in a so-far checkered carrier. He knew he would miss journalism and the *New York Times* because the paper had "been my second home."[222] The only dampening effect was that Budapest was not much on Washington's radar. Soon enough the Great Depression engulfed both countries, which turned Budapest into an interesting and challenging post for NR personally, although the circumstances did not make Hungary any more important to the United States than before.

---

[219] "The Cabinet: Manila, Budapest, Montevideo," *Time*, October 6, 1930.
[220] The quotations of the paragraph so far are from Joshua Butler Wright to Nicholas Roosevelt, September 28, 1930, Folder: Wright, J. Butler, Box 16, Nicholas Roosevelt Papers.
[221] Joshua Butler Wright to Nicholas Roosevelt, October 24, 1930, ibid.
[222] Nicholas Roosevelt to Adolph S. Ochs, October 24, 1930, Folder 7: Nicholas Roosevelt (1922–1933), Box 34, Adolph S. Ochs Papers.

Chapter 4

The American Minister to Hungary

When Nicholas Roosevelt returned to Europe in the fall of 1930, it was already burdened with the unfolding economic and financial depression. Although it had not yet reached its ugly peak, it was already clear that especially those countries that had relied to a large degree on foreign loans to finance their economy and fill gaping holes in their budgets, suddenly found no more money on the international markets. Hungary was one such country. The situation was even more serious there than in other Central, Eastern, and Southern European countries, because Hungary was mainly agricultural and could count to an overwhelming degree only on revenue from the sale of wheat. If the harvest was weak or the markets offered low prices, the Hungarian state was in trouble. Another problem was debt. After the successful League of Nations reconstruction (1924–26), Hungary ignored warnings and kept picking up fresh loans and becoming more and more indebted. In addition to overborrowing, the Hungarian population had one of the biggest per capita foreign debt services in all of Europe.[223] This was the country at which NR arrived as American minister, officially Envoy Extraordinary and Minister Plenipotentiary.

Hungary was not alone in being of little interest to the United States. Its high expectations to the contrary, the United States showed little interest in any of the countries of Central Europe—with the conspicuous exception of Germany. As long as there was political stability, and Prime Minister Bethlen provided exactly that, Washington was satisfied with the regular reports of its ministers, who provided information on the most important domestic and foreign policy issues. These

---

[223] League of Nations, *The League of Nations Reconstruction Schemes in the Inter-War Period* (Geneva: Economic, Financial and Transit Department, 1944), 150.

reports rarely crossed the threshold of serious interest in the State Department. The American loans flowing to Hungary in the second half of the 1920s were private loans for which the government never assumed any responsibility. Therefore, Budapest did not count as an eminent diplomatic mission, but it was nevertheless a post that looked interesting, and since financial and economic troubles seemed to be engulfing more and more countries, it made sense that the Department asked NR to focus on such issues in Hungary as well as in the neighboring countries.

No sooner had NR been appointed minister than Hungarian attention turned toward him. This interest was not because of him, personally, but rather it was due to what he represented: the United States, the country that did not sign the Treaty of Trianon; the country that Hungary looked to as a possible source of hope and aid in achieving revision, even if no palpable proof or any indication had been forthcoming that Washington would be interested in it. In a word, the United States—the country that supposedly was for democracy and justice; the country that had provided charity and loans in the past ten years—was seen as the only possible savior to address Hungary's ills. When Jeremiah Smith, Jr. of Boston became the League of Nations' commissioner general in 1924, Hungarians were jubilant that an American would fill the post. They had courted the former American ministers as well, Theodore Brentano and Joshua Butler Wright, and since the end of the war almost no Hungarians could be convinced that the United States neither took any responsibility for the region nor wished to fight for detached Hungarian minorities. There were few stronger mirages in Hungary in the first half of the twentieth century than the general belief that America would come to Hungary's help. So, when NR was named the latest minister, Hungarians turned to him as the embodiment of this Hungarian illusion. In addition, his family name made him seem even more familiar, and since Theodore Roosevelt had received a hero's welcome in Budapest in 1910, a close family relation—in an official capacity—could count on a similarly warm welcome.[224]

> Charmingly hospitable, the Hungarian people quickly win the hearts of their visitors. Pride in Hungary's past, passionate indignation at the injustice done to Hungary by the Treaty of Trianon, ambitious for Hungary's future, eagerness to be friendly and to show foreigners all the best in their country are shared by Hungarians of all classes. As a diplomatic post none more agreeable

---

[224] On Theodore Roosevelt's visit to Hungary in 1910, see, Peterecz, "The Visit of the Most Popular American of the Day: Theodore Roosevelt in Hungary," *Hungarian Studies* 28, no. 2, (2014): 235–54.

than Hungary can be imagined, and during the years I spent there, none more interesting.²²⁵

The lines quoted above are the opening lines of an unpublished manuscript that later served as the basis of two chapters in his 1953 memoirs. NR recorded his Hungarian reminiscences in the manuscript, and while there is nothing overtly false in these and other words he later wrote concerning Hungary, the fact remains that some of his recorded thoughts on the same topic differed between 1930 and 1953. Therefore one must treat his official memoirs with care and rely more on his diary notes, letters, and reports while on the scene as they more truthfully reflect his ideas. One opinion that remained intact throughout his life though was his conviction that old feudalistic traits were deeply embedded in Hungarian society: "Here the Occident ended and the Orient began," and "Budapest was the meeting place of two civilizations." He found the capital to be "outwardly modern and western. But the plains to the East sheltered a strange mixture of feudalism and the Orient—a people youthful and somewhat primitive, but bred in traditions that are alien to Western Europe."²²⁶ In his 1953 memoirs he struck the same critical tone when he wrote that outwardly the upper class was Westernized but they could not shed their eastern qualities: "The love of face and appearance, the unquestioning acceptance of caste and position, the preference for pleasant pretenses over unpleasant truth" were typical of these people.²²⁷ In sharp contrast, "the Hungarian peasants were living under conditions but little removed from those of the serfs in Russia of the nineteenth century," which "was, of course, a survival of feudalism."²²⁸

After his appointment as minister to Hungary, NR made the necessary preliminary rounds in order to get as up to date as possible concerning recent Hungarian affairs. Although he had watched the events in the first few months of 1919 up close and personal, since then his main attention had mainly been drawn to Western Europe and the Far East, therefore he needed a crash course on the current issues. He discussed the past ten years' questions regarding Hungary with Hamilton Fish Armstrong of the Council on Foreign Relations, and Ulysses Grant-Smith, who was the chargé before the first American minister, Theodore Brentano, was appointed to Hungary in late 1921.²²⁹ However, the most important available person having

---

[225] Nicholas Roosevelt, "Hungary," (unpublished), Box 45, Nicholas Roosevelt Papers.
[226] Ibid.
[227] Nicholas Roosevelt, *A Front Row Seat*, 188.
[228] Ibid., 189, 190.
[229] Diary entry, October 1 and 10, 1930, Hungary 1930–1933, Box 21, Nicholas Roosevelt Papers.

relevant and up to date information about Hungary, especially regarding the country's financial and economic situation, was Jeremiah Smith, Jr.

Smith was the League of Nations' commissioner general during the 1924–26 financial reconstruction of Hungary and a celebrated friend of the country, then from 1927 a member of the League's Financial Committee. Therefore, he was perhaps the most authentic person to say useful things to NR before the latter's departure. As recorded in NR's diary, his long conversation with Smith about Hungary and Hungarians gives a typical American characterization of the country: Smith called attention to Hungarians' strong nationalistic feelings but also to "their sense of inferiority;" he praised their energy and honesty but at the same time spoke of their "childishness;" he warned about "the old timers and their medieval characters."[230] Although the economic and financial picture had worsened since the end of the reconstruction program, Smith was characteristically optimistic about the near future on that account.

Naturally an important person in the eyes of Hungarians—after all, he represented the United States—as soon as the appointment was announced journalists from both Hungarian and Hungarian-American newspapers sought NR out. They were mostly interested in his views concerning Hungary's borders and whether he thought revision of the peace treaty could be achieved. These journalists wished to project a picture of the next American minister as someone who would be sympathetic to Hungary's situation. NR fended off any such efforts saying that he could not touch political questions and emphasizing that he felt a great deal of sympathy toward the country and its citizens.[231] Some journalists insisted that good things were in store for the relationships between the two countries, partly because NR was himself a good and well-known journalist, which would automatically mean greater publicity for Hungary. One of the Hungarian dailies even reported that NR had said he was going to use American newspapers for the benefit of Hungary.[232] The bar was raised even higher when he was quoted as saying, "Among the many East European races I see the Hungarian as the most valuable and outstanding."[233] No wonder the papers believed that "the service of America's new minister gives the highest hopes to Hungary."[234] NR did write a few most welcome lines to Hungarian newspaper readers: "An old Friend, returning to Budapest with a sympathetic mind,

---

[230] Diary entry, October 15, 1930, ibid.
[231] Diary entry, October 1, 1930, Hungary 1930–1933, Box 21, Nicholas Roosevelt Papers.
[232] *8 Órai Újság*, September 28, 1930, 2; *Az Est*, October 12, 1930, 1.
[233] *Pesti Hírlap*, October 12, 1930, 34.
[234] Ibid.

anxious to make Hungary better known in America and America better known in Hungary."[235]

A few days prior to his departure for Budapest, NR was the guest of honor at a dinner given by the Hungarian-American Chamber of Commerce and the Hungarian Foundation. The master of ceremonies for the evening was Philip Marshall Brown of Princeton University, a former diplomat and NR's fellow member on the Coolidge Mission in 1919. John H. Finley of the *New York Times* introduced Roosevelt to the audience and had nice things to say about him as a journalist. James T. Shotwell, a history professor at Columbia University, was also among the guests and he praised NR's realism concerning international affairs. He, however, also praised the Hungarian-American community and said that hopefully Hungary would get back its lost territories.[236] Hungary was represented by the charge d'affaires, Miklós Végh, and the secretary of the Hungarian Legation, in addition to György Ghika, Hungarian Consul-General of New York, who conveyed the official good wishes of the Hungarian government. NR gave a speech as well, one that he had previously cleared with the State Department. In it, in addition to trade and tourism, he identified the biggest problem of the two countries as the scant knowledge each had of the other. Therefore, as a remedy, he was willing to do the utmost so that "Hungary and the Hungarian problem would be better known in America."[237] This might have been interpreted as indicating that he would use his journalistic past and wide array of connections in the service of Hungary.

NR sailed for Europe and after a few stops in London, Paris, and Geneva, he arrived in Hungary on November 9. Aside from the daily challenges of the job, there were pecuniary hardships for Roosevelt from the very beginning. Most political appointees, which he was, were supposed to be able to carry their weight financially. Wealthy people could donate large sums to election campaigns, which often was repaid with an appointment to a capital city. Hungary was not high on anyone's list, however, and NR had not received his appointment in return for his financial contributions to Hoover's presidential campaign. His salary was $10,000 annually, but there were considerable expenses for social entertainment, and the $5,000 yearly expense allowance, of which the U.S. government paid about half, helped little. NR found himself short of money throughout his time as minister in Hungary, and in every letter that he wrote to his mother he complained about his finances. He tried

---

[235] Ibid.
[236] *Amerikai Magyar Népszava*, October 25, 1930, 1.
[237] Ibid., 4. Also see, Diary entry, October 27, 1930, Hungary 1930–1933, Box 21, Nicholas Roosevelt Papers.

Nicholas Roosevelt, of New York, newly appointed United States Minister to Hungary, is shown as he sailed from New York, Oct. 25, 1930, to take up his duties. (AP Photo)

to cut back on costs but regularly asked her for money. As a counterweight to these problems, he "was lucky to be surrounded by a staff that was as agreeable as it was competent."[238]

Although NR was a political appointee, he did have some experience in the diplomatic world during and after World War I. Also, he spoke fluent French and German, which meant that he did not have to rely on interpreters when discussing issues with Hungarians or other diplomats. As a result, he was not considered a total outsider by the official staff at the American Legation in Budapest. The successive secretaries of the Legation, Somerville Pinkney Tuck, Rudolph E. Schoenfeld, and David Williamson after some transition time accepted Roosevelt and built a very good working relationship with him. He was also helped by his personal secretary, Edward LaFarge, who had travelled with NR from the United States.[239] Consequently, NR could reassure his predecessor that he "found everything in

---

[238] Nicholas Roosevelt, "Hungary," (unpublished), Box 45, Nicholas Roosevelt Papers.
[239] Ibid.; Nicholas Roosevelt, *A Front Row Seat*, 190–91.

excellent order, and everybody in the Legation most helpful in the process of educating me and transforming me from a newspaper man into a so-called diplomat."[240]

In view of the competent staff and the relatively small amount of work, NR gave himself two months to get "thoroughly broken in" and to become familiar with various data and the personalities that counted.[241] Accordingly, in the first weeks he acquainted himself with the most important people in Budapest and called on every major player: ministers of commerce and finance, people in the Foreign Office, and leading journalists. First and foremost the person to meet was Miklós Horthy, the regent. NR's predecessor assured him that he would find Horthy "a delightful, vigorous, honest, straightforward and with whom you may have many points of mutual interest, if you are fond of sports, and who is really a sincere friend of the United States."[242]

He gave his letter of credence to Horthy on November 12, and thus gained his first impression of the regent, which later many more followed. Both in his unpublished notes about his Hungarian stay and in his published memoirs, NR wrote in detail about the ceremony of presenting the credentials. However backward or feudal he and many other Americans may have found this region and its peoples, they were fairly fascinated with the old traditions and uniforms that they found both alien and charming at the same time. Horthy immediately brought up two topics: his fondness for the United States and Americans who had helped Hungary in the past years, and hunting, his greatest passion. Later, his fervent anti-communism was added to NR's assessment of Horthy's principal character traits.[243]

Roosevelt also painted small vignettes of other leading Hungarian politicians, and his descriptions were always acute and entertaining. Some of them he had already met in 1919, like Pál Teleki and Albert Apponyi, but there were also new faces. The long-time prime minister, István Bethlen, for example, together with many aristocrats in Hungary, "gave an impression of fatigue, as if they lacked energy and virility," and whose political weapons were "indirection, evasion, subterfuge, secrecy."[244] Still, "Bethlen was a man of rare charm. Slight, slender, sinewy, he had

---

[240] Nicholas Roosevelt to Joshua Butler Wright, November 13, 1930, Folder: Wright, J. Butler, Box 8, Nicholas Roosevelt Papers.
[241] Nicholas Roosevelt to Prentiss B. Gilbert, December 13, 1930, Folder: Gilbert, Prentiss B., Box 6; Nicholas Roosevelt to Castle, November 21, 1930, Folder: Castle, William R. Jr., Box 2, Nicholas Roosevelt Papers.
[242] Joshua Butler Wright to Nicholas Roosevelt, December 6, 1930, Folder: Wright, J. Butler, Box 16, Nicholas Roosevelt Papers.
[243] Nicholas Roosevelt, "Hungary," (unpublished), Box 45, Nicholas Roosevelt Papers; Nicholas Roosevelt, *A Front Row Seat*, 192–93, 200.
[244] Nicholas Roosevelt, "Hungary," (unpublished), Box 45, Nicholas Roosevelt Papers.

the air of a man who had live much on horseback—as, indeed, he had. The head was a most interesting one—small, long, not very high, with a tanned brow and face that was deeply wrinkled even though still youthful. He was quiet but incisive, reserved and, at least with me, never friendly."[245]

By the end of the year, he had settled in in Budapest and in his job, adjusted to the circumstances, and picked up the rhythm of work and lifestyle typical for an American minister in Central Europe. One thing that he found striking was the lack of official information on what was going on in Europe. As he complained in a letter, the issues of the *New York Times* in the second half of November were responsible for "having given me more news of Europe in these numbers than I have been able to obtain by reading English, French, Austrian, Czech, Swiss and Hungarian papers."[246] Maybe this lack of reliable news from the European newspapers added to his feeling of isolation. On the pages of his diary at this time, he showed a mixture of rare self-doubt and characteristic egoism. On the one hand, he was not totally convinced that he should be in Hungary as American minister. On the other hand, he proudly recalled his diary entries during 1915, when he served at the Paris Embassy, and "how right I was and how clearly I foresaw things even at that age," and how he possessed "a real flair for understanding international affairs, and if so there is perhaps some good in my being here at the focal center where a new wave perhaps brewing."[247] Modesty was never one of his main virtues and it is not overstating to say that he thought of himself as the voice of omniscience—whether in his reports, lectures, articles, or private letters. He rounded out his working hours with sport and some limited socializing. He often played tennis and golf, went skiing in the winter, played poker and visited the opera, and sometimes went hunting. When he could gather partners, he played cello and he fondly remembered playing Beethoven trios with other diplomats.[248]

When NR arrived in Hungary in the late fall of 1930, the major issue was naturally the worsening economic and financial situation and the growing distress it caused. The booming 1920s, especially in the United States, had come to a sudden end in late 1929. The October Wall Street crash was more than a bellwether: it signaled the soon all-encompassing economic woes on a global scale. As far as Hungary

---

[245] Ibid. On his views of the various Archdukes and archduchesses in Budapest, Nicholas Roosevelt, *A Front Row Seat*, 195–99; and other Hungarian aristocrats, 199–205.

[246] Nicholas Roosevelt to Adolph S. Ochs, December 10, 1930, Folder 7: Nicholas Roosevelt (1922–1933), Box 34, Adolph S. Ochs Papers.

[247] Diary entry, December 31, 1930, Hungary 1930–1933, Box 21, Nicholas Roosevelt Papers.

[248] Nicholas Roosevelt, "Hungary," (unpublished), Box 45, Nicholas Roosevelt Papers; Nicholas Roosevelt, *A Front Row Seat*, 194.

was concerned, the major problem arose from its structural weakness. Being a heavily agricultural country, Hungary's well-being was to a very considerable degree conditioned on the quantity and quality of its harvest, which in turn was dependent on weather, and even in good years and with a bountiful harvest there was the question of international wheat prices. Consequently, Hungary's convertible currency stemmed from a somewhat vulnerable sector and the volatile market beyond its borders. Indeed, when prices began to decrease, then dramatically fall, Hungary found itself in a dangerous situation economically and financially.

Another long-running illness was also plaguing the country. Capital poor, traditionally Hungary had been relying on foreign capital to finance much of its lagging economy. After World War I, revolution then counterrevolution, and a punishing peace treaty, the country's financial circumstances were abysmal. It took the financial reconstruction under the aegis of the League of Nations started in 1924 to remove the country form its shaky position. The League-controlled program was successful, and after its completion in 1926 it seemed that Hungary had been put on a safe course. However, despite warnings from various quarters, Hungary stepped onto the dangerous road of taking on new loans and so much overborrowing that when the international money markets suddenly trembled, as in late 1929, then later seriously weakened, the country found itself so much in debt and with so little access to hard currency, fresh credits or loans, that financial disaster was coded in its system. This was the general picture when NR arrived in November 1930.

Perhaps this was the worst possible moment for someone to assume NR's post. Despite the United States' reputation as the beacon of hope, both politically and financially, the reality was that the U.S. showed little if any willingness to help Europe stand on its feet. It refused to accept that Europe's indebtedness to America should not be separated from the troublesome question of war reparations. Private American money did pour to Central and Eastern Europe, but these were not government loans and were not always wisely put out on the market either. In the 1920s, the United States raised its tariff wall, so Europeans could seldom sell their products on the American market, and with the passing of the Smoot-Hawley Tariff Act in the early summer of 1930 to protect American businesses, import duties caused a serious economic downturn in Europe. Therefore, when NR arrived in Budapest, he could only be witness to a country writhing in economic and financial pain, but he lacked any palliative, let alone a cure that his country could or was willing to offer. NR could only embody another chapter of hollow promises. And, of course, there was also the long-standing revisionist propaganda whose major target was America too. Harsh times were always more fertile soil for revisionist voices, yet with the severe economic conditions, the Hungarian government, that had played a safe hand under Bethlen's long reign, had to focus on finding a way out of its economic near collapse. In light of all this, the new American minister had to watch the situation carefully and balance between the forces that he was subjected to.

In the brewing disaster—which would begin in full force in May 1931—Roosevelt relied both on some members of his staff, such as the commercial attaché, who called attention to the misleading data in the monthly reports issued by the Ministry of Finance, and on Hungarian experts such as Eugene Havas. Havas was still only thirty-one years old when NR arrived in Budapest, but he was already an intellectual force to reckon with. He was an eminent economist, who for years had been the Budapest correspondent of the London-based *The Economist*, a leading weekly on the continent, and in 1928 his book on Hungarian financial and economic matters was published in England.[249] He was one of the few people helping NR understand the deepest underpinnings of Hungarian financial issues, and, in contrast to the official Hungarian reports, he provided raw facts about the growing crisis in addition to being a "gadfly, urging me to see people of all sorts and arranging meetings with politicians, journalists and others of every political shade so that I should have as complete as picture as possible."[250] The other person proving to be of great help was Royall Tyler. The American self-made financial expert served as the League's man in Budapest between 1924 and 1929 concerning the financial reconstruction. At the time of NR's arrival, he was on the payroll of Hambros Bank of London as a roving financial ambassador who often touched base in Budapest. From 1931, he would again become the League's man in Budapest. NR and Tyler were in close contact throughout NR's tenure in Hungary.[251]

Despite his later positive memories of Hungarians, NR did not initially have a high opinion of Hungarians at the time of his posting, at least that is what his initial diary entries convey after his first few months at his post. He found, for instance, the traditional Hungarian folk dance, the Csárdás, "strikingly barbaric and primitive" and similar to the Navajo Indians' dances, except for the clothing they wore. He also took issue with the Hungarians' "lament and façade. It is not well to look behind it, either, for it is disillusioning." He added that Hungarians were "keenly aware of their closeness on level to the more Eastern people, and this is why they

---

[249] Eugene Havas, *Hungary's Finance and Trade 1927* (London: General Press, 1928).
[250] Nicholas Roosevelt, "Hungary," (unpublished), Box 45, Nicholas Roosevelt Papers.
[251] For more detail about Royall Tyler's life and work in Hungary, see, *Royall Tyler and Hungary: An American in Europe and the Crisis Years, 1918–1953* (Reno, NV: Helena History Press, 2021).

make such a great hue and cry about the inferiority of the latter and their own superiority and thousand year history etc." This led him to the conclusion that "for the present I am less enthusiastic than I was."[252] This "sense of failure" became a constant on his part for a while.[253]

This feeling toward his hosts in general was not helped by the fact that the overall circumstances in Hungary as well as in the Central European region did not show any sign of improvement, and soon enough the crash took place. A scholar's assertion that the "economic history of 1931 is an almost uninterrupted catalogue of disasters" was apt regarding Hungary.[254] Although the Bethlen government tried for a while to avert financial disaster, their choice not to face reality in time, or to look the other way, may have caused even more serious injury to Hungary's economy and finances. NR, for his part, tried to influence Bethlen to do something. The prime minister seemed to pay little heed to troubling budget deficits, and the American minister, since he could not directly intervene in such a matter, made use of an indirect method. When Royall Tyler happened to be in town in early April, NR "begged him to use his influence with Bethlen to do something," but Tyler's proposal that Jeremiah Smith should return to Hungary and look into Hungarian financial matters was refused by the prime minister.[255] And on May 11, 1931, the Creditanstalt of Vienna, the largest Austrian bank, declared bankruptcy.[256] The ramifications were very quick and equally grim. The panic soon reached neighboring Hungary and Germany, and later played a role in the collapse of the gold standard that was supposed to be the main pillar of the international financial system and stability.[257] In an overwhelmingly agricultural country subject to weather and international market prices, for Hungary, carrying a foreign debt totaling at 4.3 billion pengő ($860 million), such circumstances clearly foreshadowed disaster once the banking sector also cracked.[258]

---

[252] Diary entry, February 8, 1931, Hungary 1930–1933, Box 21, Nicholas Roosevelt Papers.
[253] Diary entry, March 27, 1931, ibid.
[254] Gianni Toniolo, with the assistance of Piet Clement, *Central Bank Cooperation at the Bank for International Settlements, 1930–1973* (Cambridge: Cambridge University Press, 2005), 84.
[255] Nicholas Roosevelt, "Hungary," (unpublished), Box 45, Nicholas Roosevelt Papers.
[256] On the crisis, see, Aurel Schubert, *The Credit-Anstalt Crisis of 1931* (Cambridge: Cambridge University Press, 1991); Iago Gil Aguado, "The Creditanstalt Crisis of 1931 and the Failure of the Austro-German Customs Union Project," *The Historical Journal* 44, no. 1 (March 2001): 199–221.
[257] On the financial crises in 1931, see Barry Eichengreen, *Golden Fetters: The Gold Standard and the Great Depression, 1919–1939* (Oxford: Oxford University Press, 1996), 259–87; Toniolo, *Central Bank Cooperation*, 90–100.
[258] Péter Gunst, *Magyarország gazdaságtörténete, 1914–1989* [The economic history of Hungary, 1914–1918] (Budapest: Nemzeti Tankönyvkiadó, 1996), 48.

NR's first reaction to the unfolding situation and his message to the State Department were both ominous: "This part of the world has become a political cauldron in the last two weeks, and is about ready to boil over," he wrote to his mother, while in the official report he opined that the circumstances "had gravely increased the unrest and uncertainty in this country" and it was likely "that the political as well as the economic situation in Hungary may at any moment become critical."[259] In this estimation he was not wrong. For the next two years—his remaining tenure as minister in Budapest—Hungary balanced on the threshold of total financial collapse.

Short-term credits soon disappeared, and Hungary managed to get by throughout the summer only with recourse to the Bank of International Settlement. An envoy of the BIS, René Charron, who worked in Budapest during the earlier financial reconstruction, arrived in Budapest and had confidential talks with Bethlen. He forced a program on the prime minister so that Hungary could somehow make it through the next period. Bethlen promised to introduce the necessary reforms, and a syndicate of Hungarian banks signed an agreement with the BIS. The secret plans were duly passed on to NR by Charron, and in turn the State Department learned about them almost in real time.[260] This episode fell on July 4, the American Independence Day, so at the traditional reception at the Legation for patriots, NR had to alternate "between standing at the door and shaking hands with stray Americans and going into the library to check up on the wording of the cable that was being crafted."[261] To his mother he mentioned with some malice that "too many Hungarians came—persons who really had no claim to come at all. We served only lemonade, ice tea and ice coffee, with sandwiches etc., but everything in the house was cleaned out."[262] In the same letter he also bragged about his omniscience regarding the serious financial situation: "I was one of the very few people who already months ago predicted it and wrote lengthy dispatches about it and insisted that there was but one solution. I am of course much interested to see my predictions verified and my interpretations proved correct."[263]

---

[259] Nicholas Roosevelt to Mrs. J. West Roosevelt, May 14, 1931, Folder: Roosevelt, Mrs. J. West (mother) 1930–1933. Box 12; Nicholas Roosevelt to Henry L. Stimson, No. 101, May 15, 1931, Folder: Dispatches from Hungary 1930–1933, Box 69, Nicholas Roosevelt Papers.
[260] Diary entry, July 4, 1931, Hungary 1930–1933, Box 21; Nicholas Roosevelt to Henry L. Stimson, No. 128, July 7, 1931, Folder: Dispatches from Hungary 1930–1933, Box 69, Nicholas Roosevelt Papers.
[261] Nicholas Roosevelt, "Hungary," (unpublished), Box 45, Nicholas Roosevelt Papers.
[262] Nicholas Roosevelt to Mrs. J. West Roosevelt, July 5, 1931, Folder: Roosevelt, Mrs. J. West (mother) 1930–1933, Box 12, Nicholas Roosevelt Papers.
[263] Ibid.

From late July he traveled around Yugoslavia, Italy, Austria, and Germany in order to assess the economic and financial conditions there. This was both his interest and job, but it also gave him an opportunity to escape the Hungarian capital. His opinion concerning Europe in the beginning, namely that it was a "wretched continent," became even more pessimistic by the conclusion of his tour.[264] At the end of August he informed his mother about the dark outlook "with lots of starvation and suffering—perhaps even worse." He confessed that he was "more pessimistic than ever about this old Europe, and fear we shall have several ghastly years ahead of us."[265] Perhaps the fact that Bethlen and his government resigned on August 24 may have played a part in his diagnosis. After ten years, Bethlen, the "permanent prime minister" as he was called on account of his unprecedentedly long tenure, realized that he was not able to turn things around and rather chose to pass the reins to Gyula Károlyi.

The aristocratic Károlyi had been minister for foreign affairs since the previous December, and for a very short interim period he had served as a counter revolutionary prime minister in 1919. His experience notwithstanding, he came nowhere near Bethlen's political talent and at such a critical juncture he could not fill his predecessor's shoes. His appointment to the post was more likely due to the calculation that someone would have to take the heat for the worst phase of the depression—what was needed was a dispensable political soldier. Under the prevailing circumstances, Károlyi did not have much room to maneuver. He stepped onto the path of austerity measures: state expenditures were heavily curbed, especially in the form of reduction of state officials' salaries, social entitlements, and pensions. These, however, brought scant results, and soon enough, almost all segments of Hungarian society turned against Károlyi.[266] In short, his premiership was generally understood to be crisis management until better circumstances or leaders appeared.

NR spent his longest interval in Hungary during Gyula Károlyi's tenure. He described the count as "cadaverous and stoop-shouldered, with a short grizzled beard and rheumy eyes blinking in a tired manner behind his gold-rimmed spectacles he was gentle and frank of speech—a man of obviously spotless but immensely

---

[264] Nicholas Roosevelt to Mrs. J. West Roosevelt, July 21, 1931, ibid.
[265] Nicholas Roosevelt to Mrs. J. West Roosevelt, August 25, 1931, ibid.
[266] On the times and problems of Károlyi's premiership in general, see, Márkus László, *A Károlyi Gyula kormány bel- és külpolitikája* [The domestic andforeign policy of the Károlyi government] (Budapest: Akadémiai Kiadó, 1968); Püski Levente, *A Horthy-korszak szürke eminenciása Károlyi Gyula (1871–1947)* [Gyula Károlyi, the éminence grise of the Horthy era] (Pécs-Budapest: Kronosz Kiadó – Magyar Történelmi Társulat, 2016).

weary, there was about him a certain true nobility of character."[267] Strengthening the historical judgment of Károlyi, NR observed: "He was utterly unselfish and high-minded and had had but little experience in foreign affairs or politics."[268] Naturally, due to the conditions an American minister could not do much other than report the unfolding drama in his country of post. But as an observation post, Budapest was important for Washington at this moment and later as well.

NR hit rock bottom in the fall of 1931—at least his various letters, reports, and diary entries carry a tone of total pessimism at that time. He wrote to the economic advisor of the State Department, Herbert Feis, that it seemed impossible "to stave off disaster."[269] To his mother he was even more open. Not only Hungary but the whole region was under stress and, therefore, the looming catastrophe filled him "with profound pessimism" regarding the whole of Central Europe.[270] In October he spent ten days in Switzerland, partly to see his future wife, Tirzah Maris Gates, and partly to try to gain useful information as to the possible future of Hungary's finances. After that visit, he was afraid that Hungary's situation was "beyond help, and we face, as I foretold many months ago, a winter of suffering and probably of strife. The financial problem is beyond repair, and I fear the worst."[271] He had a conversation with Tyler at Geneva and learned from him that the League of Nations was going to send its people to Budapest to investigate the circumstances and what could be done. By the end of October, Budapest struck NR as a bleak place: "More and more beggars are to be seen, and persons in rags. Starvation is round the corner for thousands, and the situation not only here but all through East Europe seems hopeless. The government and people here continue to live in world of make believe, and refuse to face facts. It is discouraging."[272] These were rare moments of absolute loss of confidence, both in the economic and financial outlook of Hungary and Europe, and in himself.

The dire circumstances, his ambition, and his interest in financial matters spurred him to come up with a plan that he could present as a grand solution to the ongoing difficulty of American creditors. American banking houses—sometimes alone, sometimes in a consortium—placed considerable amounts of money

---

[267] Nicholas Roosevelt, "Hungary," (unpublished), Box 45, Nicholas Roosevelt Papers.
[268] Ibid.
[269] Nicholas Roosevelt to Herbert Feis, September 2, 1931, Folder: Feis, Dr. Herbert, Box 5, Nicholas Roosevelt Papers.
[270] Nicholas Roosevelt to Mrs. J. West Roosevelt, September 12, 1931, Folder: Roosevelt, Mrs. J. West (mother) 1930–1933, Box 12, Nicholas Roosevelt Papers.
[271] Nicholas Roosevelt to Mrs. J. West Roosevelt, October 1, 1931, ibid.
[272] Diary entry, October 29, 1931, Hungary 1930–1933, Box 21, Nicholas Roosevelt Papers.

in Central European countries, mainly in Germany but in other countries as well. As the danger increasingly loomed that the various countries might declare a moratorium on payments on these loans, the American private banking houses faced the possibility of staggering losses. NR thought he had found a solution for their predicament. First, he believed that since many of the loans that were floated in the United States were unsound, the investment houses would have no recourse left but to write off these debts. As to the future though, the difficult job was representation. In Hungary alone he counted three dozen different American banking houses that had issued either long-term or short-term loans. He recommended that a committee be established in which all these houses were represented, and thus they could present a united front in trying to assert their interests.[273] This plan became such a bee in NR's bonnet that he regularly wrote about it to various people in government. In the late spring of 1932, for instance, he wrote the State Department a long confidential memorandum on how to safeguard investors. In this he echoed Allen Dulles's idea concerning the establishment of an association for the protection of foreign bond holders in the United States.[274] As Dulles argued in an article for *Foreign Affairs*, "with the European bondholders organized as they are and enjoying the support of their governments, they will be in a position to obtain more consideration from foreign debtor governments than we obtain unless American bondholders are organized to exert prompt pressure, with proper support from Washington."[275] It is both impossible and unimportant to declare which of the two men came up with the idea first, but since the realization of such an undertaking would have needed governmental support, it remained hypothetical.

In addition, NR thought that the United States should play a role in financially reconstructing Europe. In his view, this was "necessary not only so as to avoid the further difficulties arising from an intensification of the economic collapse of Europe, but also because we now have, after all, the world's principal reserve of capital."[276] He also had the idea that the United States ought to take part in an international consortium that would assume control over loans issued to European countries but that the United States would help especially those countries in need.[277] In

---

[273] Nicholas Roosevelt to Henry L. Stimson, No. 185, October 23, 1931, Folder: Dispatches from Hungary 1930–1933, Box 69, Nicholas Roosevelt Papers.
[274] Allen Dulles, "The Protection of American Foreign Bondholders," *Foreign Affairs* 10, no. 3 (April 1932): 474–84.
[275] Ibid., 481.
[276] Nicholas Roosevelt to William R. Castle, Jr., October 3, 1931, Folder: Castle, William R. Jr., Box 2, Nicholas Roosevelt Papers.
[277] Ibid.

other words, he had an organization in mind akin to the World Bank established during World War II.

This activity—sending data and analyses thereof together with recommending proposals of a financial and economic nature—became a regular feature of NR's ministerial activity in Hungary. In these missives he laid out for the State Department economic data regarding Eastern Europe and the foreign indebtedness of Hungary, sent in detailed data on American investments in Hungary, on the foreign indebtedness of Hungary and the other countries in the region, the need for economic cooperation among the Danubian countries, and how the great powers could help these countries by providing special treatment so that they could increase their exports, through which it would be possible for them to get hard currency and repay their debts.[278] Apparently, these ministerial reports struck a favorable chord among those who read them. Herbert Feis, for instance, referred to "the many very excellent dispatches on Hungarian financial conditions" that NR had been sending, while ambassador Joseph Grew confirmed from Tokyo that NR's reports were "regarded as the best received from any source in Europe."[279] But compliments came from circles outside the U.S. government as well. Thomas Lamont of J. P. Morgan & Co., for one, partly based upon a conversation with Royall Tyler, praised Roosevelt for "doing an excellent job at Budapest," and said he had "proved to be a careful and watchful observer for it and have on the side so informed yourself as to make you one of the world's leading experts on Hungary and the nations round about."[280] Even NR's British counterpart found positive things to write about him and characterized him as "an intelligent, active and forceful personality of wide knowledge, specially on economic affairs. Very agreeable and friendly in conversation, of quiet manner and clear conception."[281] Thus, the energy NR spent on economic and financial questions, and his observations thereof, became appreciated in important circles in the world of business and diplomacy.

---

[278] Nicholas Roosevelt to Henry L. Stimson, No. 204, November 30, 1931, N. Roosevelt to Henry L. Stimson, No. 222, January 16, 1932, Nicholas Roosevelt to Henry L. Stimson, No. 223, January 16, 1932, N. Roosevelt to Henry L. Stimson, No. 233, January 30, 1932, Nicholas Roosevelt to Henry L. Stimson, No. 358, October 10, 1932, N. Roosevelt to Henry L. Stimson, No. 360, October 17, 1932, Nicholas Roosevelt to Henry L. Stimson, No. 363, October 20, 1932, Folder: Dispatches from Hungary 1930–1933, Box 69, Nicholas Roosevelt Papers.

[279] Herbert Feis to Nicholas Roosevelt, January 27, 1932, Folder: Feis, Dr. Herbert; Joseph C. Grew to Nicholas Roosevelt, July 11, 1932, Folder: Grew, Joseph C., Box 5, Nicholas Roosevelt Papers.

[280] Thomas Lamont to Nicholas Roosevelt, March 21, 1932, Folder: Lamont, Thomas, Box 8, Nicholas Roosevelt Papers.

[281] "Report on the Heads of Foreign Missions in Budapest," in Viscount Chilston to John Simon, January 5, 1932, C 61/61/21, FO 371/15971, The National Archives, London, UK.

At this time the League of Nations finally decided that it needed to take up Hungary's case again. In light of the dire circumstances, the League's Financial Committee held its meeting in the Hungarian capital from October 16–22. In its concluding report the Committee stated that due to the reduced wheat prices Hungary was deprived of the foreign currency that would have been needed to balance the overborrowing and overexpenditure of the past few years.[282] As part of the possible solution, the League left behind two persons in the hope that they might be able to guide Hungary back onto more normalized economic and financial paths. One of them was Royall Tyler, who had already spent five years in Hungary in the 1920s and had immense local knowledge, the other was British diplomat Henry James Bruce. Tyler became the Financial Committee's representative in Hungary and an advisor to the Hungarian government, while Bruce was named advisor to the National Bank of Hungary. The various recommendations of the League and its representatives could not, however, overturn the present situation, and by the end of the year Hungary found that the only recourse to alleviate the squeeze was to declare a partial moratorium on foreign loans.

NR had predicted this move by the Hungarian government months earlier.[283] The step, therefore, was neither totally unexpected nor a shock. Indeed, weeks before the moratorium Secretary of State Stimson was informed by the Hungarian minister in Washington, László Széchenyi, that in light of the dire straits "a default as to amortization payments might become necessary."[284] NR had firsthand knowledge that the default was imminent two weeks before its declaration.[285] The default on foreign loans perfectly fit with NR's pessimistic perspective on the situation. The Hungarian government, for his part, was so short on foreign currency that this controversial step was the only one left to it. Only the League of Nations reconstruction loan was exempt for some time, but by the following June the Hungarian government defaulted on that loan as well. The Hungarian financial calamity had reached its nadir, as had NR.

In his diary Roosevelt dug much deeper and on a more personal level than in official reports or letters regarding both himself and various Hungarian persons of note. This is how we know how gloomily he looked at his own situation, Hungary's state

---

[282] "Report on the Financial Position of Hungary, Submitted to the Council on January 29th, 1932," *League of Nations Journal*, 13th Year, no. 3 (March 1932) (Part I), Sixty-sixth Session of the Council), 611–12.
[283] Nicholas Roosevelt, "Hungary," (unpublished), Box 45, Nicholas Roosevelt Papers.
[284] Memorandum of conversation with the Hungarian Minister Count László Széchenyi and Dr. Oliver Jacobi, Lawyer and Banker from Budapest, November 11, 1931, Reel 163, Henry Lewis Stimson Papers, MS 465, Yale Archives.
[285] Diary entry, December 10, 1931, Hungary 1930–1933, Box 21, Nicholas Roosevelt Papers.

of affairs, and that of Central Europe as well. In December 1931, when he had been at his post for more than a year, instead of the financial landscape he chose to analyze himself for a change. His conclusions were at least as pessimistic as anything he had written about Hungary's finances. He complained about becoming lazy, which he blamed on the baneful effect of Europe. But the core issue was his ungratified ambition: "Here I am, in my 39th year," he wrote, "ostensibly a world success but in reality the child of fortune and someone else's good name, [...but I have] grossly and completely failed in all those things that really count in life." He believed that aside from his appreciated reports on economic and financial issues, he also failed in his job as minister. He specified as the main reasons for such an observation that he had been socially inept, had not established important and close relationships with other diplomats, and, therefore, did not represent his home country to the fullest possible measure. "I have been idle, self centered [sic], indifferent and asleep at the switch. I have been away from my post as much as the law would allow," which alluded to his study tours in various European countries, although those were clearly related to his work. It also bothered him that he had started to dislike Hungarians more and more, which also did not augur well for the future. A few months earlier he had tried to convince himself to the contrary, but now his own verdict was in: "What a ghastly mess I have made of my personal life."[286]

Three months later he again tried to take the long view regarding his time in Budapest as an American minister. This time he was seemingly over the reigning mood of near desperation. He judged that "from the point of view of the work done, I can honestly say that I never did any better. I have since looked over the files of the despatches [sic] that I sent to the Department, and it is a record of which anyone could be proud." It was as if in the safe haven of his diary he wanted to convince himself that he had been useful. He took enormous pride in foretelling events. An example would be the moratorium declared by the Hungarian government, and with some hyperbole wrote, "Not even the Hungarian Government knew as much about the real conditions here as the Department of State." His ego also received a boost from the fact that his reports were indeed "excellent, and what is more, it was apparently really appreciated in Washington." He therefore felt that there might be an avenue for him in diplomacy, since he had a knack for foreign affairs, but due to his family name "my usefulness is sharply circumscribed."[287] His real sorrow was that

---

[286] The quotations are from Diary entry, December 10, 1931, Hungary 1930–1933, Box 21, Nicholas Roosevelt Papers.
[287] The quotations are from Diary entry, February 22, 1932, Hungary 1930–1933, Box 21, Nicholas Roosevelt Papers.

he was never allowed too close to the political campfire and could only sing along with the tune of those stoking the fire.

As far as Hungary and the neighboring countries were concerned, he used a similarly gloomy tone. He was "frank to admit that I see no possible way other than a fairly rapid process of sliding back into social and economic conditions of several centuries ago."[288] His reason for this opinion was that "this part of the world," as he referred to Central Europe, lacked the sober common will for cooperation, even under detrimental economic circumstances, or especially then. He considered the possibility that using "some outside pressure could force the people of Central Europe to come to their senses," but he saw no such remedy in the near or even more distant future.[289] He expected the worst to happen in late May and thought it would be useful to be "present when the kettle boils over."[290] When he took a short trip in France and the Netherlands and talked to various people there—bankers, journalists, politicians—he also detected outright pessimism. The overwhelming opinion there was that "the European situation was beyond hope of recovery and that nothing could stave off a complete collapse in Eastern Europe."[291] No wonder, as his letter to Feis at the State Department attests, that he was also "very pessimistic about any workable solution being discovered in time to save anything out of the wreck."[292] This pessimistic mood did not change throughout 1932. In November he wrote to his predecessor that the prevailing "conditions have not been as bad since 1919, but the Hungarians continue to be cheerful and hope for a better day. For my own part I am pessimistic."[293]

As an escape from and interlude to his diplomatic post in Budapest, he had a chance to glow in one of his favorite roles: public educator. He received an invitation from the Netherlands to give a series of speeches on the topic of American journalism at the University of Leyden in late April and early May. Since it was for a European audience, he focused on American journalistic traditions and contrasted them with their European counterparts. His three major observations were that (1) in the United States writing for a newspaper was more of an anonymous task and

---

[288] Nicholas Roosevelt to Herbert Feis, February 10, 1932, Folder: Feis, Dr. Herbert, Box 6, Nicholas Roosevelt Papers.
[289] Ibid.
[290] Nicholas Roosevelt to John F. Carter, Jr., March 22, 1932, Folder: Castle, William R. Jr., Box 2, Nicholas Roosevelt Papers.
[291] Nicholas Roosevelt to Herbert Feis, May 24, 1932, Folder: Feis, Dr. Herbert, Box 5, Nicholas Roosevelt Papers.
[292] Ibid.
[293] Nicholas Roosevelt to Joshua Butler Wright, November 13, 1932, Folder: Wright, J. Butler, Box 16, Nicholas Roosevelt Papers.

there were fewer big names that gave a paper prestige, (2) serving the audience with the freshest news sometimes led to inaccuracy in presenting the news, and (3) the local newspapers carried considerably more weight.[294]

Hungary's economic and financial situation remained a constant headache for the Hungarian government and the League of Nations, let alone the various creditors. Despite NR's predictions, society did not break, and no upheaval took place, but misery and hunger were indeed rife, and no end was in sight. In June, Hungary defaulted even on the Reconstruction Loan of 1924, which enjoyed immunity to the moratorium declared the previous Christmas. The country's gold reserves were depleted, and no substantial foreign currency was available due to restricted trade. Hungary had suffered more than a 50 percent decrease in its foreign trade since 1930. Under such conditions, even the League of Nations agreed, it would have been unrealistic to expect Hungary to meet its debt obligations.[295]

On the official surface, however, NR played out the role of the American diplomat. The most important aspect of his job was to be the contact person between the United States and Hungary, and especially since he was a journalist, he put an emphasis on limited public appearances and sensible cooperation with the Hungarian newspapers. Already at the beginning of his service in Hungary, he tried to strike a friendly chord with Hungarian journalists exactly because of their being colleagues.[296] In his official capacity, on occasion he had to be present at certain events. One was the annual celebration of July 4th at the George Washington statue in the City Park of Budapest. This occasion had always proved to be a headache to American ministers in the interwar years. The Hungarian hosts, more often than not, tried to use the commemoration as an opportunity to lament the Trianon Treaty and the loss Hungary suffered as a consequence. Since almost all public speeches mentioned territorial revision in one form or another, appearing on the same stage with people embracing that view might have given the impression of agreement. The American ministers or other representatives therefore always were on their guard and took immense care not to say anything that might show agreement with irredentist politics in Hungary. They tried to avoid appearing at these public shows and often sent someone from the staff to represent the Legation. For

---

[294] "Standards and Types of American Journalism," April 29, 1932, "The Technique of Newspapers in America," May 2, 1932, and "The Ethics of Influence of the Press in America," May 3, 1932, Folder: Leydon University lectures on American journalism 1932, Box 63, Nicholas Roosevelt Papers.

[295] Work of the Financial Committee during Its Forty-sixth Session (June 27–30, 1932), *League of Nations Journal*, 13th Year, no. 7 (July 1932), Sixty-seventh Session of the Council, 1275, 1453–54.

[296] Diary entry, March 25, 1931, Hungary 1930–1933, Box 21, Nicholas Roosevelt Papers.

instance, in July 1932 Consul General John Osborne represented the American Legation. That year the Hungarian organizers were very attentive and wanted to emphasize Hungarian–American friendship by opening the Washington Walkway in the City Park, and also planting trees in memory of the Hungarian soldiers who fought in the American War of Independence.[297]

George Washington in particular enjoyed immense popularity in Hungary. In the summer of 1931, for example, NR had to be present along with most of the Legation's staff at the 25th anniversary of the George Washington statue's unveiling. NR gave a speech that pleased Hungarians because in addition to praising Washington and his legacy, he also had nice things to say about his hosts. He mentioned the beautiful Great Plains of Hungary, and he found parallels between Americans and Hungarians, including similar movements of the people, conquering the wilderness, self-help as a shared trait. He also mentioned the well-developed culture that Hungarians made possible in the Carpathian Basin. There was a clear contradiction between these words and his thoughts recorded in his diary entries that were not so favorable to his host nation. His July 4th speech also hinted, very softly though, at the Hungarian view of the all-encompassing depression and warned his hosts "not to attempt to simplify the reasons for the present difficulties, and find a culprit in one event or nation."[298] Instead, he emphasized international cooperation as a possible palliative for the economic hardships.

NR also made a public appearance in February 1932, when Hungary paid attention to the bicentennial celebration of George Washington's birthday. At a meeting held on this occasion at the Hungarian Academy of Sciences, Roosevelt gave a short speech that mainly focused on the Washington's historical role. He also emphasized the necessity for cooperation between the United States and Europe, especially in light of the economic and financial depression.[299] Hungarian newspapers took advantage of the occasion to hail president Hoover and his moratorium on intergovernmental debt payments, and the saw in the American president a true successor to Washington.[300]

From time to time NR gave interviews to Hungarian dailies. These are interesting as an example of how he, as minister representing his government in an official capacity, informed the Hungarian newspaper-reading public on various

---

[297] *Pesti Hírlap*, June 24, 1932, 7; July 5, 1932, 3.
[298] *Budapesti Hírlap*, July 5, 1931, 5.
[299] *Pesti Napló*, February 23, 1932, 9; *Budapesti Hírlap*, February 28, 1932, 10; *Pesti Hírlap*, March 18, 1932, 6.
[300] *Pesti Hírlap*, July 4, 1931, 10.

issues concerning the United States and Europe. He always avoided politics but was willing to confer about issues of general interest. For example, similarly to his lectures in the Netherlands, he tried to explain the difference between continental and American journalism. The main difference, according to NR, lay in the much wider range and variety of information consumed by Americans, whereas in Europe a newspaper was trying to put forward an opinion. More generally, he thought the chasm between the United States and Europe was unbridgeable, and he believed that Europe was not being Americanized.[301] This is interesting from the aspect that in Europe as well as in Hungary, there had been voices raised against the American cultural juggernaut influencing Europe: jazz, the Charleston, Hollywood movies, etc. In 1928, for example, Hungarian editorials took up the issue and saw the danger of a predominance of American financial power that might negatively affect Hungarian culture and art.[302] From this point of view, NR's statements may have been somewhat reassuring, although during these hard times the question became, if not moot, somewhat academic. In another newspaper interview, however, he was asked about the relative lack of high culture in the United States. He fervently defended his compatriots and their lifestyle. The importance of commercialism and the general welfare, he emphasized, were not necessarily irreconcilable with culture. And although he admitted that standardization was typical in the United States, he also cited the achievements of American science, charity, or well-organized public education.[303] On yet another occasion, referring to the upcoming summer Olympics to be held in Los Angeles, he emphasized American society's orientation toward setting records.[304]

In the summer of 1932 American journalist Hubert Renfro Knickerbocker of the *New York Evening Post* was writing a book on the present state of affairs in Europe. He explored mainly the economic conditions as he covered the major countries of the continent: England, France, Germany, Italy, and lesser ones like Austria, Belgium, Czechoslovakia. He wished to devote a chapter to Hungary as well. Accordingly, he spent a few days in that country, and he was accompanied by Roosevelt on the journey from Vienna to Budapest. He probably even received a few tips from the American minister as well as to which parts of the capital were worth visiting.[305] The result of the three-month trip was the book *Can Europe Recover?* In

---

[301] *Az Est*, January 29, 1931, 7.
[302] *Budapesti Hírlap*, August 24, 1928, 1, and August 26, 1928, 1.
[303] *Pesti Napló*, April 5, 1931, 49–50.
[304] *Sporthírlap*, March 24, 1932, 9.
[305] *Pesti Napló*, July 6, 1932, 6.

the chapter on Hungary the author's main observation was that although Hungary and Hungarians were down and in a serious condition—the country was in his judgment "stripped to the bone"—the future was not as bleak as many suggested, since the countryside could feed itself, and that was "a reassuring omen for Europe."[306] Still, even if the people in the villages could eat, and their appearance showed as much, the suburbs of Budapest told a different story. There starvation and destitution were the rule, Knickerbocker wrote, and even compared to other miserable places in Europe, the Hungarian capital did not fare well: "Nowhere in the Soviet Union have I seen such wretchedness as that of the peripheral population of Budapest."[307] In Knickerbocker's view, four conditions had to be met in order to climb out of the depression in Central Europe: people should not be satisfied with anything less than a certain standard of living; the armed forces should be strong enough to keep order; there should be cooperation among the governments; and governments must lift the restrictions on trade and currency.[308] But despite such negative assessments, the author's conclusion was optimistic, and Hungarian readers must have liked it: "Hungary will recover."[309] In December Knickerbocker returned to Hungary, in all likelihood to promote his just-published book, and once again NR accompanied him to Budapest from Vienna.[310]

Another famous visitor arrived in Hungary in September: General Douglas MacArthur. The chief of staff of the United States army spent three days in Budapest on his unofficial European tour, on which France, Poland, Austria, Hungary, Romania, and Turkey were the stops. Most likely, his goal was to look around on the continent, and especially in Central Europe as to the conditions for a possible disarmament agreement later on. Although not an official state visit, the Hungarian government was very proud to host the general. Not only was he the first high-ranking American military officer to visit Hungary since 1919, but, as always, Hungarians wanted to read into this visit a manifestation of American friendliness toward Hungary. Hungary was trying to strengthen its limited military forces, and meeting with a prominent American officer gave a chance to talk about military principles and questions under unofficial circumstances.[311] During this visit, MacArthur

---

[306] Hubert Renfro Knickerbocker, *Can Europe Recover?* (London: John Lane, The Bodley Head Ltd., 1932), 61.
[307] Knickerbocker, *Can Europe Recover?*, 65.
[308] Ibid., 72–73.
[309] Ibid., 59.
[310] *Pesti Napló*, December 14, 1932, 4.
[311] Nicholas Roosevelt to Henry L. Stimson, October 5, 1932, 864.00 P.R./58, M 1206, Roll 3, Microfilm Publications, Records of the Department of State Relating to Internal Affairs of Hungary, 1930–1944,

met the minister of defense and soon to be Prime Minister Gyula Gömbös and also Regent Horthy. He inspected two small military training facilities and was the guest of honor at lunches and dinners, to which NR always accompanied him.[312] But the prominent visitor gave the American minister in Budapest a headache, as the general always demanded various items of comfort for himself that Roosevelt deemed inappropriate.[313]

By the fall of 1932, it was clear that Hungary was not going to recovery quickly if at all from the tight grip of the depression. The position of the government, and especially that of Károlyi, the prime minister, was never strong and over time showed further gradual weakening. Half a year into his tenure, more and more dissatisfaction was manifest, and attacks were made against him, including by the majority political party led by Bethlen.[314] A new man was needed at the helm, and from October 1, Gyula Gömbös was the new prime minister. Gömbös was a fervent nationalist and believer in revisionism who favored agriculture as the main component of the Hungarian economy, as opposed to heavy industry. He believed in a highly centralized government, took certain measures from Mussolini but did not think fascism was exportable to Hungary. In the domestic political arena he turned out to be a populist, while in foreign policy he proved to be a realist who laid the emphasis on his country's economic interests.[315]

Gömbös appealed to NR in many ways, and NR was "optimistic about him."[316] He liked the prime minister's "directness, vitality and obvious simplicity" and found him "immensely alive and refreshingly earthy."[317] Even more to Roosevelt's taste was that Gömbös, who had a good command of English, "always spoke to me with great freedom—even about Hungarian political affairs—and I enjoyed his racy

---

National Archives and Records Administration (hereafter cited as NARA), Washington, D. C., U.S.A.

[312] *Ujság*, September 17, 1932, 3; *Nemzeti Ujság*, September 18, 1932, 3; *Pesti Napló*, September 18, 1932, 3, and September 20, 1932, 5; *Nemzeti Ujság*, September 20, 1932, 7; *Budapesti Hírlap*, September 20, 1932, 5.

[313] On MacArthur's visit to Hungary, Nicholas Roosevelt, *A Front Row Seat*, 206–10.

[314] See, Márkus, *A Károlyi Gyula kormány*, 276–85; Püski, *A Horthy-korszak szürke eminenciása*, 73–80.

[315] On Gömbös's life and career see, Pál Pritz, *Magyarország külpolitikája Gömbös Gyula miniszterelnöksége idején, 1932–1936* [The foreign policy of Hungary during the premiership of Gyula Gömbös, 1932–1936] (Budapest: Akadémiai Kiadó, 1982); Mária Ormos, *Magyarország a két világháború korában (1919–1945)* [Hungary in the age of the world wars] (Debrecen: Csokonai Kiadó, 1998), 147–68; Jenő Gergely, *Gömbös Gyula. Vázlat egy politikai életrajzhoz* [Gyula Gömbös. Sketches for a political biography] (Budapest: Elektra Kiadóház, 1999); and József Vonyó, *Gömbös Gyula* [Gyula Gömbös] (Budapest: Napvilág Kiadó, 2014).

[316] Nicholas Roosevelt to Mrs. J. West Roosevelt, October 11, 1932, Folder: Roosevelt, Mrs. J. West (mother) 1930–1933, Box 12, Nicholas Roosevelt Papers.

[317] Nicholas Roosevelt, "Hungary," (unpublished), Box 45, Nicholas Roosevelt Papers.

bluntness."³¹⁸ Sometimes they had dinner together, and these occasions convinced the American minister that Gömbös may have been a simple soul, but he was shrewder than expected.³¹⁹ During Gömbös's tenure as prime minister Hungary slowly climbed out of the depression's hole. It was not solely thanks to him, of course, but he played an important part in strengthening the Hungarian economic and financial landscape.

Another important Hungarian figure playing a key role in this task was Béla Imrédy. Formerly a leading official at the National Bank of Hungary, he earned international prestige for his talent and now took the helm at the Ministry of Finance. Imrédy, too, appealed to Roosevelt, because he "was a realist, and hence free from the temptation of trying to shape conditions to meet theories. He was always satisfactory to deal with, albeit he never made any concessions in negotiations. It was refreshing to find a Hungarian who had no illusions about his country's position in the world."³²⁰ Gömbös indeed brought fresh blood to the politics of Hungary, and at the initial stages he was successful. NR reported to Washington that new prime minister's popularity after having been in office for just two months had only grown.³²¹ Two months later, however, he detected signs that Gömbös's popularity was waning.³²² No doubt this was because things in the country were not quickly turning around for the better.

There were two more famous Hungarians that NR often referred to in his writings. He knew both from the 1919 days, and even earlier, and both played a prominent role in Hungary's political life in the first half of the twentieth century. One of them was Pál Teleki, who made perhaps the most positive impression on NR among the roster of Hungarian politicians. Teleki was no ordinary politician, because despite the political role he was willing to play (he was prime minister in 1920–21 for a short time and assumed that burdensome position again during the first phase of World War II), he was mainly a scientist, more precisely an eminent and renowned geographer. When NR met him in 1919, he came away thinking Teleki was the brightest mind he had come across. In his memoirs he described him as "cool, clear, and frank," a man who "neither evaded nor denied facts which more biased Hungarians would have brushed aside angrily because they affected

---

³¹⁸ Ibid.
³¹⁹ Diary entry, November 30, 1931, Hungary 1930–1933, Box 21, Nicholas Roosevelt Papers.
³²⁰ Nicholas Roosevelt, "Hungary," (unpublished), Box 45, Nicholas Roosevelt Papers. On Imrédy in more detail, see Ormos, *Magyarország a két világháború korában*, 186–201.
³²¹ Nicholas Roosevelt to Henry L. Stimson, December 5, 1932, 864.00 P.R./60, M 1206, Roll 3, NARA.
³²² Nicholas Roosevelt to Henry L. Stimson, February 8, 1933, 864.00 P.R./62, ibid.

Hungary's claims adversely."³²³ Teleki was one of those rare specimens in this part of the world who, despite the "oriental" surroundings, stood out intellectually as "a western European"—clear praise on NR's part.³²⁴

The other such person, actually NR's longest acquaintance in Hungary, was Albert Apponyi. NR first met the grand old man of Hungary in St. Louis, Missouri, when Apponyi took part in the Twelfth Conference of the Inter-Parliamentary Union in 1904 and then paid a visit to Theodore Roosevelt at Oyster Bay.³²⁵ They met again in Hungary in that fateful March of 1919. Now, in the early 1930s, NR could again on occasion enjoy the company of the old and revered politician. In his memoirs, NR created a positive image of Apponyi: "He always expressed himself honestly. His exceptional knowledge and long familiarity with European events made him an unusually interesting companion. He was a charming host, always considerate and receptive. He loved music and understood it and he knew the literature of at least five nations. [...] He was a figure to be remembered as a man, as a type, and as a friend." He also portrayed him as a detached mentor of his on European, and especially Austro-Hungarian issues.³²⁶ Although these lines from his 1950s drafts for a memoir are not untrue, back in the early 1930s he was more critical of the old man. At the time of his first formal luncheon as American minister, for instance, he had a conversation with Apponyi, who proved to be "a fine old man but who repeated the same things he told me 11 years ago about Hungary."³²⁷ And NR did not like or share those thoughts about Hungary seeking revenge for lost territories.

Despite his past criticism of Apponyi, when the old man died at the age of 86 in 1933, in an unusual gesture of honor and respect, NR wrote an obituary for one of the Hungarian dailies. He perhaps did not hyperbolize when he wrote that the death of Apponyi was "a profound loss to Hungarian American relations. More than any other single individual he served to interpret the two countries to each

---

³²³ Nicholas Roosevelt, *A Front Row Seat*, 201.
³²⁴ Ibid., 202.
³²⁵ On Apponyi's tour in the United States and for his own account of the meeting with Theodore Roosevelt, see Albert Apponyi, *The Memoirs of Count Apponyi* (New York: The Macmillan Company, 1935), 155–76.
³²⁶ Nicholas Roosevelt, "Hungary," (unpublished), Box 45, Nicholas Roosevelt Papers.
³²⁷ Diary entry, January 28, 1931, Hungary 1930–1933, Box 21, Nicholas Roosevelt Papers. This was not a new charge on Nicholas Roosevelt's part. When he traveled to Europe in mid-November 1923, he had a few occasions to talk with Apponyi, and he recorded his feelings: "I had a number of interesting talks with Count Apponyi about the Hungarian situation, in which he said little that I had not often heard before from the Hungarian Royalists. He pretended to favor the fulfilment of the Trianon Treaty, but it was clear that he had many reservations and that the foremost of these was that Hungary would never rest until she had regained her lost territories. This was precisely the same attitude which he took when I saw him in Budapest in 1919." Entry without date, European trip 1923–1924, Box 21, Nicholas Roosevelt Papers.

other."³²⁸ The count had indeed been in many ways the longest link between the two countries both in the private and official spheres. More controversial were observations in the obituary such as Apponyi having been neither "misled by false doctrines nor blinded by prejudice" and an individual who had "never lost faith in the ultimate triumph of justice."³²⁹ NR emphasized that Apponyi could not have been accused of "blatant chauvinism," because he was more characterized by "reasoned patriotism."³³⁰ It is enough to look at Roosevelt's diary entries, especially from 1919, to understand that despite possibly more positive impressions garnered late in the count's life, NR's thoughts and judgments on Apponyi were often far from favorable. What is more, these negative impressions were formed exactly due to Apponyi's stance on what justice meant for Hungary or how much of a chauvinist he had been.

Given NR's strong interest in financial and economic issues, according to his memoirs, "the [State] Department wanted me to study the economic conditions in the neighbor nations and co-ordinate this information in compact, nontechnical form."³³¹ He followed this avenue and became deeply interested in the ins and outs of finance, economics, and their problems, of which there were plenty in the early 1930s.

NR also wanted to play an official role in financial and economic negotiations on the continent. He believed that his well-received reports on the subject, his relatively wide range of contacts in Europe, and his personal drive might be enough to secure him such a position. He knew, or at least anticipated, that soon enough discussion would commence on solving the reparations and debt issue, and he wanted to be one of the Americans playing a role in it. At the end of 1931 he repeatedly pleaded with Herbert Feis that if Washington decided to send people to such a conference, he should be included in the delegation.³³² This also implied that he was looking beyond his present job in Hungary and imagined for himself a more significant position vis a vis the American government. He felt that his usefulness was very limited in his host country, where things were not going well anyway. The envisioned financial collapse and social upheaval remained more of a worry, however, therefore the days of chaos of 1919 were unlikely to be repeated, which meant that Hungary's importance remained minor as well.

---

[328] The English version of the article can be read in Folder: Count Apponyi, Box 1, Nicholas Roosevelt Papers. The article appeared in Hungarian on the front page of *Pesti Napló*, February 11, 1933, 1.
[329] Ibid.
[330] Ibid.
[331] Nicholas Roosevelt, *A Front Row Seat*, 186.
[332] Nicholas Roosevelt to Herbert Feis, October 6, 1931, and Nicholas Roosevelt to Castle, December 31, 1931, Folder: Castle, William R. Jr., Box 2, Nicholas Roosevelt Papers.

When Herbert Hoover lost the election to Franklin D. Roosevelt in November 1932, NR renewed his efforts to secure a position as a financial expert for his government. He desperately wanted to be included in the upcoming London Monetary and Economic Conference to be held following summer. Its central issues were to be the revival of international trade and the gold standard together with questions of tariff and intergovernmental debts.[333] He knew that a Democratic win at the polls limited his options, and he was ready to "make almost any sacrifice" to be sent to the Conference.[334] Although his good reports and name entered into discussion as to the personnel to be sent to London, forces working against him in the State Department mentioned that he was not an economist by training.[335] Clearly, the Democrats back in power would not use Republicans in excess, and he was not willing to use his name and friendly though distant relationship with the president-elect to secure any job. As he wrote to Consul Prentiss B. Gilbert in Geneva, Switzerland: "As I have spent most of my life trying to live down my relationship to other people, I am not particularly anxious to have to begin again explaining that I do not owe a new job solely to the fact that my name is Roosevelt."[336] NR also resented the State Department's relative lack of interest in Eastern Europe. He accused the Department of being "blind to the history of Europe and persistently forget[ing] Sarajevo and the Creditanstalt. I say 'forget' in spite of the fact that occasionally they pay lip service to these two names without having any real understanding of what it was all about." In typical NR fashion he added, "I shall continue sending in occasional things for their possible edification and education."[337]

The writing, however, was on the wall. Being a "Hoover man," NR had hoped to see his political hero reelected in November 1932. But the Hoover administration's lack of effort during the years of hardships had turned many people against it, and

---

[333] On the Conference, see, Rodney J. Morrison, "The London Monetary and Economic Conference of 1933: A Public Goods Analysis," *The American Journal of Economics and Sociology* 52, no. 3 (July 1993): 310–13; George C. Herring, *From Colony to Superpower: U.S. Foreign Relations Since 1776* (Oxford: Oxford University Press, 2008), 494–95; William J. Barber, *Designs within Disorder: Franklin D. Roosevelt, the Economists, and the Shaping of American Economic Policy, 1933–1945* (Cambridge: Cambridge University Press, 2006), 34–35; Patricia Clavin, *Securing the World Economy: The Reinvention of the League of Nations, 1920–1946* (Oxford: Oxford University Press, 2013), 84–123.

[334] Nicholas Roosevelt to Prentiss B. Gilbert, November 14, 1932, Folder: Gilbert, Prentiss B., Box 6, Nicholas Roosevelt Papers.

[335] Herbert Feis to Nicholas Roosevelt, October 13, 1932, Folder: Feis, Dr. Herbert, Box 6; Prentiss B. Gilbert to Nicholas Roosevelt, November 17, 1932, Folder: Gilbert, Prentiss B., Box 6, Nicholas Roosevelt Papers.

[336] Nicholas Roosevelt to Prentiss B. Gilbert, November 14, 1932, Folder: Gilbert, Prentiss B., Box 6, Nicholas Roosevelt Papers.

[337] Ibid.

after twelve years of Republican presidency the door was wide open for a Democratic win. Franklin D. Roosevelt's landslide victory at the polls also meant a shakeup of diplomatic posts. According to custom, political appointees were expected to hand in their resignation so that the new president could fill those places with his own people. As soon as NR learned the results, he sent a consolation note to Hoover and hyperbolically opined that "you have been one of the greatest Presidents that we have had, and that in only a few years the country will recognize that no one could have done more than you have done to stem the tide of economic disaster that is engulfing the world."[338]

Although he felt sorry to leave the realm of diplomacy because he immensely enjoyed the prestige of it and was confident that he had the skills for international affairs, NR altogether did not mind leaving Budapest behind, "the interest of which I shall have just about exhausted when spring comes."[339] Looking out for future possibilities, he inquired of Arthur Krock of the *New York Times* whether there was an opening for him, but he was turned down.[340] He also wrote to Adolph S. Ochs, owner of the *Times*, and tried to get back to that paper through him, but also to no avail.[341] He clearly saw that he needed to choose between journalism and business, since the avenue to public service, at least for the next four years, was closed to him. He understood that the choice was not an easy one, because at the age of forty he was "no longer able to do things solely because they are 'interesting.'"[342]

NR tried to spend his remaining time in Hungary usefully. The most conspicuous side of this was his trips to mainly neighboring countries and having talks with some famous political leaders of the day. This was an activity that fell under the job description of a minister, but it was also done with an eye toward a possible renewal of his journalistic career. He visited King Alexander of Yugoslavia in the first months of 1933, then the trio of Benito Mussolini, Fulvio Suvich, and Guido Jung, prime minister, undersecretary of state for foreign affairs, and finance minister, respectively, of Italy, and finally Edvard Beneš, Czechoslovak minister for

---

[338] Nicholas Roosevelt to Herbert Hoover, November 9, 1932, Folder: Hoover, Herbert, Box 7, Nicholas Roosevelt Papers. For his characterization in his memoirs of Hoover as a potential president, see, Nicholas Roosevelt, *A Front Row Seat*, 235–36.
[339] Nicholas Roosevelt to Arthur Krock, November 9, 1932, Folder: Roosevelt, Nicholas, 1923, 1932, 1942–1970, Box 52, Series 2: Correspondence, 1916–1974, Arthur Krock Papers, 1909–1974, Seeley G. Mudd Manuscript Library, Princeton, U.S.A.
[340] Ibid.; Arthur Krock to Nicholas Roosevelt, November 22, 1932, ibid.
[341] Nicholas Roosevelt to Adolph S. Ochs, January 3, 1933, Folder 7: Nicholas Roosevelt (1922–1933), Box 34, Adolph S. Ochs Papers.
[342] Nicholas Roosevelt to Mrs. J. West Roosevelt, January 3, 1933, Folder: Roosevelt, Mrs. J. West (mother) 1930–1933, Box 12, Nicholas Roosevelt Papers.

foreign affairs. The American ministers serving in those countries' capitals helped arrange NR's meetings with these leaders.

Accordingly, in the second half of January 1933 he visited Belgrade and had the chance to meet King Alexander for half an hour. The main takeaway was that Yugoslavia was on bad terms with Italy, which country it accused of trying to interfere in Eastern Europe and secretly sending shipments of weapons to Hungary. There was no mention of Yugoslavia's domestic affairs during the meeting, and Hungary was discussed only as far as the economic conditions went. King Alexander struck NR as "an interesting but not particularly intelligent man, obviously a soldier first and foremost."[343]

Much longer and more interesting was his time in Rome. His talk with Fulvio Suvich was the least remarkable, since it was concerning Hungarian economic affairs and the bad relationship between Italy and Yugoslavia, and the politician mainly echoed his boss's point of view.[344] The prize of the Roman visit was his conversation with Mussolini. NR drew up his longest memorandum about this meeting. After all, Mussolini was a prime minister and Italy occupied an important place in the European power constellation of the interwar years. Its fascist system was not without praise in America, and for a long time Italy was also seen as the possible counterweight to Germany. Their conversation mainly centered on the possible future of Central Europe. Mussolini said he would favor a pact with Austria and Hungary, which he explained in economic terms. As for Hungary, he favored a revision based along ethnic lines buttressed by plebiscites, especially in the northern region (Slovakia), but he admitted that in the case of Transylvania this would be much more problematic, since that land lay far from Hungary, and many Romanians lived on the territories in-between. He stressed that the German–Polish relationship was brittle, but he estimated that Hitler needed at least three or four years before a strong Germany could see its wishes become reality.

Mussolini made three important points to NR. One, that the deep-seated hatred between any two nations in the region was not truly appreciated by Americans; two, if the smaller countries did not wish to play along in border rectification, the great powers must force them to do so even if it meant territorial sacrifice on the part of

---

[343] Report of Interview of American Minister at Budapest, the Honorable Nicholas Roosevelt, with King Alexander of Yugoslavia, on January 21, 1933, in John Dyneley Prince to Henry L. Stimson, January 24, 1933, Dispatches from Hungary 1930–1933, Box 69, Nicholas Roosevelt Papers; Nicholas Roosevelt, "Hungary," (unpublished), Box 45, Nicholas Roosevelt Papers.

[344] Memorandum of Mr. Nicholas Roosevelt's conversation with Mr. Suvich, Rome, March 14, 1933, Dispatches from Hungary 1930–1933, Box 69, Nicholas Roosevelt Papers.

those smaller nations; and three, that if it came to war again, that would be utterly fatal and devastating for the continent.[345] Mussolini was essentially right in all his observations. Exactly one year later the Austrians, Hungarians, and Italians signed the Rome Protocols, supposedly an economic agreement but in fact a regional pact against both Germany and Yugoslavia.[346] Hitler did indeed need a few years before really starting to flex the muscle of the Third Reich; the Munich Agreement and the First Vienna Award, both in 1938, proved that the great powers dictated the diplomatic initiatives on the continent and the small states had no option but to acquiesce to them; and World War II brought destruction that probably went even beyond what Mussolini might have imagined. In NR's opinion, somewhat contradicting his own expectations, Mussolini possessed an "ability to analyze situations [that was] exceptional," and "had true genius."[347]

To complete the roster of Italian officials, he talked to Finance Minister Guido Jung in mid-March in Budapest. This was right after NR returned from Rome. Their conversation focused principally on economic and financial questions. The Italian, who was "one of the most intelligent, clear-headed and dispassionate men" Roosevelt had met in Europe, argued that the debt burden of the Danubian countries should first be alleviated, then their currencies must be strengthened, and only then would it be possible to tackle the economic and trade issues of the region.[348]

A month after these conversations with the Italians, NR's last major interview with a prominent Central European politician came just a few weeks before his departure. When he visited Prague, he had a chance to talk with Edvard Beneš,

---

[345] Memorandum of Mr. Nicholas Roosevelt's conversation with the Chief of the Government, Rome, March 13, 1933, in Enclosure No. 1 to dispatch No. 1837 of March 14, 1933, from the Embassy in Rome, Folder: Dispatches from Hungary 1930–1933, Box 69, Nicholas Roosevelt Papers.

[346] In March 1934 the Rome Protocols were signed between these three countries. The agreement had an economic emphasis, but it was clearly a regional pact against both Germany and Yugoslavia. The Germans and the Yugoslavs understandably were not happy with it, while all other countries in Europe basically welcomed it. The Protocols were popular in Hungary since, at least on paper, it made possible larger wheat sales to Austria and Italy, while also kindled the hope of a possible treaty revision with Italy's help. For the text of the Protocols, see, *League of Nations Treaty Series. Publication of Treaties and International Engagements Registered with the Secretariat of the League of Nations*, vol. 154, (Lausanne: Imprimeries Réunies S.A., 1934–1935), 281–303. See also, György Réti, "Gömbös és a Római Hármas Egyezmény, 1934" [Gömbös and the Rome Three Power Pact], *Történelmi Szemle* 36, nos. 1–2 (1994): 159–65; Gergely, *Gömbös Gyula*, 125–26; Petra Hamerli, *Magyar-olasz diplomáciai kapcsolatok, Magyar-olasz diplomáciai kapcsolatok és regionális hatásaik (1927–1934)* [Hungarian-Italian diplomatic relations and their regional effects] (Budapest: Fakultás Kiadó, 2018), 210–17.

[347] Nicholas Roosevelt, "Hungary," (unpublished), Box 45, Nicholas Roosevelt Papers.

[348] Memorandum of Conversation of Mr. Nicholas Roosevelt with Finance Minister Jung of Italy on March 15 and 17, Budapest, March 20, 1933, Folder: Dispatches from Hungary 1930–1933, Box 69, Nicholas Roosevelt Papers.

Czechoslovak minister for foreign affairs and the principal force behind the Little Entente, the alliance of Czechoslovakia, Romania, and Yugoslavia, founded right after the peace treaties of Paris after World War I in order to keep Hungary in check. Throughout the interview, this was the dominant point: the Little Entente was the only viable entity, both economically and politically, and apparently Beneš could imagine Hungary coming into the fold, but he wanted to hear nothing about revision.[349] Compared to his meeting with the Czechoslovak politician ten years earlier, NR now found Beneš "somewhat in eclipse," seemingly "an exhausted man" who "had lost his grip."[350] His conversations with these prominent figures, and some other lesser ones, convinced NR that Central Europe was perhaps beyond repair, for which not only the economic conditions but the nature of the region's inhabitants were equally responsible. He also included mention of the interviews with Alexander, Mussolini, and Beneš in his memoirs,[351] as the public's memory of most of these men was still fresh, and could interest American readers.

His last weeks in Hungary were about preparation for his departure. He was convinced that only a weaker person would follow him, especially if the choice was left to the Democratic Party machine. With much derision, he noted to his colleague in Geneva that he was "looking forward to learning whether my successor here will be one of the Tammany boys or a Jewish gentleman from the East Side, born in Budapest and selected because his uncle was associated with Bela Kun and the Communists and he is therefore certain to be persona [non] grata to the Horthy regime."[352] This language clearly demonstrates his bitterness at being forced out of diplomacy if not necessarily out of the Hungarian post.

Naturally, NR made efforts to secure a prominent position where his experience concerning economic and financial questions could be put to use. First, there seemed to be an opening at the League of Nations. He somewhat excitedly informed his mother that Royall Tyler had told him confidentially that the League of Nations was considering him for a job similar to Tyler's in Hungary, but in Bulgaria.[353] Alexander Loveday, director of the Financial Section and Economic Intelligence

---

[349] Conversation of Mr. Nicholas Roosevelt with Dr. Eduard Beneš, Czechoslovak Minister for Foreign Affairs, Prague, April 11, 1933, Folder: Dispatches from Hungary 1930–1933, Box 69, Nicholas Roosevelt Papers.
[350] Nicholas Roosevelt, "Hungary," (unpublished), Box 45, Nicholas Roosevelt Papers.
[351] Nicholas Roosevelt, *A Front Row Seat*, 213–17.
[352] Nicholas Roosevelt to Prentiss B. Gilbert, February 25, 1933, Folder: Gilbert, Prentiss B., Box 6, Nicholas Roosevelt Papers.
[353] Nicholas Roosevelt to Mrs. J. West Roosevelt, February 6, 1933, Folder: Roosevelt, Mrs. J. West (mother) 1930–1933, Box 12, Nicholas Roosevelt Papers.

Service of the League of Nations, initially thought NR could serve in Romania, but his service in Hungary made that unworkable for Bucharest, therefore Sofia, Bulgaria, remained another option. Also, the Economic Committee was not satisfied with the current American delegate, Lucius Eastman, and there seemed to be an opening there as well.[354] Roosevelt, however, would have liked to become a member of the League's Financial Committee.[355] This was not only because it involved his interest and work in financial issues in the past few years, but also because it was "only a part time job; carries in Europe a big prestige," and "it will be much easier to make a good American connection with that as a starter, than merely as an ex-Minister."[356] The people at the Bank of England also wished to see him in a League role, but he convinced himself that Bulgaria "would mean being isolated for two or three years in a remote corner of the world."[357] In the end, therefore, he did not become member of the League of Nations organization.

NR also took steps to secure a U.S. government position. He mainly eyed Norman H. Davis's post and asked Prentiss Gilbert's help in arranging his possible succession to Davis.[358] Davis was chairman of the American delegation to the General Conference for the Reduction and Limitation of Armaments under the auspices of the League of Nations held in Geneva, Switzerland. The Conference opened in February 1932 and adjourned in December that year but was reconvened in May 1933 with Davis as chairman of the American delegation. Davis held the rank of ambassador to convey presidential authority at the Conference. The Conference was a failure, though mainly because Germany withdrew in October 1933.[359] Gilbert indeed talked to Davis about Roosevelt as a possible successor to him, but Davis said that he thought there was no real chance for Roosevelt to secure

---

[354] Prentiss B. Gilbert to Nicholas Roosevelt, March 27, 1933, Folder: Gilbert, Prentiss B., Box 6, Nicholas Roosevelt Papers.
[355] Nicholas Roosevelt to Prentiss B. Gilbert, March 31, 1933, ibid.
[356] Nicholas Roosevelt to Mrs. J. West Roosevelt, March 31, 1933, Folder: Roosevelt, Mrs. J. West (mother) 1930–1933, Box 12, Nicholas Roosevelt Papers.
[357] Nicholas Roosevelt to Eugene Havas, June 23, 1933, Folder: Havas, Eugene, Box 6, Nicholas Roosevelt Papers.
[358] Nicholas Roosevelt to Prentiss B. Gilbert, March 22, 1933, Folder: Gilbert, Prentiss B., Box 6, Nicholas Roosevelt Papers.
[359] On the Disarmament Conference, see, Department of State, *Peace and War: United States Foreign Policy 1931–1941* (Washington: United States, Government Printing Office, 1943), 9–12; Arnold A. Offner, *American Appeasement: United States Foreign Policy and Germany, 1933–1938* (Cambridge, MA: Belknap Press of Harvard University Press, 1969), 20–53; Zara Steiner, *The Triumph of the Dark: European International History, 1933–1939* (Oxford: Oxford University Press, 2011), 36–56. On Davis's career, see, J. M. Galloway, "The Public Life of Norman H. Davis," *Tennessee Historical Quarterly* 27, no. 2 (Summer 1968): 142–56.

the job due to the method by which a new member was chosen.[360] So, on the eve of his leaving Europe, there were no prospects for NR to continue his work on the Old Continent.

His departure from Hungary took place in early May 1933, by which time Hungary seemed to have left behind the worst of the economic depression and started its long climb out of the deep hole. Royall Tyler's latest report to the League at least contained small signs of improvement, like the possibility of a smaller deficit in the upcoming fiscal year and the increase of the country's export values after three years of negative figures.[361] Roosevelt therefore could inform the State Department in his last report from Budapest that Tyler's latest conclusions on Hungarian financial affairs "furnished a note of optimism which has been lacking for eighteen months, albeit the improvement noted was slight."[362]

On March 4, 1933, at the time of Franklin D. Roosevelt's inauguration, according to custom NR submitted his resignation, which was duly accepted.[363] He was "frankly, quite ready to get away. I have no wish to remain longer unless there is some compelling reason."[364] Although it had "been a most interesting experience, with many pleasant aspects," and he did "not regret an hour of it," being minister in Hungary "was beginning to pass its period of utility."[365] This tone of optimism was echoed in an interview he gave to one of the Hungarian dailies. In it he talked about American tourists' interest in Hungary and predicted that many of them would visit Hungary. The country's most appealing features, he thought, were Hungarian culture and the way its citizens actually lived. As for his own experience, he highlighted Hungarian music, concerts, folk songs, and gypsy music, saying that "Hungarians literally flooded me with their kindness, readiness to help, and hospitality in every part of the land. I do not know any other nation that so fervently desires to welcome foreigners so kindly."[366] During his farewell dinner for Hungarian journalists,

---

[360] Prentiss B. Gilbert to Nicholas Roosevelt, May 1, 1933, Folder: Gilbert, Prentiss B., Box 6, Nicholas Roosevelt Papers.
[361] Royall Tyler's Sixth Quarterly Report, April 22, 1933, OV33/12, Bank of England Archive; *League of Nations Journal*, 14th Year, no. 7 (July 1933), Seventy-third Session of the Council, (Part I), 829.
[362] Nicholas Roosevelt to Cordell Hull, May 6, 1933, 864.00 P.R./65, Roll 3, M1206, NARA.
[363] Nicholas Roosevelt to Franklin D. Roosevelt, March 4, 1933, Folder: Resignation, Box 64, Nicholas Roosevelt Papers; *Amerikai Magyar Népszava*, April 4, 1933, 1. Interestingly, Theodore Roosevelt, Jr., who had served as governor of Puerto Rico (1929–1932) and then as governor general of the Philippine Islands (1932–1933), also sent his letter of resignation to the new president, Franklin D. Roosevelt..
[364] Nicholas Roosevelt to Mrs. J. West Roosevelt, March 31, 1933, Folder: Roosevelt, Mrs. J. West (mother) 1930–1933, Box 12, Nicholas Roosevelt Papers.
[365] Nicholas Roosevelt to Mrs. J. West Roosevelt, April 14, 1933, ibid.
[366] *Budapesti Hírlap*, April 30, 1933, 5.

his "colleagues," he struck a very friendly note, as could have been expected. He promised to remain a friend of Hungary, just like Jeremiah Smith, Jr., and said he believed that Hungary was over the most difficult period and the way forward was encouraging.[367] In his very last interview with a Hungarian paper, he reiterated that Hungary would be on the right track, and that he liked Hungarians and admired their endurance.[368] When he left the Hungarian capital, some dignities paid their respect at the railway station, including the Hungarian Minister for Foreign Affairs, Kálmán Kánya, a representative of Prime Minister Gömbös, and the British and Italian ministers, among others.[369]

His successor was John Flourney Montgomery, who had helped Franklin D. Roosevelt's election campaign financially.[370] NR left a memorandum for him on the various personalities he thought might be useful for Montgomery to know: Horthy, Gömbös, Imrédy, Sándor Khuen-Héderváry, Gábor Apor, Philip Wiesz, Béla Schóber, three leading journalists and other professionals, the foreign ministers in Budapest, and a short description of each. It also contained a list of the staff of the Legation and the house.[371] He took with him back to the States two Hungarian sheep dogs, Chloe and Puli. The two black pulis he believed were the first of their breed to reach America, and he planned to set up a breeding farm for them on Long Island. One of the dogs, however, perished early the next year, and he gave up this plan.[372]

This is how NR's two and a half years of diplomatic mission ended, and he found himself back on home soil where he had to carve out a new beginning.

---

[367] *Pesti Napló*, May 6, 1933, 5.
[368] *Pesti Napló*, May 7, 1933, 6.
[369] *Az Est*, May 10, 1933, 5.
[370] On Montgomery's Hungarian tenure between 1933 and 1941, see, *Discussing Hitler. Advisers of U.S. Diplomacy in Central Europe 1934–1941*, ed. and with an introduction by Tibor Frank (Budapest, New York: Central European University Press, 2003).
[371] John Flourney Montgomery to Nicholas Roosevelt, July 13, 1933, Folder: Montgomery, John F., Box 9, Nicholas Roosevelt Papers.
[372] *Az Est*, May 10, 1933, 5; *New York Times*, June 2, 1933.

Chapter 5

Nicholas Roosevelt in the New Deal and World War II

Nicholas Roosevelt arrived in the United States on the *Washington* on June 1, 1933. This made modest waves, though quite a few papers had reported briefly on his resignation in April and on his return to America. Some even mentioned that he brought the first Hungarian sheep dogs to the country.[373] As for the Hungarian-American community, it celebrated the ex-minister as Hungary's friend, which role he also assumed in his public appearances among this group. A few days after his arrival, at a dinner in his honor in New York organized by the Colonel de Kovats Society of America, he declared that "from now on I see myself as Hungary's unofficial ambassador in America, and I will take every opportunity to make the American people better understand both the problems of Hungary and the great qualities of the Hungarian people."[374] Obviously, this was what the gathered guests wanted to hear, and György Ghika, the Hungarian consul general in New York, answered that "we almost feel that Nicholas Roosevelt today belongs to us, Hungarians."[375]

Such prestige among Hungarian-Americans, however, did not provide a living, and this was the central question for NR, since he found himself in debt. He regularly complained to his mother about pecuniary problems while in Budapest. Although during his tenure he had managed to rent his house back home, the costs of representing the United States in a European capital, being part of the social season with its inevitable lunches, dinners, and receptions, meant that he exhausted his resources and had to borrow from his mother. Now out of job and no immediate prospect, he had to secure a steady income as soon as possible. His pet project, the

---

[373] See, for example, *Detroit Michigan Free Press*, June 3, 1933.
[374] *Amerikai Magyar Népszava*, June 19, 1933, 1.
[375] Ibid.

109

planned American Bondholders' Protective Association to help American investors with their losses abroad, had not taken form, and government service was out of the question, the avenue open was relatively narrow. It was almost a given that he had no recourse but to return to journalism, which he did in the fall. Most importantly, in the next years he assumed the coveted role of public educator: he wanted to inform and teach Americans about certain issues both domestic and foreign.

He made the first steps in that direction soon after his return home. On June 28, 1933, the first of his radio programs "Watch Eastern Europe" aired on the NBC affiliate WJZ. In it he mainly concentrated on the Austrian–German relationship and said that he found the revival of the Habsburg monarchy a stillborn idea.[376] Even Walter Lippmann praised his show and thought "the form which you have invented is admirable."[377] He was planning to do one show a week and he also started freelance newspaper work for various papers, like the *New York Times*, but these provided only ad hoc paychecks, and he needed something more stable.[378] This finally happened when on November 1, 1933, he rejoined the *Herald Tribune*, "the leading Republican journal in the East," as an editorial writer.[379]

Soon after his return from Hungary, he reported both to the State Department and the president about his experience in Central Europe. He proudly reported to his mother that a few days later when he incidentally met Stimson, the ex-secretary of state declared that Nicholas had made a success at Budapest, and his "dispatches, especially on financial subjects, were the best received at the Department."[380] As for his meeting with Franklin D. Roosevelt, it was a friendly affair, and he recorded it in his memoirs. The president invited him for a swim in the new swimming pool at the White House. His impressions of the president were all positive. He found his namesake "youthful, charming, plausible, he was full of the fun of life," with "buoyancy of spirit, magnetism, and restlessness," but he emphasized the president's superficiality, especially when compared to Theodore Roosevelt.[381] This strengthens

---

[376] *Amerikai Magyar Népszava*, June 27, 1933, 1, and July 1, 1933, 3; Nicholas Roosevelt to Mrs. J. West Roosevelt, June 26, 1933, Folder: Roosevelt, Mrs. J. West (mother) 1930–1933, Box 12, Nicholas Roosevelt Papers.

[377] Walter Lippmann to Nicholas Roosevelt, August 10, 1933, Box 99, Folder 1832, Roosevelt, Nicholas (Mr. & Mrs.) (1931–1944), Series III, Correspondence, Selected Correspondence, 1931–1974, Walter Lippmann Papers, MS 326 HM 257, Yale Archives.

[378] Nicholas Roosevelt to Mrs. J. West Roosevelt, June 26, 1933.

[379] Nicholas Roosevelt, *A Front Row Seat*, 239.

[380] Nicholas Roosevelt to Mrs. J. West Roosevelt, June 26, 1933.

[381] Hungary, Box 11 Roosevelt, Franklin D., Nicholas Roosevelt Papers. This passage on the meeting with the president found itself with only minor changes into his memoirs of twenty years later. See, Nicholas Roosevelt, *A Front Row Seat*, 221.

the image that has often been tied to FDR: youthful, booming with energy, almost nonchalant, all this despite, or on account of, his being forced to use a wheelchair. It is not recorded what the two were talking about, but probably it was small talk rather than substantial political conversation, though FDR wrote to NR's mother that Nicholas "did a splendid piece of work in Budapest and I am proud of him."[382]

Later on, however, despite their initial good relationship and his high esteem of the president, NR became a fervent critic of the New Deal and the president's policies. It is worth investigating this complicated relationship between these two Roosevelts.

The first known letters between the two are from the time when Franklin Roosevelt was the Democratic governor of New York state. The young, ambitious politician assumed that office on January 1, 1929, thinking it a suitable springboard to a possible presidency.[383] The two met in the summer of 1928, and NR was quite enthusiastic about Franklin: "What a fine fellow he is, so intelligent and cultivated, and with so much character."[384] Despite the fact that NR was a proud Republican, he actually voted for FDR in the governor's race. He wrote to FDR that "You have the greatest opportunity of any Democrat in years to do something for your party—which doesn't interest me—and for your country—which does interest me. If you will speak out vigorously and fairly, without truckling to the peanut politicians, you will go far."[385] The central point of comparison for NR was Theodore Roosevelt. No matter how much he idolized that cousin in his younger years, he had come to understand that more tact was needed in order to win political office than Teddy had exhibited. That is why he warned FDR as he did. FDR appreciated NR's letter and the tone of it, and in response he expressed his hope "that you will keep on writing me in just the same way whenever you want to."[386] This was an invitation a man like NR could not refuse, and he did write to FDR on various issues. Sometimes it was family history, but more often it pertained to American domestic and foreign policy. They also exchanged ideas on conservation policy, another lifelong passion of NR's that he inherited to a large degree from TR.

---

[382] F. D. Roosevelt to Laura Henrietta d'Oremieulx, June 25, 1933, Box 11, Roosevelt, Franklin D., Nicholas Roosevelt Papers.

[383] On Franklin Delano Roosevelt's governorship, see, Jean Edward Smith, *FDR* (New York. Random House, 2007), 223–46). Perhaps somewhat unfortunately but also understandably, FDR's tenure at Albany has never become the focus of historians.

[384] Nicholas Roosevelt to Laura Henrietta d'Oremieulx, August 31, 1928, Box 11, Roosevelt, Franklin D., Nicholas Roosevelt Papers.

[385] Nicholas Roosevelt to F. D. Roosevelt, January 15, 1929, ibid.

[386] FDR to Nicholas Roosevelt, January 28, 1929, Ibid.

In 1930, for instance, their letters touched upon the ongoing London Naval Conference and the question of a possible future presidency for FDR. Regarding the Conference FDR was more optimistic than dissatisfied; as for a future bid for the presidency, he was not yet committed. NR warned him not to let himself be talked into running in 1932 and advised that FDR talk to him first and decide only then.[387] FDR avoided giving a straight answer to the question. Instead, he complained that 1932 had "become a positive nightmare to me and the whole family," and he wanted to focus instead on his current job.[388] It is true that initially Democrats in general and FDR in particular thought that he would only have a chance in 1936. However, already at this time—the first months of the recession-soon-to-become-depression—it was clear that there indeed was a chance of taking the White House back from the Republicans.

During NR's years as minister in Budapest, the letters between the two Roosevelts came to a virtual halt. The only time they exchanged letters was in early 1932—when the shadows of the presidential campaign were looming ever larger. Although FDR downplayed his possible nomination by the Democratic Party and appeared disinterested in getting it, and in addition described the presidency as "the most difficult and thoroughly annoying job in the world," his ambition was unquestionably to become president.[389] Concrete proof that family ties played a positive role between these two Roosevelts, despite their respective party affiliations, is that FDR asked NR to take some part in the campaign "if, by some lucky or unlucky chance, I should be the Democratic nominee."[390]

Of course, Franklin Roosevelt not only secured his party's nomination but went on to win a landslide victory on November 8, 1932. NR congratulated the president-elect the very next day (as he was stationed in Budapest, he could not do this on the day of the election). The letter he sent was correct from all angles: "I am proud of you for the sake of the family, and that because of this as well as because of my personal feelings toward you I wish you the best of good luck and success in the trying years that are ahead of you." Then he added that he felt this way "despite the fact that I am a Republican and a Hoover man, and shall doubtless continue to

---

[387] Nicholas Roosevelt to F. D. Roosevelt, April 30, 1930, Box 69, Folder, Roosevelt, Nicholas, 1913–1920, Franklin D. Roosevelt Library, Hyde Park, NY, U.S.A.
[388] FDR to Nicholas Roosevelt, May 19, 1930, Ibid.
[389] F. D. Roosevelt to Nicholas Roosevelt, January 25, 1932, Box 69, Folder, Roosevelt, Nicholas, 1913–1920, Franklin D. Roosevelt Library.
[390] Ibid.

differ with you in many things as I have done in the past."³⁹¹ He also emphasized that he would not seek political favors for anyone or be a vehicle for any such demands.

With Franklin Roosevelt assuming office in March 1933 and launching the first phase of his New Deal to tackle the economic depression, NR was "enormously pleased with the way he has taken hold of things and that I think he has got off to a splendid start."³⁹² After the dispassionate and languid response to the Depression on Hoover's part, now it was "a relief to see somebody at the helm again who is not afraid to be a leader."³⁹³ To his mother NR put it this way: "One feels that he has what poor Hoover lacked, and what the country so much needs—leadership. It looks as if he would do much to restore our confidence again."³⁹⁴ The historical analysis confirms that vigorous action was indeed needed in order to support the structure of the American economy and even more importantly, the American people, who were in dire straits.

At least during the first year of FDR's first term, NR can be said to have been a zealous supporter of the president's policies. For example, he wrote a personal letter on October 3, 1933, in which he congratulated the president on his address to the American Legion in Chicago.³⁹⁵ NR also visited FDR on October 29 and December 12, 1934, on both occasions for a fifteen-minute talk—the regular allocated time for visitors.³⁹⁶ In the late spring of 1935, he warmly congratulated the president on a historic veto message FDR delivered before a joint session of Congress.³⁹⁷ The veto was of the Patman "Greenback" Bonus Bill, which would offer cash payment of World War I adjusted service certificates, which were not due before 1945. FDR's veto on May 22, 1935, was the first time a president had delivered a veto message in person to Congress, and it was also broadcast on radio—that is how NR was able to follow it. Although in both chambers there was a majority to override the presidential veto, in the Senate it did not reach the required two-thirds

---

³⁹¹ Nicholas Roosevelt to F. D. Roosevelt, November 9, 1932, Box 11, Roosevelt, Franklin D., Nicholas Roosevelt Papers.
³⁹² Nicholas Roosevelt to Louis Howe, March 22, 1933. Howe passed the letter on to FDR on April 22, 1933, Folder, Roosevelt, Nicholas, Franklin D. Roosevelt's, Papers as President, Official Files, Franklin D. Roosevelt Library.
³⁹³ Ibid.
³⁹⁴ Nicholas Roosevelt to Mrs. J. West Roosevelt, March 10, 1933, Folder: Roosevelt, Mrs. J. West (mother) 1930–1933, Box 12, Nicholas Roosevelt Papers.
³⁹⁵ Folder: Roosevelt, Nicholas, Franklin D. Roosevelt's, Papers as President, Official Files, Franklin D. Roosevelt Library.
³⁹⁶ http://www.fdrlibrary.marist.edu/daybyday/daylog/october-29th-1934/ and http://www.fdrlibrary.marist.edu/daybyday/daylog/december-12th-1934/, accessed April 26, 2022.
³⁹⁷ Nicholas Roosevelt to F. D. Roosevelt, May 22, 1935, Folder, Roosevelt, Nicholas, Papers as President, President's Personal Files, Franklin D. Roosevelt Library.

majority. The veto message was seen as a signal of a resurgent FDR, who had, after some lackluster efforts in the previous six months, again found his energy as president.[398] Five days after the veto decision, the Supreme Court in the Schechter case invalidated the National Industry Recovery Act (NIRA), the backbone of the New Deal. In the words of historian Arthur M. Schlesinger, Jr., with these two events, "Franklin Roosevelt returned to the game of leadership."[399]

In sharp contrast to the First Hundred Days in 1933, with the later phases of the New Deal, NR started to sour on his distant cousin and his policies.[400] He never shied away from declaring that there was a difference of worldview between them. As a lifelong Republican, brought up in the TR household NR sucked in the basics of a reform-minded conservative take on politics. Also, NR belonged to the Oyster Bay branch of the family on Long Island, and FDR was the heir to the Hyde Park branch. This latter point did not create friction between these two Roosevelts; but FDR's policies did. The *New York Herald Tribune*, for which NR worked, started to attack the New Deal continually as a socialist undertaking and a mockery of American traditions.

A detailed analysis of NR's articles concerning FDR and his New Deal is unnecessary, but a few examples will suffice to show the opposition between what the president represented—both as a politician and his policies—and what NR thought would be more beneficial for the United States.

The first serious salvo of what became a small-scale crusade was fired in the fall of 1934 in the columns of the *New York Herald Tribune*, a mainly conservative, Republican-leaning daily paper.[401] In early September NR wanted to believe that Americans were losing their belief in the president because they had realized that FDR did not "know his own mind and that he prefers to listen to inferior and inexperienced advisers rather than to sound and seasoned men."[402] This was more

---

[398] See, Turner Catledge, "War Veterans and Bonus Politics," *Current History* (1916–1940) 42, no. 4 (July 1935): 360; Kenneth S. Davis, *FDR: The New Deal Years, 1933–1937. A History* (New York: Random House, 1979), 513–14; for the text of the veto message, see, Samuel I. Rosenman, ed., *The Public Papers and Addresses of Franklin D. Roosevelt*, Vol. 4. (New York: Random House, 1938), 182–93.

[399] Arthur M. Schlesinger, Jr., *The Politics of Upheaval* (Boston: Houghton Mifflin Company, 1960), 290. Indeed, six weeks later Congress passed the National Labor Relations Act, the Wagner Act, which passed Supreme Court scrutiny.

[400] For his retrospective and mainly not too positive characterization of FDR and the New Deal, see, Nicholas Roosevelt, *A Front Row Seat*, 222–34.

[401] On the newspaper's history, see, Richard Kluger, *The Paper: The Life and Death of the New York Herald Tribune* (New York: Alfred A. Knopf, 1986). On the period when Nicholas Roosevelt worked there, see, Ibid., 239–406.

[402] Nicholas Roosevelt, "The Real Roosevelt," *New York Herald Tribune*, September 2, 1934.

wishful thinking than stable analysis. A month later NR returned to the New Deal and somewhat reluctantly admitted that the policy so far had worked. He declared that it was a novelty, it was not partisan, it contained promise and hope, and because of "the great personal charm and engaging optimism of Franklin D. Roosevelt the program was virtually irresistible."[403] Frustrating perhaps as it may have been personally, he confessed that the president was one "of the most astute politicians in our history."[404] Three weeks later NR's article took issue with FDR's many broken promises and asserted that the propaganda machinery was churning out statements that were not factual. "Like leader, like followers," he concluded.[405]

After a longer hiatus he returned even more vehemently to attacking the New Deal. He went so far, perhaps because it was an election year, as to call FDR's policies under the New Deal a "miscellaneous assortment of half-baked, semi-socialistic, semi-Fascist theories which are lumped together."[406] He regularly condemned the New Deal as a planned economy, therefore, it was comparable to the Soviet Union's method, which meant to him that it was dictatorial. In other words, it was a socialist undertaking and by definition un-American. Accordingly, in another piece he argued that the New Deal had killed off many of the basic American traits, people had become too dependent on government, and the Republicans must turn things around.[407] As the election of 1936 loomed ever closer, he intensified the attacks. NR portrayed an apocalyptic future if FDR was reelected. He warned his readers that the "American system is in danger. Do we wish to preserve it, or shall we accept the New Deal substitute which is perilously much like the autocracies in Europe?"[408] Up until the November elections, he expounded his case against the president. In the heat of the campaign, he contributed a series of articles titled "The Roosevelt Record," each an indictment of government policy and the president's character as leader. He accused him of misleading and outright lying to the American people, preferring the spoils system to the merit system, breaking a score of campaign promises, making steps toward so strong a centralization of executive power that it was

---

[403] Nicholas Roosevelt, "Our Tangled Politics," *New York Herald Tribune*, October 7, 1934.
[404] Ibid.
[405] Nicholas Roosevelt, "Truth and the New Deal," *New York Herald Tribune*, October 28, 1934.
[406] Nicholas Roosevelt, "Attempt Noted to Lift New Deal from Shoulder of the President," *New York Herald Tribune*, January 26, 1936.
[407] Nicholas Roosevelt, "'Cleaning Up' After New Deal Held Chief Republican Problem," *New York Herald Tribune*, June 7, 1936.
[408] Nicholas Roosevelt, "America Held Facing a Choice of Federal or Central Power," *New York Herald Tribune*, June 28, 1936.

bordering on dictatorship, and keeping people on the dole instead, thereby killing individualism—that sacred American attribute.[409]

He also wrote a short book attacking the idea of a social experiment that was not part of the New Deal but was inextricable from the financial and economic calamities of the 1930s. Frances E. Townsend was an elderly citizen living in California who urged that poverty among the elderly must be tackled nationwide. Soon a movement and an organization were born, and a plan was formulated whose most important element was that each retired person should receive $200 a month from the federal government on condition that the amount be spent within that month. The argument was that this measure would both alleviate poverty among retired Americans and boost the sagging U.S. economy. NR responded intensely to what he saw as an irresponsible social initiative.

After he attacked the Townsend Plan in the newspapers, NR's short book dissected its major stipulations and tried to prove that they were full of egregious errors economically and were outright unworkable.[410] He had a double argument against the Plan. First, financially it would have been more harmful than beneficial. By adding transaction-sales taxes onto basically every level of production and on all levels of local, state, or federal taxes, this would create conditions contrary to the basically nice idea of putting money into needy old people's pockets. It only "would cripple business. Factories would close. Unemployment would be rampant."[411] Therefore consumption would not grow nationwide, but working people would be drowned in staggering new taxes so that older citizens could purchase items. This argument led to deeper indignation that stemmed from a social perspective. As a believer in rugged individualism a la Hoover, NR detected in the Townsend Plan "the insidious poison of dependence" on government handouts.[412] This principle would introduce "enforced idleness," and in the long run the Plan would create out of the earlier honest worker "a parasite" living off society.[413] He did not deny the need for steps to be taken to do something for the elderly who were either too weak to continue to work or found themselves out of a job. "A sound policy of old-age pension is essential and deserves the most careful attention," he admitted, but he

---

[409] These articles appeared between October 13 and 26, 1936, *New York Herald Tribune*.
[410] Nicholas Roosevelt, "Townsend Pension Plan Branded Great 'Let's Pretend' of Politics," *New York Herald Tribune*, January 5, 1936; Francis E. Townsend and Nicholas Roosevelt, "Townsend Pensions: Sense or Nonsense? A Debate," *Forum and Century* 95, no 5 (May 1936): 282–87.
[411] Nicholas Roosevelt, *The Townsend Plan: Taxing for Sixty* (Garden City, NY: Doubleday, Doran & Company, Inc., 1936), 34.
[412] Ibid., 59.
[413] Ibid, 62.

maintained that it ought to be done very differently, since the "Townsend Plan is a delusion and a snare."[414] It must be noted that the Roosevelt administration did not embrace the Townsend Plan either and instead introduced the historic Social Security Act in 1935.

This again well represents how seriously NR took his role as a watchdog over governmental actions as well as various currents in society at large. He believed that serious journalism had to take on what it saw as an attack on the American way and system. And since the liberal and groundbreaking New Deal program offered the targets, he did not slowdown in challenging the soundness of the president's economic policies.

NR's criticism of FDR's New Deal perhaps reached its apogee with an article he wrote for the *American Mercury*, a widely recognized intellectual monthly magazine that was founded by Henry L. Mencken and George Jean Nathan in 1924. According to M.K. Singleton, the historian of the first decade of the magazine, it could boast of "essentially a skeptical, anti-Puritan, urban, and sophisticated editorial viewpoint,"[415] was "truly formidable," and "perhaps no other magazine of comparable circulation has so strongly caught the national imagination."[416] Frederick Lewis Allen of *Harper's* in his best seller about the 1920s said of Mencken's project:

> Its contents were explosive [...] it poured critical acid upon sentimentality and evasion and academic pomposity in books and in life; it lambasted Babbitts, Rotarians, Methodists, and reformers, ridiculed both the religion of Coolidge Prosperity and what Mencken called the "bilge of idealism," and looked upon the American scene in general with raucous and profane laughter.[417]

Another historian of journalism called the *Mercury* the voice of "skepticism and iconoclasm," an outlet that proved to be "an opinionated and caustic commentator" of the twenties and beyond.[418] It had a modest circulation of almost 80,000 before the Great Depression. In October 1936, when a new management decided

---

[414] Ibid., 67.
[415] M. K. Singleton, *H. L. Mencken and the American Mercury Adventure* (Durham, NC., Duke University Press, 1962), 242.
[416] Ibid., 246.
[417] Frederick Lewis Allen, *Only Yesterday: An Informal History of the Nineteen-Twenties* [1931] (New York and Evanston: Harper & Row, Publishers, 1957), 231.
[418] Theodore Peterson, *Magazines in the Twentieth Century* (Urbana: The University of Illinois Press, 1956), 377.

to cut the price in half, from 50 to 25 cents, the sagging circulation climbed back to pre-depression levels.[419]

The years of frustration with what he saw as a blatant rape of the American system in the shape of the New Deal had been bubbling up in NR since at least 1934. Now, the *American Mercury* offered the perfect vehicle for him to vent this frustration and he did not hold back. In the June 1936 issue, he wrote an account of the upcoming Republican National Convention and primarily criticized FDR. NR described the president as someone who promised everything to everybody to ensure his popularity but knew very well that he would not deliver on those promises: "His system is simple—to give supporters and enemies alike the impression that he agrees with them 100 per cent," he wrote.[420] FDR was "without doubt the glibbest promiser we have ever had," and he, NR, believed there was a great demand "for a man of courage and honesty, who will say what he thinks, do what he says, and never hesitate to take a course which threatens unpopularity when to do so is obviously necessary for the nation's welfare."[421] Probably this was the article that Walter Lippmann commented on in a letter to NR dated May 22, 1936. The article had come out in the June issue, but there was no other article by NR in the *American Mercury* earlier that year. In all likelihood either the issue came out a few days earlier or the letter was misdated by a month. In any event, Lippmann agreed with what he had read. He had also become disappointed in FDR and, as he wrote to NR, "I am afraid I am going to have to resign my job of defending Franklin from his fifth cousin. I can stand no more of him."[422] In fact, Lippmann had chosen to change parties and voted for the Republican nominee, Alf Landon, not because he had great hope in him, but because this was his protest vote against FDR.[423] NR naturally also voted for Landon, but as he quipped in his memoirs, while "Roosevelt had one of the great magic radio personalities of our times, Landon was a master at making people tune in on another program [...] in a contest which was being decided largely by radio listeners."[424]

---

[419] On the history of the magazine and its circulation, see, Peterson, *Magazines in the Twentieth Century*, 377–81; Singleton, *H. L. Mencken and the American Mercury Adventure*; Brooks E. Hefner, and Edward Timke, eds., *Circulating American Magazines*, James Madison University, http://sites.jmu.edu/circulating/, accessed April 28, 2022.

[420] Nicholas Roosevelt, "Wanted: An Honest President," *The American Mercury* 38, no. 150 (June 1936): 196.

[421] Ibid., 197, 200.

[422] Walter Lippmann to Nicholas Roosevelt, May 22, 1936, Folder 1832: Roosevelt, Nicholas (Mr. & Mrs.) (1931–1944), Box 99, Series III, Correspondence, Selected Correspondence, 1931–1974, Walter Lippmann Papers, MS 326 HM 257, Yale Archives.

[423] Ronald Steel, *Walter Lippmann and the American Century* (Boston and Toronto: Little, Brown and Company, 1980), 317–19.

[424] Nicholas Roosevelt, *A Front Row Seat*, 239.

In the November issue of the *American Mercury* NR further attacked FDR. This was the month of the presidential election and the article was an even more scathing criticism of both the man running for reelection and his New Deal program. Already in the beginning he set the tone:

> This chameleon-like quality has made it possible for Franklin Delano Roosevelt to pose as a great Liberal at the same time that he is fostering reactionary activities. Because he does not think things through, he is unaware that the New Deal is basically paternalistic. No doubt he sincerely believes he is a plumed Progressive. Yet he is, in fact, the conscious leader of world reaction in America today.[425]

The president had extraordinary "sensitiveness to currents of popular thought," but his mind was "mercurial rather than profound," and this was coupled with "supreme self-confidence" in a leader who enjoyed "power for its own sake."[426]

The major point of attack on the New Deal was that the executive had taken over powers that traditionally did not belong to it and in the process had corrupted American democracy: "He has made a rubber stamp of Congress and has established government by decree. All these things tend towards paternalism—and away from the American system."[427] A benevolent and paternalistic government with an affable president who deluded people was outright dangerous in his view. In the final analysis,

> Mr. Roosevelt has all the "front" of the perfect Liberal. This makes him all the more useful to those reactionaries who, in the name of a New Deal and a More Abundant Life, are following in America the course that has destroyed democratic Liberalism in Europe. Mr. Roosevelt has identified himself with the reactionaries. This is why true progressives now oppose him.[428]

The 1936 presidential election was an unprecedented victory for Franklin Roosevelt and his policies: he garnered more than 60 percent of the popular vote, while in the Electoral College he had 523 votes awhile the Republican Alf Landon

---

[425] Nicholas Roosevelt, "Franklin Delano Roosevelt," *The American Mercury* 39, no. 155 (November 1936): 329.
[426] Ibid., 329, 330.
[427] Ibid., 330.
[428] Ibid., 331.

had 8. Such a landslide victory proved that NR represented only a small elite who on various grounds—mainly intellectual and ideological—opposed the president's policies.

FDR's "court-packing" plan the next year further alienated NR from the president's policies. After his landslide victory Franklin Roosevelt announced his plan to increase the number of judges sitting on the Supreme Court to 15 with compulsory retirement at 70 years of age. The move was unmistakably an effort to ensure that the composition of the highest court would be changed until it became more liberal and curb the practice of the past two years during which the Supreme Court had struck down many major pieces of New Deal legislation. There was a widespread outcry, even among Democrats, against what many interpreted as changing the Constitution to suit the chief executive's wishes.

NR joined this loud chorus. Already in January, when the first hint came from the White House that a plan was afoot to overhaul the Supreme Court, NR charged that such a scheme was against the Constitution and the political traditions of the country.[429] Although the Constitution did not specify the numbers, since 1869 there had been nine justices. He again attacked FDR's character for cooking up the plan. He wrote that "indirection, lack of candor, readiness to ignore promises, and a lighthearted unwillingness to consider the far-reaching effects of his proposals are characteristics of Mr. Roosevelt's mental processes."[430] Reforms were one thing, and, in Theodore Roosevelt fashion, NR believed in them. Indeed, in many a piece he badgered the Republican Party to be more up to date if it wanted to fight FDR and the Democratic Party successfully. But reforms and changing the Constitution by decree were two very different things for NR, and he interpreted the reelected president's move as harmful and warned his readers that "democracy is in grave danger in this country."[431]

In the end, in July the Senate struck down the "court-packing" bill but the Supreme Court started to judge the various New Deal bills in a more liberal way. President Roosevelt did not need to resort to extraordinary measures, but he had clearly suffered a political setback. In the long run, however, victory was his, and during his long presidency the composition of the federal Supreme Court became

---

[429] Nicholas Roosevelt, "Roosevelt 'Hint' to Court Held Misconception of Its Function," *New York Herald Tribune*, January 17, 1937.

[430] Nicholas Roosevelt, "'Smartness' of Court Plan Held Typical of Roosevelt Character," *New York Herald Tribune*, February 14, 1937.

[431] Nicholas Roosevelt, "Roosevelt May Be No Dictator, But What of His Successors?" *New York Herald Tribune*, February 21, 1937.

overwhelmingly liberal and proved to be a major ingredient in establishing the welfare state in the United States.[432]

When it came to foreign policy, NR held his distant cousin in much higher esteem, though not everything was according to his taste in this field either. He criticized FDR's Russian policy, for example, especially the recognition of the Soviet Union in 1933.[433] Nevertheless, when it came to military preparedness, he was in accordance with the president. NR preached the logic of needing a stronger naval force to deter any future threat, which was similar to what, albeit cautiously, Franklin Roosevelt did in the second half of the 1930s.[434] In the wake of a trip FDR made to South America between November 17 and December 15, 1937, NR began to write in a different spirit than earlier that year. The presidential trip was intended to improve and strengthen the "good neighbor policy" vis a vis Latin American countries, which he had declared in his inauguration address in March 1933. He attended the Inter-American Conference for the Maintenance of Peace in Buenos Aires, which was meant to build a quasi-coalition for future exigencies in light of the worsening situation in Europe and to establish the basis of a hemispheric defense mechanism. Parallel to that conference, the Anti-Comintern Pact was signed between Germany and Japan, which added further impetus to the idea of collective security in the Americas.[435] NR found a lot to commend in the president's realism in trying to be prepared for any situation and building up the navy.[436] He also found it important to write a personal letter to the president as well. In this he pointed out, "Even those of us who have been so much out of sympathy with the New Deal methods cannot but recognize that your Latin American policy has been, in the main, excellent."[437] To be fair, then, NR offered respect if he felt it was merited.

In addition to NR's attacks on FDR's domestic policies, his other journalistic output is also worth investigating, because it sheds light on his thinking and on

---

[432] In more detail about the "court-packing" plan, see, Leonard Baker, *Back to Back: The Duel between FDR and the Supreme Court* (New York: The MacMillan Company, 1967); William E. Leuchtenburg, *The Supreme Court Reborn: The Constitutional Revolution in the Age of Roosevelt* (New York, Oxford: Oxford University Press, 1995), 82–162.

[433] Nicholas Roosevelt, "Unrecognizing Russia," *New York Herald Tribune,* February 7, 1935.

[434] Nicholas Roosevelt, "Show of Naval Might Is Held Essential to Guard Commerce," *New York Herald Tribune,* August 16, 1936.

[435] On FDR's Good Neighbor policy and his trip to South America, see, Frank Freidel, *Franklin D. Roosevelt: A Rendezvous with History* (Boston: Little, Brown and Company, 1990), 209–20.

[436] Nicholas Roosevelt, "Roosevelt Navy Policy Enables U.S. to Dictate Its Own Neutrality," *New York Herald Tribune,* December 5, 1936.

[437] Nicholas Roosevelt to FDR, December 6, 1936, Folder, Roosevelt, Nicholas, in Franklin D. Roosevelt's, Papers as President, President's Personal Files, Franklin D. Roosevelt Library.

the issues that he was interested in, sometimes rather passionately. While the most common theme was criticism of the New Deal, there were other topics, sometimes related, that he wanted to educate readers about. Once more on the roster of the *New York Herald Tribune* but having pieces appear in other papers and magazines as well, he often touched upon the economic and diplomatic issues he had experience with.

He started with an analysis of the debt situation in Central and Eastern Europe for *Foreign Affairs* in October 1933. In this piece he emphasized the delicate situation concerning accumulated debt, lack of credit, defaults of loans, and the counterproductive aims of debtor countries trying to sell goods abroad while creditors were wishing to collect debts. As a possible solution, he once again stressed his pet theme that "creditors must cooperate in working out a plan which is fair to different classes of creditors and which at the same time gives the debtor nations a chance to recover."[438] Then he focused on the home front and had a ten-article series on the question of economic recovery in the Mid-Western states, the plight of the farmers, and possible solutions. In the *Herald Tribune* he argued that the American standard of living must be maintained but perhaps not through the methods of the New Deal, which controversially paid subsidies to farmers for reduced amounts of produce.[439] Such serialized articles remained characteristic features for some time. In quick succession in December 1933, he published two such series. In the first, "The ABC of Inflation," he again relied to a large degree on his still recent experience of Europe, and especially in Hungary. He emphasized that altogether he was very much against inflation, because in the long run he deemed it truly baneful, especially for political reasons.[440] Then before Christmas in another economy-related series, "What of the Nation's Credit?," he criticized the U.S. government for what he saw as its failed gold and inflation policy and mistaken debt policy, and for endangering the country's credit with its fiscal policy.[441]

In the following years, in addition to his regular criticism of the New Deal, he mainly focused on foreign affairs. First, *The Christian Science Monitor* commissioned him to write about the situation in the Foreign Service, a topic on which he had fresh experience. The title set the basic tone of the nine-article series: "Diplomacy in Rags." The thesis was that the diplomatic corps was seriously underpaid, and this phenomenon scared otherwise talented people away from that very important field.

---

[438] Nicholas Roosevelt, "Salvaging the Debts of Eastern Europe," *Foreign Affairs*, Vol. 12, no. 1 (Oct. 1933): 140.
[439] *New York Herald Tribune*, November 12, 13, 14, 15, 16, 17, 18, 19, 20, and 21, 1933.
[440] *New York Herald Tribune*, December 3, 4, 6, and 7, 1933.
[441] *New York Herald Tribune*, December 13, 14, and 15, 1933.

The first installment wrote about the very low salary for people working in the diplomatic corps abroad, which salary the government cut by 15 percent. The article caused a stir, and both Henry L. Stimson and Cordell Hull, former and present secretaries of state, respectively, spoke up. There was also positive bipartisan congressional reaction by the Foreign Affairs Committee. The House of Representatives, independently of the article, took up the case as well, and by an overwhelming majority voted for compensating government officials serving abroad with a 40 percent increase in their pay.[442]

In the first months of 1934 another foreign affairs topic that NR dealt with in detail was the situation of Austria. Just trying to climb out of the devastating effects of the depression, Austria found itself more and more at a crossroads of European power plays and domestic political turmoil. The German-speaking republic had never stood on firm legs since its birth after World War I. The Paris peace treaties forbade the Anschluss, that is, the union of Germany and Austria, but many Austrians saw this as an inevitable step toward prosperity. With the League-coordinated financial reconstruction program launched in late 1922 the financial issues were solved, and for the rest of the decade Austria was in many ways the poster child of a new Central Europe. With the deepening depression and the collapse of the Creditanstalt in May 1931, however, Austria weakened again, and with the rise of Hitler in Germany, the domestic political ferment gained strength. Trouble was brewing and NR had personal experience of this. He often visited Vienna while serving as minister in Budapest, and toward the end of his time there, he became convinced that the Nazi movement was in ascendancy.[443] Engelbert Dollfuss became chancellor in May 1932 at the age of 39, and the political situation deteriorated further under him. He dissolved Parliament, outlawed the extremists' political parties, assumed dictatorial powers in 1933, and established what he termed Austrofascism in an attempt to navigate toward Italy as a counterweight against Germany.[444] Starting in January and continuing through the summer, when things came to a head with the assassination of Dollfuss on July 25, NR regularly devoted space

---

[442] *The Christian Science Monitor*, February 14, 15, 16, 17, 19, 20, 21, 23, and 24, 1934.
[443] Nicholas Roosevelt, "Hungary," (unpublished), Box 45, Nicholas Roosevelt Papers.
[444] On Dollfuss's life and political career, see, Günter Bischof, Anton Pelinka, and Alexander Lassner, eds., *The Dollfuss/Schuschnigg Era in Austria: A Reassessment.* (Contemporary Austrian Studies 11) (New Brunswick, NJ and London: Transaction Publishers, 2003); Johannes Messner, *Dollfuss: An Austrian Patriot* [1935] (Norfolk, VA: Gates of Vienna Books, 2004); Wolfgang Maderthaner and Michaela Maier, *"Der Führer bin ich selbst": Engelbert Dollfuß – Bennito Mussolini Briefwechsel* (Vienna: Erhard Löcker Verlag, 2004); Gudula Walterskirchen, *Engelbert Dollfuss: Arbeitermörder oder Heldenkanzler* (Vienna: Molden, 2004).

to the issue of Austria. In these articles he mainly focused on the plight of Austria and what a German orientation would mean to the neighboring countries and to Europe at large. His analysis was prescient: "The 'Anschluss' means the rewriting of the map of Europe, with Germany almost in sight of the Adriatic. It implies the end of Czechoslovakia, the dismemberment of Poland and the revival of German domination throughout all central and eastern Europe from the Bosporus and the Black Sea through to the English Channel and the Baltic."[445] Indeed, even if after Dollfuss's death the Anschluss was put off for the time being and an imminent war was avoided—largely because Germany was not strong enough to launch one—the events of 1938 and 1939 proved NR one hundred percent right.

He also wrote about other Central European countries: Hungary, Poland, and Yugoslavia. He dealt with the problem of the League of Nations and minorities after Poland refused to uphold the minority treaties to which it was a signatory, on the tensions between Croats and Serbs, and an account of the diplomatic turmoil in the wake of the assassination of King Alexander of Yugoslavia in Marseilles in October 1934.[446] In these articles, sometimes openly and at other times indirectly, he criticized the League for failing to maintain peace on the continent, thereby feeding into the fifteen-year-long American narrative that the United States was better off without the League. Although the respective American administrations of the interwar years kept a close eye on the workings at Geneva, for domestic political reasons the idea of joining the organization was never seriously entertained in Washington. NR also wrote about Mussolini, whom he assessed positively as a realist statesman in Europe.[447] When the Ethiopian–Italian dispute broke out and soon deteriorated into a war, he agreed, for a change, with the U.S. president's staying out of the diplomatic tension, since "abstention from 'involvement' in the localized quarrels of foreign states must continue to be one of the fundamentals of American foreign policy."[448] This again shows that when FDR's policies struck him as sensible, he did not shy away from praising them. This happened mainly in the foreign policy domain; on the domestic front, he remained an acerbic critic.

In the columns of *Foreign Affairs*, NR revisited the Philippine question. In the spring of 1934 Congress passed the Tydings–McDuffie Act, which stated that

---

[445] Nicholas Roosevelt, "Germany Defies Austria," *New York Herald Tribune*, February 3, 1934.
[446] Nicholas Roosevelt, "Poland Defies the League," *New York Herald Tribune*, September 15, 1934; "Where East Meets West in Yugoslavia," *New York Herald Tribune*, October 11, 1934; "Yugoslavia Indicts Hungary," *New York Herald Tribune*, November 24, 1934; "The Tension in Europe," *New York Herald Tribune*, December 9, 1934.
[447] Nicholas Roosevelt, "Mussolini—the Holder of the Scales," *New York Herald Tribune*, January 6, 1935.
[448] Nicholas Roosevelt, "Keeping Out of Trouble," *New York Herald Tribune*, July 29, 1935.

after a ten-year period the Pacific country would regain its independence. Early the following year, in accordance with the Act, a Constitution of the Philippines was approved and ratified, thereby establishing the Commonwealth of the Philippines. NR again expressed his belief that the American policy on the archipelago was mistaken. He argued that Washington had to make up its mind about either staying in the Philippines or leaving it behind. Granting independence was premature in his view, but since the original American undertaking did not succeed, that is, the Filipinos had not embraced an American-style democracy, there was no other option for the U.S. but to face the consequences and leave them to their own devices. He thought that not seeing the original plan through would mean that the Open Door policy in China would be given up together with a secure commercial position for America in the Far East, while the balance of power in the larger region would also be upset, not to mention the loss of prestige to American foreign policy. His conclusion was that the United States must leave the Philippines immediately.[449] On a less serious but still important note, he regularly urged making more high quality wine in America instead of only imitating European wines, and he welcomed the introduction of a 50 percent tariff reduction on foreign beers.[450]

In 1936 NR ended his long status as a bachelor and married Tirzah Maris Gates. She was born in New York, but the Gates family was from California, and in the early twentieth century became successful in local politics there. Her father, Egbert James Gates, served as Republican state senator from 1912 until his death in 1923. Tirzah attended Leland Stanford Jr. University and was twenty-nine years old at the time of the wedding, which took place in a small private ceremony in Pasadena on June 5. The couple then moved to Long Island before settling in Big Sur, California, after NR's retirement for health reasons after World War II.[451] While in Hungary as American minister a few years before his marriage, NR wrote to his mother about Tirzah, as a way of introduction. In that letter, when engagement became seemingly timely, he characterized his future wife as "not only handsome and charming, but has all the earmarks of the 'grande dame' and would make an admirable

---

[449] Nicholas Roosevelt, "Laying down the White Man's Burden," *Foreign Affairs*, Vol. 13, No. 4 (Jul. 1935): 680–86.

[450] Nicholas Roosevelt, "Where Are American Wines?" *New York Herald Tribune*, October 14, 1934; "American vs. Foreign Wines," *New York Herald Tribune*, June 27, 1935; "Why Not Our Own Wines," *New York Herald Tribune*, January 2, 1937; "All Hail to Foreign Beers!" *New York Herald Tribune*, January 19, 1935.

[451] "Miss Tirzah Maris Gates and Nicholas Roosevelt Are Wed in Pasadena Residence of Bride," *The Brooklyn Daily Eagle*, June 6, 1936, 4; "The Life Summary of Tirzah Maris," https://ancestors.familysearch.org/en/K1DP-W4D/tirzah-maris-gates-1906–1961, accessed May 3, 2022.

Miss Tirzah Maris Gates, Pasadena socialite, became the bride of Nicholas Roosevelt, former American Minister to Hungary, and a distant relative of Franklin D. Roosevelt, in Pasadena, Calif., June 5, 1936. The couple is shown after the ceremony (AP Photo)

chatelaine for this or any other legation or embassy."[452] He also informed his mother that Tirzah was "not *rich*, but has a comfortable income which would go a long way towards making it possible to hold much more expensive posts than this one."[453] That is, she was wealthier than NR, and he was clearly hoping at the time to have a future diplomatic post at some more prestigious station.

As the second half of the 1930s progressed, NR devoted more space to Germany and Hungary in his articles. He wrote about Hitler's aim, bringing all Germans under Berlin's rule, which he thought would mean "a Germany supreme on the Continent," that is, a further destabilizing factor for the precarious peace in Europe.[454] He detailed the Czechoslovakian crisis not long before Hitler took large

---

[452] Nicholas Roosevelt to Mrs. J. West Roosevelt, October 1, 1931, Folder: Roosevelt, Mrs. J. West (mother) 1930–1933, Box 12, Nicholas Roosevelt Papers.
[453] Ibid.
[454] Nicholas Roosevelt, "What Hitler Wants," *New York Herald Tribune,* February 5, 1937; "Hitler's Ultimate Objective," *New York Herald Tribune,* September 20, 1938.

swaths of that country in the fall of 1938, thanks to the Munich Pact.[455] He also predicted that the acquisition of the Sudeten Germans would be only a first step, and it would not satisfy Hitler.[456] He also criticized Great Britain and France, the democracies that he judged as accomplices in creating lawlessness in international relations, whose effects Americans would feel with time.[457]

As for Hungary, he stressed two factors. First, he hailed the Hungarian resumption of its debt payments to America after a six-year moratorium.[458] Second, he analyzed Hungarian foreign policy vis-à-vis Germany and revision. He understood that Hungary had no choice but to be friendly to Germany, although Horthy did not sympathize with Hitler, and nor did the majority of Hungarians.[459] But Germany also needed Hungary for geographical and agricultural reasons, while the stricter governing style of the new prime minister, Béla Imrédy, struck him as indicative of the spread of Hitlerian ideology into eastern Europe—"a backward step in European history."[460] In addition, with German backing the revisionist aims of Hungary could be satisfied. He opined that if Hungary got back parts of Slovakia, it would demand Transylvania, and a vicious cycle would set in, inevitably leading to war.[461] Predictably enough, a few weeks after the Munich Pact was signed, through the auspices of the First Vienna Award—by the decision of Germany and Italy—Hungary received territories in the north, where the majority of the population was ethnic Hungarians.[462] NR actually praised the Hungarian government for wanting to achieve this enlargement by negotiation and not by force, and for not acting as a brute after once taking parts of Slovakia.[463]

In connection with the Hungarian-American community, a year before the war broke out NR agreed to say a few words at the dedication of the Hungarian Garden in Cleveland. He concentrated on three points in his address: the Hungarian immigrant adding value to the United States; the importance of the American character

---

[455] Nicholas Roosevelt, "Hitler's Latest Gesture," *New York Herald Tribune*, July 24, 1938. The most thorough account of the Munich Crisis is Steiner, *The Triumph of the Dark*, 610–68.
[456] Nicholas Roosevelt, "Hitler's Ultimate Objective," *New York Herald Tribune*, September 20, 1938.
[457] Nicholas Roosevelt, "The Triumph of Lawlessness," *New York Herald Tribune*, September 25, 1938.
[458] Nicholas Roosevelt, "Hungary, Honest Debtor," *New York Herald Tribune*, August 28, 1937; "Hungary Pays on Account," *New York Herald Tribune*, June 16, 1938.
[459] Nicholas Roosevelt, "Hungary Salutes Germany," *New York Herald Tribune*, August 23, 1938.
[460] Nicholas Roosevelt, "Hitlerizing Hungary," *New York Herald Tribune*, September 6, 1938.
[461] Nicholas Roosevelt, "Re-drawing Europe's Map," *New York Herald Tribune*, September 25, 1938.
[462] Hungary received about 4,600 square miles with almost a million ethnic Hungarians. For a comprehensive study on the First Vienna Award see, Gergely Sallai, *Az első bécsi döntés* [The First Vienna Award] (Budapest: Osiris, 2002).
[463] Nicholas Roosevelt, "Hungary's Portion," *New York Herald Tribune*, October 15, 1938; "An Admiral on a White Horse," *New York Herald Tribune*, November 14, 1938.

and system; and the bad situation of having authoritarian European governments. As always, he knew how to charm his audience, especially when he claimed that Hungarians were "one of the finest, toughest and most lovable races of Europe. [...] I only wish I might be able to claim a Hungarian ancestor." Contrary to his observations while being American minister at Budapest, now he praised the Hungarian character "which we in this country cherish—a great vitality, an unshakeable integrity, a respect for hard work, and a passionate love of the land." This also served as an explanation why the immigrant Hungarians had become such a valued asset to America. He added that he believed that immigrants represented a positive addition American society and only made it stronger. Somewhat contradicting his earlier documented views again, now he professed that Americans were not the "chosen people" and that the mixed blood of American society was a positive thing. What he emphasized regarding America was its unique will and capacity to be "not only the asylum for the oppressed of Europe" but also to ensure the individual development of the immigrants, and the United States "has not only been tolerant to dissenters but that has steadily held on high the torch of intellectual freedom." This led him to the question of the spread of authoritarian systems in Europe. He believed that Americans needed to be careful not to allow such views to confuse them and instead they ought to remain dedicated to "those principles and standards by which the American nation became great." By this he meant the American system of limited government and high degree of individualism.[464]

As the possibility of a new war became ever more tangible as 1939 went on, NR remained committed to writing about his former diplomatic host country. He judged that Hungary had "become the political nerve center of Eastern Europe," and could be a good litmus test of what was going to happen elsewhere in the region.[465] He praised Horthy for his conservativism and for standing up for Hungary's independence, and wrote that these two factors secured the stability of the country and perhaps that of some of the neighboring countries.[466] Just prior to the outbreak of World War II, he held the opinion that it would be a difficult task to preserve Hungary's independence, and that to some degree it would need to cooperate with Germany. It was the proportion of that collaboration that was going to be a challenge.[467]

---

[464] The quotations in the paragraph are from "America in the Making," Remarks of Nicholas Roosevelt at the Dedication of the Hungarian Garden in Cleveland, July 10, 1938, File: Mss – Speeches and Statements, Box 62, Nicholas Roosevelt Papers.
[465] Nicholas Roosevelt, "Threatened Hungary," *New York Herald Tribune,* February 7, 1939.
[466] Nicholas Roosevelt, "A Bulwark Against Germany," *New York Herald Tribune,* June 20, 1939.
[467] Nicholas Roosevelt, "Hungary in the Axis," *New York Herald Tribune,* August 12, 1939.

As a small token of his commitment to Hungary, NR was on the American Advisory Board of *The Hungarian Quarterly* between 1936 and 1940. This magazine was the high-quality propaganda tool of revisionist Hungary as former prime minister Bethlen imagined it, quite closely following the thematics and layout of *Foreign Affairs*. Although Bethlen was the instigator, the actual work mainly fell on the shoulders of the competent editor, József Balogh. The target audience was the elite of Great Britain and the United States. The journal was launched in 1934 and contained essays in English by both English speaking and Hungarian authors, and it was supposed to prove that Hungary had an ancient Christian culture akin to those of the English speaking countries. In order to facilitate wider recognition and a larger pool of possible future contributors, the journal managed to organize and set up advisory boards both in London and Washington, D.C. The major reason NR joined the committee was that it did not entail much work, and he believed that by doing this he can help Hungary to reach a wider audience, but this should not be interpreted to indicate that he shared the idea of revisionism. When Hungary joined the Axis Powers in the fall of 1940, many of the committee members resigned their post, NR included.[468]

In the meantime, NR's writing expanded to include books as well. The books he had authored in the second half of the 1920s were generally praised for their contents. A new book, on which he had been working for a number of years, was in many ways a sweeping treatise on what American democracy was about.[469] The new volume had both domestic roots (the New Deal, which was trying to change the United States in which NR had grown up) and foreign challenges in an unstable and less secure international environment that, if it came to an explosion, would threaten the security of the United States as well. Even the title of the book, *A New Birth of Freedom*—perhaps the most famous line of Lincoln's Gettysburg Address of 1863—clearly signaled that the author saw the American democratic model at its best as connected to the spiritual legacy of Abraham Lincoln and the Republican Party.

---

[468] On the history of the journal and especially the work of Balogh, see, Tibor Frank, "Literature Exported: Aspects of *The Hungarian Quarterly* (1936–1944)," *Studies in English and American*, 4 (Budapest: Eötvös Loránd University, 1978): 255–82; Tibor Frank, "Editing as Politics: József Balogh and *The Hungarian Quarterly*," *The Hungarian Quarterly* 34, no. 129 (Spring 1993): 5–13; Tibor Frank, "Patronage and Networking: The Society of *The Hungarian Quarterly*, 1935–1944," *The Hungarian Quarterly* 50, no. 196 (Winter 2009): 3–12.

[469] When he showed the manuscript to Hamilton Fish Armstrong in the spring of 1935, for example, the main editor of *Foreign Affairs* found many faults in the text and thought it was not ready for publication. Hamilton Fish Armstrong to Nicholas Roosevelt, April 22, 1935, Folder 22: Roosevelt, Nicholas, Box 53, Series 1: Correspondence, 1893–1973, Hamilton Fish Armstrong Papers, 1893–1973, Seeley G. Mudd Manuscript Library.

The content was basically an argument against the "all-powerful state" and setting forth the virtue of the American system, even if the latter had possible flaws. NR analyzed the Constitution, American representative democracy, the relations of the member states and the federal government, the expansion of presidential powers, and other related issues. He practically penned a political science study about individual rights, the danger tyrannies pose for democracies, and the role of government. He sided with the idea of limited government, warned against sweeping reforms and revolutions, and attacked, without mentioning names, the present Democratic government for trying to wield too much power. "Federalism is rooted in self-reliance and cooperation," he wrote, while "centralization accepts dependence as inevitable. Under a federal system men and localities have a voice in their own government. Under a central system, they do as they are told."[470] He saw the solution in decentralization, giving greater power to local political entities, and again strengthening self-reliance as one of the basic American characteristics and as a pillar of present and future success. He argued for the capitalist system but also called attention to its vices and argued for checking its abuses. He was not against modernization of government but could not agree with turning against old and tested principles. He also argued against collectivism in any form, especially against planned economies.

Although he could not have entertained in his wildest dreams the astronomic debt the United States would accumulate in the twenty-first century, the considerable debts of his day scared him and made him fear, like many pundits at least since the 1980s, that "the nation is heading toward a fatal calamity."[471] He similarly complained of the decline of the influence of the church, the breakdown of traditional family life, the deterioration of educational standards, and what he saw as the whole nation getting lazy by relying too much on government. Instead, he argued that the nation needed "a rebirth of self-reliance, a new faith in the God-given independence of spirit of every man, woman and child, and a new understanding of the eternal value of integrity, truth and honor. Without staunch moral standards in government and business as in personal affairs, life in America will be sterile."[472] In the final analysis, according to NR, "There must be a new faith in the old ideals—spiritual as well as political—if the dreams of those who founded and helped build America are to come true."[473]

---

[470] Nicholas Roosevelt, *A New Birth of Freedom* (New York: Charles Scribner's Sons, 1938), 118.
[471] Ibid., 163.
[472] Ibid., 259.
[473] Ibid., 274.

This train of thought hearkened back to a speech he gave at the University of Virginia in 1935. In a discussion titled "The Constitution and the New Deal," NR struck a correspondingly grave and pessimistic tone. Although he admitted that the overall situation had improved since Franklin D. Roosevelt assumed the presidency, he clearly saw danger in the highly centralized New Deal. His main condemnation was that the economy showed signs of centralized planning similar to socialist undertakings in the Soviet Union thereby stifling free competition and killing off a building block of the American system. "A planned economy," he argued, "implies changing the American system of government. It means substituting an economic dictatorship for a political democracy. I, for one, regard this as a threat to the very foundations of our civilization."[474]

Aside from the many insights in *A New Birth of Freedom*—some of them politically motivated, others perhaps superficial, although from a Republican who came of age under Theodore Roosevelt absolutely understandable—the most memorable passage was the one dealing with the question of populism. He must have had FDR in mind in characterizing present-day demagogues and describing how to be a successful politician. Some observations still ring true today, and maybe more strongly than ever.

> Your success will depend largely on your ability to smile and to promise everything to everyone. Learn, therefore, to be a good handshaker and mixer and to kiss the babies. Agree with everyone about everything. Do not forget that most men are more interested in your promises than in your achievements. They want to believe that you are their friend—that you want to do the right thing by them. Never miss a chance, therefore, to make plain your eagerness to improve the individual lot of the underprivileged. Promise them everything they want and, if you are really wise, try to do for them some of the things they desire most. Your efforts will convince them of your good will. This will make them your friends, and they will repay your friendship by voting for you. [...]
>
> What you need is as many votes as possible. Do not look for numbers among the educated and the wealthy. They are few—very few. Look, rather, to the masses. Advocate anything which may be popular with them. Ingratiate yourself with them. Assure them that they are not getting their due, and repeat, over and over again, that you will help them.

---

[474] Nicholas Roosevelt, *Two Amazing Years*, Washington, D.C.: American Liberty League, 1935, 14.

When it comes to a campaign, begin by maligning your opponent in well-chosen private conversations. Denounce his acts in public and attack his motives. If possible, dig up some discreditable incident in his private life. Do not be too particular about the truth of what you charge, but be sure you paint a rosy picture while you are about it. Remember that a denial or correction never catches up with the original slander, and that it flatters many men to hear evil of their leaders. [...]

Never admit that you will increase any taxes except those that you can pin on the wealthy. Advocate every reform that has any chance of proving popular, and do not feel under any obligation to carry it out if you are elected. You can always count on the short memory of the public. [...]

If you make a blunder, never admit it. Blame one of your subordinates and, if necessary, discharge him publicly for the mistake which you yourself made. [...]

Under no circumstances tie yourself irrevocably to any particular course of action. [...] You are, to use another simile, like the quarterback on a football team, and must be ready to change your play in accordance with the progress of the game. [...] It is your job to be always just a little ahead of public opinion, and public opinion changes quickly. But under no circumstances get too far ahead. The people are not interested in the future—only in to-day.

In your speeches, do not be specific. The voters like generalities—especially if they are phrased in fine-sounding, benevolent terms. Avoid facts. They may be used against you by your enemies. If, however, it is necessary to give an appearance of definiteness, do not be squeamish about mere accuracy. Make a positive statement, with figures to support your case, even if neither the facts nor the figures are as you say they are. Only a few people will check on you, and by the time your opponents have discovered your misrepresentation, the people will have lost interest. If not, you can make another speech to divert them.

In these days of radio, it is not what you say, but how you say it, that counts. Few people will ever read your speeches, but millions will listen to you on the air. [...] The voters will believe you if you talk as if you yourself believe what you say.[475]

---

[475] Nicholas Roosevelt, *A New Birth of Freedom*, 30–34.

In other words, the framers of the Constitution could not have dreamed of the present political climate, and what had transpired in 150 years created circumstances that NR deemed negative. He argued that Americans could find their way back to the original path only by following the basic tenets of the early republic.

In a favorable review, James F. Ellis wrote that the book had "penetrating insight and the clear-cut analysis of controlling factors," it was written in a "non-partisan" manner producing "a very readable volume" and "an excellent interpretation of political trends."[476] Thomas Lamont of J. P. Morgan & Co. and a long-time acquaintance of the author, reacted to the book in a private letter a few months later. In a friendly way he collected on eight pages a number of points on which he wished to differ with Roosevelt's various observations. Although by and large he agreed with the main thrust of the book, he mainly took issue with passages where NR criticized big business. Here he complained of "too broad generalizations" and "unwarranted assumptions," but overall he praised Roosevelt for the work.[477]

Another book followed in quick succession, a product of his trips in Latin America. In December 1938, he was sent by a group of American business interests to Lima, Peru, to study the Pan-American Conference held there. The Pan-American idea and conferences started with Secretary of State James G. Blaine at the end of the 1880s. The United States promoted closer ties among the nations of the American continents for its own national security reasons and financial interests, but the latter of these motives clearly made the countries south of the United States wary. In late 1938, Washington's basic attitude was to ensure that in case of another major war erupting in Europe, the Latin American countries would join in the defense of the Western Hemisphere. NR summed up his observations in a small pamphlet published by the National Foreign Trade Council, Inc. In it he emphasized that the basis of a Good Neighbor Policy was economic cooperation between the United States and the Latin American countries. The former needed the raw materials of these countries, while the latter wanted American capital and finished products. He stressed that if the Good Neighbor Policy were to work, it must be a two-way policy and not a one-sided American endeavor.[478] He repeated this thesis in an address at the National Foreign Trade Convention a year later. He

---

[476] James F. Ellis, "*A New Birth of Freedom* by Nicholas Roosevelt," *The Journal of Politics* 1, no. 3 (Aug. 1939): 322–23.
[477] Thomas Lamont to Nicholas Roosevelt, July 13, 1939, Folder: Lamont, Thomas, Box 8, Nicholas Roosevelt Papers.
[478] Nicholas Roosevelt, *Wanted: Good Neighbors* (New York, The National Foreign Trade Council Trade Council, Inc., 1939).

again emphasized the relation between American investment and Latin American demand for everything from toothpaste to powdered milk, thus helping American exports. However, he argued this investment policy should be implemented fairly on both sides, the investor and the host country.[479] In the same year he also published a small book on Venezuela. It was basically a travel book with many pictures, probably most of them taken by NR. He wrote mainly about the oil industry there and various related things, with an American economic angle as the vantage point.[480]

World War II did break out and the United States and the president had to react to the dangerous international situation. At the outbreak of hostilities NR had nothing but praise for FDR. He appreciated FDR's fireside chat of September 3, 1939, in which the president declared U.S. neutrality but stressed that individual conscience demanded taking sides, however cautiously. With this move the president thus outlined America's role in the first phase of the war.[481] But afterwards, in a score of articles up until Pearl Harbor, NR mostly criticized the president. He attacked FDR's personal style of diplomacy, which prevented everybody else from knowing the whole picture, and which practice NR did not find democratic.[482] But this only grew worse, as FDR seemed to zigzag and showed "his inability to follow a simple course consistently." NR considered this "one of his greatest failures in domestic as in foreign affairs."[483] When, however, the question of building up the navy and modernizing the army came to the fore, NR once more found himself applauding FDR.[484] Still, the general tone of his articles remained critical, mainly on account of the preparedness program, which he judged chaotic.[485]

Before the United States joined World War II, but when Europe had already plunged into mayhem, NR assumed perhaps his favorite role: that of a public educator teaching fellow Americans the truth about the world as he perceived it. There were two topics in particular about which he could spread his gospel: journalism and international affairs.

On the 150th anniversary of the ratification of the Bill of Rights, the first ten Amendments to the U.S. Constitution, at an event organized by the Citizenship

---

[479] Nicholas Roosevelt, Creative Dollars Abroad: An Address Delivered by Nicholas Roosevelt at the 27th National Foreign Trade Convention, the Americas' Session, at the Palace hotel, San Francisco, California, July 30, 1940 (New York City, 1940).
[480] Nicholas Roosevelt, *Venezuela's Place in the Sun: Modernizing a Pioneering Country* (New York: Round Table Press, Inc., 1940).
[481] Nicholas Roosevelt, "The President's Appeal," *New York Herald Tribune,* September 5, 1939.
[482] Nicholas Roosevelt, "Personal Diplomacy," *New York Herald Tribune,* March 31, 1940.
[483] Nicholas Roosevelt, "Bungled Diplomacy," *New York Herald Tribune,* April 3, 1940.
[484] Nicholas Roosevelt, "War Marches Near," *New York Herald Tribune,* April 14, 1940.
[485] Nicholas Roosevelt, "Our Galloping President," *New York Herald Tribune,* June 20, 1940.

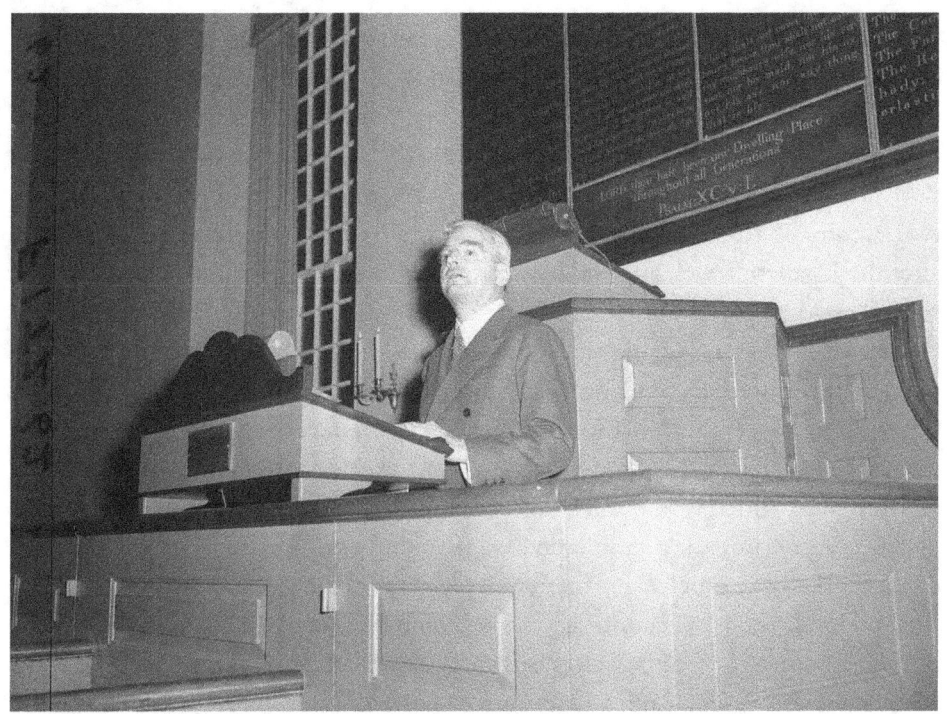

Nicholas Roosevelt, speaks at the celebration in St. Paul's Church, Dec. 15, 1944, in Mt. Vernon, NY, commemorating the 153rd anniversary of the ratification of the Bill of Rights.
(AP Photo/Tom Fitzsimmons)

Educational Service, NR gave an address on one of the freedoms listed in the First Amendment: freedom of the press. This speech was also entered into the *Congressional Record* by Senator Arthur Capper of Kansas on October 9, 1941. In it NR defended freedom of the press, which was "inseparable from freedom of speech and freedom of the air," and its essential role was "freedom to think, and freedom to hold and communicate an opinion." The European scene gave a perfect platform to emphasize that under dictatorship the life-giving truth was suppressed by the limited and censored press, and once there was free and uncontrolled journalism and a free press, a dictatorship could not exist long. Only through a free press could there be informed public opinion, which was also an indispensable element of democracy. So, as "long as the means of expression remain unhampered by Government control," Roosevelt ensured his audience, "the American way of life can be made to prevail."[486]

---

[486] *Congressional Record*, 77th Congress, 1st Session, Appendix, Washington: United States Government Printing Office, 1941, 4571–72.

Just prior to Pearl Harbor, when most Americans dealing with foreign affairs clearly saw that it was a question of when and not if the United States had to enter the war, NR started to give a series of lectures on international affairs at Mills College in California. This was a regular activity during the winters, and, by his own calculation, he gave "several hundred lectures from 1934 to 1940."[487] Intriguingly, the last two lectures on his tour in November–December 1941 took place only a few days after the Japanese attack and the United States becoming a belligerent power. But since these were typed-out lectures and not impromptu talks, he reflected little on the present moment. In these six lectures he was clearly trying to educate his audience, mainly university students, and started by assuring his listeners that though the war might seem far off for most of them, the effects of the ongoing carnage would gravely affect the United States. A German victory would mean an American garrison state, which would run counter to the long-standing constitutional model of the country providing various civilian freedoms and liberties. He believed that danger lurked at home "from three sources—indifference, ignorance and defeatism."[488] But, he said, the country's history should be enough to cure anyone of such pessimism, since the United States had always evolved and progressed when facing a challenge. In his November 12 lecture he again showed foresight, although for a close observer of international affairs it might not have been very difficult at that moment. He told his audience "it is through events in the Far East that we may well be drawn into this war."[489] Less than a month later Pearl Harbor was attacked.

In his lecture the following day he drew a contrast between totalitarian regimes, especially Germany's, and democracies. Here he relied to a large extent on his first-hand experience in Central Europe. He characterized the old type of revolutions as being for political liberalism, while the latest ones were carrying water for reactionaries. It was no matter whether it was called "Nazism, or Fascism or Communism, or state socialism, or planned economy. They are all forms of reaction, manifestations of pessimism."[490] Their major sin was that "their guiding principle is that the individual is too stupid to run his own affairs and that, therefore, he must be told what to do."[491] This, together with the doctrine of economic self-sufficiency

---

[487] Nicholas Roosevelt, *A Front Row Seat*, 246. For his reminiscences on these speaking engagements, ibid., 246–54.
[488] Nicholas Roosevelt, "On the Brink of Chaos," November 12, 1941, Folder: Lectures—Mills College 1941, Box 63, Nicholas Roosevelt Papers.
[489] Ibid.
[490] Nicholas Roosevelt "The Nature of the World Revolution," November 13, 1941, Folder: Lectures—Mills College 1941, Box 63, Nicholas Roosevelt Papers.
[491] Ibid.

preached by Germany, was in stark opposition to the democratic, but especially the American experience. He also shared with the audience one of his favorite anecdotes. According to the source of the story, György Festetics, a Hungarian aristocrat who served in World War I, had received orders to arrest the editor of a clandestine newspaper in northern Italy, but twice let the man escape. The editor turned out to be none other than Mussolini, the later Fascist dictator of Italy.[492]

In another session two weeks later he analyzed the United States' position in the international arena and how to curb the chance of a similar world conflagration in the future. On the one hand, he warned that "complacent irresponsibility" on part of America must stop, and the nation and its leaders must fully understand that security would not be achievable just by having the shield of two oceans and staying out of others' problems, because physical distance was not enough anymore to remain unaffected.[493]

In light of the League of Nations' stumbling and failing efforts in the 1930s to prop up collective security, NR expressed his belief in an expanded version of Theodore Roosevelt's "international police power" idea, which the former president articulated for the Western Hemisphere in 1904. The lessons of Manchuria, Ethiopia, and Hitler's voracious land grabs in Europe made it clear that aggressors understood only force. To ensure that such a collective force would be available, the key was to gather the global principal powers who through their military and economic strength could rapidly project power anywhere to keep in check any aggressor that would wish to disturb the peace. And when saying that "unless the United States is willing to take its share of responsibility for world peace another war cannot be prevented," he had the United States and Great Britain in mind for that police role.[494] Only these two countries, because at that moment the Soviet Union was fighting for its own survival, and NR did not think of China or any other country as possibly being a large power.

This deterrence by force, together with global free trade and a federalized Europe was to create, in NR's reading of the situation, a new international order where peace would thrive. Obviously, for all this to happen the traditional isolationist outlook in the United States had to be forgotten, therefore the long-held Washingtonian principle of non-alliance with other countries, especially European nations, must be altered. In some ways, he was ahead of official U.S. foreign policy, given that

---

[492] Ibid; Diary entry, March 20, 1932, Hungary 1930–1933, Box 21, Nicholas Roosevelt Papers.
[493] Nicholas Roosevelt, "Partners for Peace," November 27, 1941, Folder: Lectures—Mills College 1941, Box 63, Nicholas Roosevelt Papers.
[494] Ibid.

the Truman Doctrine, which was structured along similar lines, was not declared until 1947. NR also thought that this should be the one and only criterion for Washington: to keep the peace. He was not for spreading abroad American ideals, such as FDR's "four freedoms."[495] NR reiterated that he was "not suggesting that we should impose our will, or our form of government, or our ideals, on the rest of the world. I am not referring to such projects as spreading four—or ten—or fifty—freedoms throughout the globe. I am referring only to a single objective—the prevention of the outbreak of another war, be it small or large."[496] NR's ideas were actually similar to Franklin. D. Roosevelt's concerning the use of force as insurance that there would be no aggression in the future. In a sense, NR's stance proved to be the bridge between TR's policing the Western Hemisphere and FDR's four policemen idea beginning in 1942. Initially, FDR was also for an Anglo-American police duo.[497] However, soon the president began to think in more cooperative terms and believed that there should be four policemen: the United States, Great Britain, the Soviet Union, and China. In other words, it would not be an international organization that would be the guarantor of international peace, but sheer military power. He wanted to see most countries disarmed and if anyone still toyed with aggression, sheer force would be the solution. As he expressed it to the Soviets, "If any nation menaced the peace, it could be blockaded and then if still recalcitrant, bombed."[498] This thinking started to take shape from 1942 on and became a cornerstone of international relations. Of course, the Cold War overwrote the possibility of harmonious cooperation of these four countries, but the idea nonetheless was a healthy one.[499]

In his last two speeches, a few days after Pearl Harbor, NR dealt with some basic features of the American way of life: the Constitution, democracy, and immigration.

---

[495] In January that year President Roosevelt in his State of the Union address spoke of four freedoms as the basis of a peaceful world: freedom of speech and expression, freedom from want and from fear. Franklin D. Roosevelt, State of the Union, January 6, 1941, https://voicesofdemocracy.umd.edu/fdr-the-four-freedoms-speech-text/, accessed May 13, 2022.

[496] Nicholas Roosevelt, "Partners for Peace," November 27, 1941.

[497] Warren F. Kimball, *The Juggler: Franklin Roosevelt as Wartime Statesman* (Princeton, NJ: Princeton University Press, 1991), 85.

[498] *F.R.U.S.*, 1942, Vol. 3, 569.

[499] On FDR's foreign policy evolution and arriving at the four policemen concept, see, Kimball, *The Juggler*, 83–105; John Lamberton Harper, *American Visions of Europe: Franklin D. Roosevelt, George F. Kennan, and Dean G. Acheson* (Cambridge: Cambridge University Press, 1994), 77–131; Robert Dallek, *Franklin D. Roosevelt and American Foreign Policy, 1932–1945: With a New Afterword* (Oxford: Oxford University Press, 1995), 317–484; Townsend Hoopes and Douglas Brinkley, *FDR and the Creation of the U.N.* (New Haven, CT: Yale University Press, 1997), 43–129; John Lewis Gaddis, *The United States and the Origins of the Cold War, 1941–1947* (New York: Columbia University Press, 2000), 1–31.

He highlighted the most important features of the Constitution and expressed his fear that too much power had lately been accumulated in the hands of the president.[500] As for democracy, he was pessimistic because of the changes that had taken place within society. He argued that Americans had become too dependent on too many things, that is, he once more attacked the New Deal as being contrary to the American system of rugged individualism. When it came to immigration, he talked about the significance of immigration historically and defended the latest wave, which was arriving mainly from Central, Eastern, and Southern Europe, as not inferior to older waves. He closed his last talk with a reference to Lincoln, because, as he told the audience,

> The American dream is not yet fully realized. There is still much to be done. But it calls for hard work, self-sacrifice, and courage. Never before has the need for these qualities been greater, for it is only through them that we can realize Lincoln's vision that this country shall have a new birth of freedom, and that "government of the people, by the people, and for the people shall not perish from the earth.[501]

With the Japanese attack on Pearl Harbor, the United States found itself a belligerent nation again in another world war. Although the nature of the attack gave reason for indignation, the more informed segment of the American public—NR included—knew that it had been only a matter of time before their country had to become a party to the war. NR was too old for active duty, but his skills could be utilized in spheres other than service on the front: his weapon was the pen.

World War II offered Nicholas Roosevelt an opening into another chapter in his checkered involvement with history. Even before but especially after the outbreak of World War II, President Franklin Delano Roosevelt tried to steer public opinion, and he made efforts to prepare isolationist Americans for the fact that they might not escape being drawn into the conflict. With Pearl Harbor, the possibility of the United States staying out of the war inevitably disappeared, and the nation stood as one behind the president. An important point for the government was how to inform its citizens, how to educate them about America's role in the war, its war aims, and its approach to peace and the postwar world. FDR liked to sit in the middle of a large web of his own creation constructed of various government

---

[500] Nicholas Roosevelt, "Know America First," December 10, 1941, Folder: Lectures—Mills College 1941, Box 63, Nicholas Roosevelt Papers.
[501] Nicholas Roosevelt, "The American Tradition," December 11, 1941, ibid.

offices together with private and public aides. He listened to them, but also followed public opinion and his own hunches and endeavored to shape the information that was to reach the public. To coordinate this effort, by executive order in June 1942, Roosevelt called into being a large-scale propaganda effort that was to last for the remainder of the war. The Office of War Information was a mainly civilian propaganda arm of the U.S. government for the next three years.[502]

The matter of government-sponsored propaganda was not without controversy. Although at the beginning of the twentieth century the word "propaganda" was largely synonymous with information, the experience of World War I changed that. During that time, both the British propaganda effort and the American version of state propaganda claimed an important role in disseminating information and forming public opinion among American citizens. Just a few days after the United States joined that war in April 1917, President Woodrow Wilson created the Committee on Public Information (CPI). Led by George Creel, it launched the first large-scale propaganda effort orchestrated by the U.S. government. The CPI tried to shape how Americans perceived the conflagration and bloodshed in Europe and America's role in the fight. With its various branches producing written materials, pictures and posters, movies, and thousands of talks across the country, the CPI disseminated Wilsonian views and ideas. Beyond the home front, the CPI actively propagated a positive image of America and Wilson throughout Europe as well.[503]

By the 1930s, however, both the assessment of the CPI and the word "propaganda" started to acquire a negative image. The findings produced by the Nye Committee (1934–1936), together with the growing propaganda machines of Nazi Germany and the Bolshevik Soviet Union all pointed to the way that state propaganda had detrimental effects on individuals' perception of reality, and therefore it was anti-democratic. The United States by definition had to be different.[504] Seen in this light, it is

---

[502] Some of the most important sources concerning the OWI during World War II are Lester G. Hawkins and George S. Pettee, "OWI: Organization and Problems," *Public Opinion Quarterly* 7 no. 1 (Spring 1943): 15–33; Sydney Weinberg, "What to Tell America: The Writer's Quarrel in the OWI," *Journal of American History* 55 no. 1 (June 1968): 73–89; Allan M. Winkler, *The Politics of Propaganda: The Office of War Information, 1942–1945* (New Haven: Yale University Press, 1978); Clayton D. Laurie, *The Propaganda Warriors: America's Crusade Against Nazi Germany* (Lawrence: University Press of Kansas, 1996).

[503] On the CPI see, George Creel, *How We Advertised America* (New York: Harper & Brothers Publishers, 1920); Alan Axelrod, *Selling the Great War: The Making of American Propaganda* (New York: Palgrave Macmillan, 2009), 65–217.

[504] For the official findings of the Nye Committee, named after its chair, Senator Gerald Nye of South Dakota, see, Report of the Special Committee on Investigation of the Munitions Industry. The Nye Report, U.S. Congress, Senate, 74th Congress, 2nd Session, February 24, 1936, 3–13. https://www.mtholyoke.edu/acad/intrel/nye.html, accessed April 20, 2022.

understandable that President Roosevelt played a careful game vis a vis how to set up a propaganda body after the country found itself in the war in December 1941. There was little doubt in Roosevelt's mind that Americans needed to be educated about the various issues in the global conflict in which the United States had become the latest and one of the major participants. But he was equally aware that he needed to avoid the pitfalls set up by memories of the CPI on the one hand, and on the other how the autocratic European countries carried out their—quite influential—propaganda. The solution for FDR lay in setting up the Office of War Information.

The OWI did not arise out of the blue. It had predecessors that paved the way for the larger and more all-encompassing agency. Roosevelt was a keen politician and understood both the need for and possible advantages of a centrally disseminated propaganda wave that would engulf Americans. But not only did FDR follow a cautious approach to propaganda, he also had his own idiosyncratic organizational style, which led to a haphazard beginning. When the war broke out, FDR's first move in this sphere was to establish the Office of Government Reports in September 1939; this was followed by the Division of Information of the Office of Emergency Management in March 1941; and still before Pearl Harbor, the Office of Facts and Figures under Archibald MacLeish was set up in October 1941. Another executive order called into being the Office of the Coordinator of Information in July 1941, which was responsible both for propaganda and intelligence. On June 13, 1942, the president signed Executive Order 9182, which combined the abovementioned offices into the Office of War Information, with a focal point of domestic information. At the same time, Roosevelt also set up the Office of Strategic Services, which would be the branch dealing in clandestine operations and psychological warfare outside the United States.[505]

The Office of War Information had extended responsibilities. On the one hand, it had to coordinate "the war informational activities of all Federal departments and agencies," while it was also entrusted with formulating and carrying out "through the use of press, radio, motion pictures and other facilities, information programs designed to facilitate the development of an informed and intelligent understanding, at home and abroad, of the status and progress of the war effort."[506] The new agency had a Domestic Branch and an Overseas Branch, responsible for domestic

---

[505] On the antecedents and establishment of OWI, see, Hawkins, "OWI: Organization and Problems," 16–19; Winkler, *The Politics of Propaganda*, 8–37; Weinberg, "What to Tell America," 73–81; Laurie, *The Propaganda Warriors*, 50–111.

[506] Steven Casey, *Cautious Crusade: Franklin D. Roosevelt, American Public Opinion, and the War against Nazi Germany* (New York: Oxford University Press, 2001), 61.

and foreign propaganda, respectively.[507] Its main purpose, of course, was propaganda. As historian Leo Margolin noted shortly after the conclusion of World War II: "Both the Office of War Information and the military and naval Psychological Warfare branches, which OWI serviced with material and personnel, were strictly in the business of using propaganda as a weapon of warfare. We did not carry the torch of democracy. Our only interest was winning the war."[508] This is a hard-nosed but realistic assessment of the primary war aims of the United States in World War II.

The Office of War Information oversaw a motley crew of thousands of people, including journalists, printers, advertisers, playwrights, film makers, actors, radio broadcasters, managers, and academics—most of them liberal in outlook. This latter perception—that is, that these people were zealous New Dealers—was a key factor why Congress was inimical to the OWI and pulled the purse strings tight, but the State Department, the War and Navy Departments were also antagonistic toward it. Elmer Davis, who was a well-known and widely respected CBS radio commentator, was chosen as the OWI's Director, while Milton S. Eisenhower was associate director, the three assistant directors being Gardner Cowles, Jr. (Domestic Branch), Robert Sherwood (Overseas Branch), and Archibald MacLeish (Policy Development). Under the assistant director were the deputies responsible for one territory each.[509] Unfortunately, Davis proved to be not a very efficient bureaucratic leader, and confusion also worked against the organization. As historian Sydney Weinberg quipped, "the function of the OWI was never quite clear to many of its officials, to the public, and apparently even to the President himself."[510] In addition, or rather as a consequence, there were constant disagreements within and without the organization as to its proper role.[511] The most visible output of the OWI was its weekly magazine, *Victory*. The 30-plus-page issues informed Americans about war production, price controls, rationing, labor, housing, transportation, war-related statistics, photographs, cartoons, etc. The idea was to report the news, but obviously there was an agenda for the whole undertaking. The agency functioned throughout the war and was abolished by Harry Truman's executive order on August 31, 1945.

NR, was recruited personally by Elmer Davis, and worked for this organization for eight months. Soon after the United States became a party to the war he

---

[507] On the two branches and their work, see, Winkler, *The Politics of Propaganda*, 38–111.
[508] Leo J. Margolin, *Paper Bullets: A Brief Story of Psychological Warfare in World War II* (New York: Froben Press, 1946), 66.
[509] *Victory: Official Weekly Bulletin of the Office of War Information* 3, no. 28, (July 14, 1942): 32.
[510] Weinberg, "What to Tell America," 73.
[511] On the OWI's organization, ideas of work, and problems, Winkler, *The Politics of Propaganda*, 38–72; Laurie, *The Propaganda Warriors*, 112–27.

had offered his services in a letter to the president, who appreciated the initiative. "Thanks ever so much for your kind letter which I have noted with the deepest interest," answered FDR. "We will certainly use you and your wide knowledge if we can, and of course you know that I appreciate your cooperative spirit in offering your service."[512] The director of the Domestic Branch was Gardner Cowles, Jr., a well-known journalist of the era, who was co-founder, co-publisher, and editor of *Look* magazine, among other outlets. He had a handful of deputies overseeing various aspects of information coordination. NR was appointed to the post of deputy director of the news bureau concerning military information. According to Staff Order 7, issued on October 10, 1942,

> Each deputy will be responsible for developing and maintaining an adequate information problem on each subject in the field assigned to him. [...] It will be [his] [...] duty to [...] define information policy, develop a proposed coordinated program [...] present the proposed policies [...] to the Board in writing, [...] determine, through the use of intelligence service, how well the information objective is being attained and to suggest necessary adjustments.[513]

The holder of this post acted as a liaison officer between the OWI and the War and Navy Departments. The title was News Bureau Chief, and Robert W. Horton held it first, followed by Lt. Commander Paul C. Smith, who resigned in mid-August of 1942. He was succeeded by NR in December.[514] This was an important position and carried weight for Director Davis, too, since it involved daily meetings with the army and navy representatives where information policy for the war effort was discussed.[515] Secretary of War Stimson noted in his dairy that NR was "very anxious to help, and he is enthusiastic and will be a good helper I believe."[516]

---

[512] Franklin D. Roosevelt to Nicholas Roosevelt, January 12, 1942, "Roosevelt, Nicholas," in Franklin D. Roosevelt's, Papers as President, President's Personal Files, Folder, Roosevelt, Nicholas; Franklin D. Roosevelt Library.
[513] Hawkins, "OWI: Organization and Problems," 24.
[514] *Victory*, Vol. 3, no. 33, (August 18, 1942): 2; *Information Digest*, OWI News Bureau, November 12, 1942, 9; Hawkins, "OWI: Organization and Problems," 23; A. H. Feller, "OWI on the Home Front," *The Public Opinion Quarterly* 7, no. 1 (Spring 1943): 60; Major George Fielding Eliot to Henry A. Wallace (Vice President), December 10, 1942, Box 15, Office of War Information 1943, Nicholas Roosevelt Papers.
[515] Hawkins, "OWI: Organization and Problems," 23.
[516] Diary entry, December 10, 1942, Reel 8, Vol. 41, Henry L. Stimson Diaries, Henry Lewis Stimson Papers, MS 465, Yale Archives.

In this capacity NR dealt with radar, food waste in the army, prisoners of war, African Americans in the armed services, war plants, the battle of the Pacific, and bacterial warfare.[517] But most importantly, his job was to make sure that news would flow from the War and Navy Departments. However, cooperation between these departments and the OWI was anything but smooth and productive, and he remembered these months as "the most frustrating and futile job in my life."[518] This was due to too much security on the part of the navy as to its activities not long after Pearl Harbor, which led to it not providing enough and accurate news, which in turn produced a low public relations profile. NR was to alter that if he could.

One example of such secrecy was regarding radar, a critical development in warfare technology during World War II. The Joint Security Control Board initiated discussions with the Office of Censorship and the Office of War Information on a revision of the army's and navy's radar news policy. The talks culminated in a statement prepared by NR on behalf of the OWI that contained all of the information that the government felt comfortable revealing about radar. Nathaniel R. Howard, Head of the Press Division of the U.S. Office of War Censorship, reviewed the proposed statement on April 17, 1943, and wrote to his boss, Byron Price, former executive news editor of Associated Press and now director of censorship: "It would let us peg the radar issue close to where we have it, and I told Mr. Roosevelt we were entirely satisfied." So, the statement was accepted and was released on April 25, 1943. It contained a short history of radar, on what scientific principles it worked, and what military advantages it offered, especially in locating enemy ships and planes. True to propaganda measures in wartime, only one paragraph gave any information about the role of radar in Allied military operations, when it mentioned the Battle of Britain. The reasoning for being so tight-lipped was that more information might compromise Allied war efforts. As a result, "it has been decided that no further items on the subject will be released until the army and navy are convinced that the enemy already has the information from some other source."[519]

The limited powers of the OWI in disseminating the news as it saw fit—to a large degree thanks to the resistance of the War and Navy Departments—left NR frustrated at his post. One example of frustration was the clash regarding a news

---

[517] *Preliminary Inventories*, Number 56: Records of the Office of War Information, Washington, National Archives, 1953, 18. For his summary of the work he did for OWI, see, Nicholas Roosevelt, *A Front Row Seat*, 255–64.
[518] Nicholas Roosevelt, *A Front Row Seat*, 255.
[519] The content and the quotations in the paragraph are from Michael S. Sweeney, *Secrets of Victory: The Office of Censorship and the American Press and Radio in World War II* (Chapel Hill & London: The University of North Carolina Press, 2001), 196.

release that had two versions: the original, which the OWI wanted to bring out, and a rewritten version by Admiral Ernest Joseph King, who had recently been promoted to Commander in Chief of United States Fleet, and was, in NR's words, "as impervious to reason in matters of public relations as he was responsive and brilliant in his all-important duties of winning the fighting war."[520] Although the original piece was accepted by both the Joint Chiefs of Staff and the War Department, King unilaterally altered the text, and Roosevelt judged that the new version "would be turned down by all but the dullest and dumbest editors."[521] In his eyes the Admiral's alteration was "as unwarranted and indefensible as it would be for me to tell Admiral King how he should dispose the fleet in the Pacific."[522] He complained about this issue to Rear Admiral Richard E. Byrd because, as NR explained in a handwritten note two decades later, "Byrd alone among high ranking naval officers understood our problem."[523] At that time, however, the only place to give vent to his anger was in private or semi-official letters.[524]

NR was also exasperated that in the popular press the OWI was blamed for slow releases of various news items, when actually it was the Army and Navy Departments that withheld or only painfully slowly agreed to give out information concerning various aspects of the war effort. As he summarized the navy's procedure in his memoirs,

> The technique was simple: to listen to every suggestion from the O.W.I. with cordial appreciation and gratefulness; to promise prompt and enthusiastic support in submitting the suggestion to the high command; and, after a more than reasonable delay, designed to give the impression that the high command was studying it from every possible angle, to report regretfully that the suggestion had been turned down.[525]

NR used private channels to soothe his irritation, such as a personal letter in reaction to an article by Frank R. Kent who accused the OWI of slowing down the news getting out, and in particular called Elmer Davis an incompetent leader of

---

[520] Nicholas Roosevelt, *A Front Row Seat*, 263.
[521] Nicholas Roosevelt to Rear Admiral Richard E. Byrd, March 2, 1943, Box 15, Office of War Information 1943, Nicholas Roosevelt Papers.
[522] Ibid.
[523] Nicholas Roosevelt's handwritten note, June 15, 1964, Ibid.
[524] See, for instance, Nicholas Roosevelt to Arthur Hays Sulzberger, April 17, 1943, Folder 6: Office of War Information, Box 224, Arthur Hays Sulzberger Papers.
[525] Nicholas Roosevelt, *A Front Row Seat*, 257.

the organization. NR's personal letter to Kent refuted the charge and blamed the lack of prompt news releases on the resistance of the Army and Navy Departments. On the other hand, he argued that the OWI had actually taken steps to expedite getting and disseminating messages. He also complained about the vagueness as to the OWI's powers in the Executive Order: "Time and again we have asked the War and Navy Departments' Public Relations Bureau to release stories promptly. Time and again they have either imposed interminable delays or refused to give out any information. [...] our failures have been largely due to our inadequate powers."[526]

Kent in his response maintained that he had always found the Army and Navy Department prompt in reacting to his requests, therefore, the blame stayed with the OWI. Equally, he was not willing to change his negative opinion of the Director. He described Davis as "preposterously pompous but underbred and bad mannered," who "personally, cannot help not being a gentleman, as a public official he might easily help being an ass."[527] NR's response was not only a summary of his frustration with the situation but also a good description of the situations that hurt the OWI's efforts to fulfill its mandate. He attacked the Army Public Relations Division for not cooperating with him and his organization. He was fully convinced that "they resent the very existence of OWI. I know that some of them dislike Elmer very much. Probably many of them dislike me. All of them would feel happier if OWI were to be closed up because its very existence is an implied reflection on the inadequacy and incompetence of the Public Relations Bureaus of the two Departments in the earlier months of the war."[528]

In September 1943, after eight months of hard work and ample disappointment, NR quit his job and left the OWI. Already the previous May he signaled to Davis that probably by the end of the summer he would reach the possible maximum expected of him "under the present limited powers of the OWI to induce the army and navy to expedite and amplify the flow of war news."[529] The next three months neither changed the relationship between the OWI and Army and Navy Departments nor provided any hope that it might be altered for the better. NR felt that the only logical and acceptable option for him was to resign, and on September 2 his third and last stint working for the U.S. government ended on a low point.

---

[526] Nicholas Roosevelt to Frank R. Kent, July 22, 1943, Box 15, Office of War Information 1943, Nicholas Roosevelt Papers.
[527] Frank R. Kent to Nicholas Roosevelt, July 24, 1943, Ibid.
[528] Nicholas Roosevelt to Frank R. Kent, August 2, 1943, Ibid.
[529] Nicholas Roosevelt to Elmer Davis, August 13, 1943, Box 15, Office of War Information 1943, Nicholas Roosevelt Papers.

Chapter 6
Retirement and Reminiscing

Although Nicholas Roosevelt left the OWI in 1943, he remained in contact with the organization. For example, he drew up a memorandum for Arthur Hays Sulzberger, the publisher of the *New York Times*, on an OWI War Advertising Council meeting in Washington for "off the record" use in early spring 1944.[530] When Sulzberger was asked by the OWI to prepare a text of roughly 1,000 words to be broadcast in China as a propaganda effort on the part of the United States, the publisher asked for NR's opinion again. Partly because of his earlier frustration with the OWI, and partly due to his realism, he gave a scathing criticism of the organization and the issue in question. "This is a racket," he wrote. "People in the O.W.I. exhaust what few brains they have in trying to think up names of persons to sign canned material to be broadcast in English to China, which has very few receiving sets and only a fraction of a percent of whose people understand English."[531]

For the remainder of the war NR returned to journalism, this time working for the *New York Times*. Arthur Crock, a veteran journalist on the paper and a long-time acquaintance of Roosevelt's, brought up to Sulzberger the subject of using NR's services, and Sulzberger gave the idea the nod.[532] Early in 1944, the newspaper bought the radio station WQXR-AM and FM. Initially under the call letters W2XR, in 1936 the AM station became the nation's first commercial classical music

---

[530] Nicholas Roosevelt to Arthur Hays Sulzberger, March 13, 1944, Box 224, Arthur Hays Sulzberger Papers.
[531] Nicholas Roosevelt to Mrs. L. K. Lang, September 25, 1944, Folder 6: Office of War Information, Box 224, Arthur Hays Sulzberger Papers. Sulzberger drew up a text to be broadcast in China, October 10, 1944, ibid.
[532] Arthur Krock to Nicholas Roosevelt, November 26, 1943, Roosevelt, Nicholas, 1923, 1932, 1942–1970, Box 52, Series 2: Correspondence, 1916–1974, Arthur Krock Papers, 1909–1974, Seeley G. Mudd Manuscript Library, Princeton, U.S.A.

station; the call letters were changed to WQXR at the end of that year. In 1939 the FM enlargement took place.⁵³³ Arthur Sulzberger named NR as vice-president and his assistant and official liaison to the station.⁵³⁴ Throughout 1945 and 1946 in this new capacity, NR was in frequent, sometimes daily, contact with John V. L. Hogan, original owner and founder of the station, and Elliott M. Sanger, co-founder and active manager of the station, concerning various technical or content-related issues. There were questions of wavelength, or how often the *New York Times* should be mentioned on the air, how many times there should be news bulletins, or what commercials the station should run that would ensure profit but would not reflect badly on the station and the paper.⁵³⁵ NR recognized early on that the government's oversight of the airwaves and of some of the stations' content in the form of the Federal Communications Commission challenged the constitutional guarantee of free speech and freedom of the press.⁵³⁶ This new activity agreed with NR much more than the OWI days, and the end of the war found him still in this job—although not for long.

He also remained relatively close to Hungarian affairs. First, he was asked by John F. Montgomery, who served as American minister in Hungary between 1933 and 1941, to join American Hungarian Relief, Inc. This organization was financed by and working through the United Nations Relief and Rehabilitation Administration (UNRRA), and it was licensed by President Harry Truman's War Relief Control Board. It collected private donations and gave the money to UNRRA to buy then send medical applies, clothes, and other vitally needed items to Hungary. At first the supplies shipped by American Hungarian Relief were distributed within Hungary through the representative of the International Red Cross there. When the American Military Mission began to function in Hungary, American Hungarian Relief requested that it undertake the distribution and this had been done. The UNRRA provided $4 million to the Hungarian government.⁵³⁷ NR had already been informed about the organization through János Pelényi, former Hungarian minister at Washington, who resigned his post in 1940 and remained in the United

---

533 For a short history of the station, which the newspaper owned until 2007, when it sold it to Radio Disney, see, "About WQXR," https://www.wqxr.org/about/, accessed May 23, 2022.
534 Nicholas Roosevelt *A Front Row Seat*, 276; "Nicholas Roosevelt is Dead; Writer and Diplomat Was 88," *New York Times*, February 17, 1982.
535 To this latter point see, for example, Nicholas Roosevelt's memorandum to Arthur Sulzberger, November 28, 1945, Folder 9: WQXR, Box 276, Arthur Hays Sulzberger Papers.
536 Nicholas Roosevelt to Arthur Hays Sulzberger, June 10, 1946, Folder 8: WQXR, Box 276, ibid.
537 File: American Hungarian Relief, Inc., United Nations Relief and Rehabilitation Administration (UNRRA), 1943–1946, https://search.archives.un.org/american-hungarian-relief-inc-2855, accessed September 6, 2022.

States. NR, for his part, however, refused to sign on. His reasons were that he was suspicious of the various political forces in Hungary, while he thought the Russians also could not be trusted that relief aid would reach the real target, the Hungarian people in need.[538]

However, when a situation proved to be more personal, he became actively involved. István Wolf had faithfully served the various ministers at the American Legation in Budapest since its opening in 1922 and throughout the interwar years. With the Hungarian war declaration on the United States in December 1941, when the Legation closed, Wolf needed to find other employment. After the war, with Hungary, but especially Budapest in devastated shape, people were fighting for survival among the ruins. István Wolf was no exception, and he appealed to his old acquaintances in order to find a job. Since Roosevelt had really liked him during his minister years, he wanted to help, in cooperation with John Montgomery. First, NR turned to the State Department and asked whether it could be arranged that Wolf be employed as a night watchman, and some money could be sent to him too.[539] After receiving a noncommittal answer a few days later, he vented his anger to his fellow ex-minister: "I hope you will make it a penitentiary offense for anyone to take the negative approach. I have worked periodically for the Department during the last thirty years and have never yet known anyone in it who ever approached any problem from the point of view of doing something. The idea is always how to avoid doing it."[540]

After this round of disappointments, NR turned with his request to Arthur Schoenfeld, who had just been appointed minister to Hungary, and later to Assistant Secretary of State for Western Hemisphere Affairs Spruille Braden, who in NR's view was "more likely to get action than that other stuffed shirt," i.e., Dean Acheson.[541] Schoenfeld, after making rounds to find out the situation with Wolf, informed Roosevelt that during the war Wolf had worked for the Hungarian Sugar Refinery Company, then for the Hungarian-American Oil Company, and finally at the Swiss Legation before a mine crippled him. In addition, at present there was no available opening at the reopened American legation.[542] However, in view if his

---

[538] Nicholas Roosevelt to John F. Montgomery, July 12, 1945, Folder: Montgomery, John F., Box 9, Nicholas Roosevelt Papers.
[539] Nicholas Roosevelt to Dean Acheson, February 4, 1946, File: Montgomery, John F., Box 9, Nicholas Roosevelt Papers.
[540] Nicholas Roosevelt to John F. Montgomery, February 11, 1946, ibid.
[541] Nicholas Roosevelt to Arthur Schoenfeld, February 13, 1946, N. Roosevelt to Spruille Braden, May 9, 1946, and N. Roosevelt to John F. Montgomery, May 9, 1946, ibid.
[542] Arthur Schoenfeld to Nicholas Roosevelt, April 30, 1946, ibid.

past long service, the legation soon found a clerk position for Wolf, and the former butler started to work in mid-May.[543]

In the meantime, NR suffered a third bout of pneumonia in 1946 and feared that he might not survive another one. The conditions in New York were unfortunately conducive to respiratory diseases. Accordingly, he made a profound decision and at the age of 53, and he resigned from the *New York Times* on September 30, 1946. He had informed Sulzberger a few months earlier that his usefulness was up at the paper and because on account of his health issues he must often be away, his WQXR liaison job was also finished by then, and in addition he planned to write books.[544] Also, his mother had died the previous year, so one more link was missing to make him stay. He sold his Long Island estate and moved to Big Sur, California, to the former vacation house that became their permanent home. In his memoirs he gave a vivid description of their home on the California coast, which at the time was not as much in the nation's awareness as it is today.[545]

Around 1950, there was no color television, and technicolor movies were still not that common, so the vast expanse and changing colors of the Pacific were not known to many Americans.[546] The nearest source of household supplies was miles south in Monterey, and once a week the Roosevelts traveled there to shop. So, after three decades of journalism, diplomacy, and educating the public, NR's active career was over. This definitely did not mean, however, that he was going to succumb to hollow inactivity. As he indicated to Sulzberger at the time of his resignation, he was planning to write additional books and focus mainly on his memoirs.

In the seclusion of Big Sur, NR could devote time to his cooking passion, and enjoying the natural surroundings, but his major undertaking in the latter part of the 1940s was putting on paper his reminiscences about the first half of the twentieth century. He rightfully claimed that he had witnessed many momentous events first hand, was involved in historical occasions, and knew many of the most important players during that time. And without a doubt, his résumé is impressive: the 1912 presidential campaign, World War I, the Paris Peace Conference, Coolidge Mission, Hungarian Bolshevik takeover, Central European issues in the 1920s, the Far East and his appointment as Vice General to the Philippines, his diplomatic mission to

---

[543] Arthur Schoenfeld to Nicholas Roosevelt, May 15, 1946, ibid.
[544] Nicholas Roosevelt to Arthur Hays Sulzberger, April 9, 1946, Folder 16: Roosevelt, Nicholas, 1926–1931, 1944–1962, Box 64, and Nicholas Roosevelt to Chairman of the Board of Directors of the Interstate Broadcasting Company, September 13, 1946, Folder 8: WQXR, Box 276, Arthur Hays Sulzberger Papers, New York Times Company Records, New York, U.S.A.
[545] Nicholas Roosevelt, *A Front Row Seat*, 279–80.
[546] Nicholas Roosevelt, *A Front Row Seat*, 281–85.

Hungary as American minister in the early 1930s, a close observer and critic of the New Deal, member of the OWI during World War II. In addition, he knew such people as Theodore Roosevelt, Franklin Delano Roosevelt, Herbert Hoover, Henry Stimson, Allen Dulles, to mention the most famous persons he had been in contact with, sometimes to a considerably degree of intimacy. NR was convinced that his experiences were worth being published for a reading audience hungry for recent history. And especially with the Cold War setting in and the frontlines seeming to have hardened between the two superpowers and their respective allies, NR also wanted to take stock of what had been unfolding in the past decades.

After a relatively short time he wrote to Sulzberger that he was close to finishing the manuscript, which he was planning to call *A Front Row Seat*.[547] The title supposedly came from Archibald Coolidge, who uttered these words to NR when the latter left for Europe in March 1917.[548] This was a well-chosen title for the book that was finally published in September 1953.

A Front Row Seat turned out to be an interesting and readable volume. NR wrote with skill, and aside from recounting the many adventures he had been a participant in, he used his journalistic skill to a great extent. Also, he had a unique sense of humor, sometimes quite sarcastic and hovering on the border of insult, but it added to the text's enjoyment factor. More importantly, the 1953 memoir, like so many autobiographies, gives not a mirror image but a distorted image of what took place earlier. In his memoirs, NR used the following technique with regard to the original manuscript of 1919, for instance. He summarized certain things based upon the additional knowledge he had gathered in the intervening thirty years, but he also rewrote some passages and even quotations. This did not alter the original meaning, but the text was carefully tailored to suit the needs of contemporary circumstances. There were episodes that he had originally chronicled in just a few lines or did not even write down but in 1953 he extended the space given to those episodes, because with hindsight he considered them more interesting to a readership in Cold War America. The most important change, however, and at the same time the most painful, is the memoir's lack of the original diary entries, thus masking the author's original thoughts. This does not mean that in 1953 NR wrote something altogether different than what he thought in 1919 or at other times, but the text did go through a large dose of sanitation. Therefore it is of significance to be familiar

---

[547] Nicholas Roosevelt to Arthur Hays Sulzberger, February 20, 1950, Folder 16: Roosevelt, Nicholas, 1926–1931, 1944–1962, Box 64, Arthur Hays Sulzberger Papers.
[548] Nicholas Roosevelt, *A Front Row Seat*, 101.

with NR's original thoughts, which were much more straightforward and detailed, and thus truly counts as historical text.

In 1953 NR could reflect on those dramatic years with hindsight, therefore he already judged many things from a historical aspect. He highlighted certain things accordingly, while other episodes and persons were basically deleted, although this drastic editing may have been due to the page limit he had to work with in the case of his memoirs. Nevertheless, the two texts are at points very different from each other. It is worth remembering the many vast changes since 1919: the United States Senate did not ratify the Versailles Peace Treaty, so America did not become a member of the League of Nations, and, as a consequence, after a short romance it largely withdrew from European political and diplomatic issues; the 1920s brought economic prosperity to large swaths of Americans many of whom enjoyed the comforts of new technological achievements; in 1929 the break came and economic devastation and long stagnation set in in the 1930s; the New Deal tried to alleviate the pain of the depression and introduced certain elements of the future federal governing style; in Europe and Asia there were signs of state aggression and general international instability; World War II surpassed any earlier known armed conflict and the United States had become a superpower by its end and took on an unprecedentedly active role in shaping the international landscape; in 1947–48 the Cold War began, and in 1950 the Korean War broke out, which came to an uncertain conclusion in the year NR's memoir came out. All these events and changes put a few things in different perspective for NR concerning his ideas in 1919 or 1930, and also gives some explanation for the discrepancies between the diaries and the memoir.

In *A Front Row Seat*, for example, there is no trace of the anti-Semitic opinions NR so often expressed in his dairy entries and sometimes in letters throughout the decades. When he wrote about Adolph S. Ochs and Arthur Hays Sulzberger, long-time publishers of the *New York Times* and his bosses at certain periods of his journalistic career, he showed no sign of antipathy because of their Jewish origins. Whether it was due to the personal and professional veneration he felt for both men, or his views had changed profoundly with World War II, would be only speculation. In any event, the Holocaust and the foundation of Israel in 1948 did not leave room for such views in a published book. Nevertheless, his private letters and diary entries continued to reflect his dislike of Jewish people, especially if they were of European origins.

Even in the sanitized version that attempted to court prominent publishing houses and in turn a large readership, the manuscript did not prove to be a hot item on the market. New York-based Scribner, one of the most prestigious publishers in the United States, had earlier brought out two of NR's books, *The Restless Pacific* and *A New Birth of Freedom*, but refused to print this book, as did other publishers in New York. They simply did not believe there would be enough interest in such a book among the reading public. NR complained that the reason for the rejection was that these publishers "would have to sell their yachts, fill up their swimming pools, and take their children out of college if they published it, because not a single soul would by [sic] a copy."[549] He also thought that his ongoing criticism of FDR might have discouraged a big-name publisher. These considerations may indeed have played a part, but in all likelihood his name did not have enough allure in the tumultuous early 1950s to make it a safe bet for publishing houses. In the end the book was published by the University of Oklahoma Press.

In *A Front Row Seat*, NR systematically reviewed some of the outstanding chapters of the past forty years through his own experiences. He tried to balance the past, his involvement, and what he thought the readers would be interested in and produced an interesting addition to the many volumes on the history of the first half of the twentieth century whose authors had been much closer to these events. He found that two things stood out as the most profound changes regarding the United States. One was how his nation had been transformed "from a comparatively small, unimportant member of the international community into the most powerful nation in the Western world."[550] Since the Soviet Union had also made a comparable leap in status, but stood in opposition to almost everything America stood for, the nascent Cold War defined the international landscape as NR was writing and beyond. His second observation concerned domestic policy and he noted that the outstanding development at home was "the changed concept of the function of government in the United States."[551] Just as he did during the New Deal years in the 1930s, he found fault with the trend toward a welfare state because he thought such conditions would rob people of initiative and enterprise, but he admitted that it had proven to be popular and people seemed to want more of it.

The book actually got favorable reviews, though certain important magazines like *The New Yorker* and *Time* did not list it.[552] Arthur Krock, for one, penned a positive review for the *New York Times*, and despite their long-standing

---

[549] Nicholas Roosevelt to Harold Phelps Stokes, November 30, 1953, Folder 89, Roosevelt, Nicholas, 1932, 1953, 1957, n.d. Series I. Correspondence, Box 3, Harold Phelps Stokes Papers, Yale Archives.
[550] Nicholas Roosevelt, *A Front Row Seat*, 281.
[551] Ibid., 283.
[552] Nicholas Roosevelt to Harold Phelps Stokes, November 30, 1953.

acquaintance, Krock would not have praised it if he had not liked what he read.[553] Another reviewer offered more mixed opinions. John M. Blum also highlighted its readability, its engaging style, and especially NR's reflections about Theodore Roosevelt and other family members. However, he took issue with NR's seemingly little-changed notions of international affairs during the early years of the twentieth century, and chided him for closely echoing TR. His conclusion was that NR "gives the historian a lesson in prose, for he is always readable, but he needs some lessons in history. Historians will, therefore, read his book less for information or for wisdom than for enjoyment."[554] NR did not have appealing to historians in mind when writing the book. He wanted to project his own take on history and believed that certain perspectives and approaches should not change even if the times had. Therefore, criticism of how he treated history probably did not bother him. He wanted to tell a good story with interesting characters embedded in his own history. His memoirs must be read carefully and with further investigation of what really took place at certain events. Because of the many distortions throughout the memoirs compared to his earlier materials, it is difficult to agree with a recent reviewer of the volume, who studied Hungarian revisionist aims and the mistaken hope that the United States would help. She judged it "an authentic historical source."[555]

It was fortunate for NR that he finished the memoir when he did and managed to have it published, because in January 1953 he suffered his fourth bout of pneumonia and this restricted his activity primarily to reading. From the age of sixty, he had to lead a physically limited life for of the rest of his years. At least the political landscape became to his liking with Dwight D. Eisenhower's election victory in the fall of 1952. After twenty long years the executive branch was back in Republican hands. As he wrote to Allen Dulles, an old acquaintance from the Paris Peace Conference days who was about to assume the position of director of the Central Intelligence Agency (CIA), he supported Eisenhower but was inactive in the election campaign. Although another Republican in the CIA asked if NR was interested in getting back into government service, he was against the idea. The only post he would have accepted was the embassy in the Netherlands, but he

---

[553] Arthur Krock, "In the March of History," *New York Times*, September 6, 1953.
[554] John M. Blum, "*A Front Row Seat* by Nicholas Roosevelt," *The Mississippi Valley Historical Review* 40, no. 3 (Dec. 1953): 555.
[555] Éva Mathey, "Nicholas Roosevelt in A Front Row Seat: Hungary in the 1930s as Reflected in the Memoirs of an American Diplomat," *Acta Neerlandica* 15 (2019): 152.

understood it was a long shot, and indeed the serving ambassador, Selden Chapin, was succeeded by H. Freeman Matthews, both of them career diplomats.[556]

Though NR had to get accustomed to a semi-reclusive life, especially compared to his busy career in the previous four decades, it did not mean he stopped being engaged with certain fields that he was deeply interested in. There were abortive attempts to bring out new books. He finished the manuscript for two books, *Economic Forces in the Development of American History* (1951) and *Stream of Liberty* (1954), but they were never published. However, his first book on cooking, *Creative Cooking,* appeared in 1956 and was followed by another on the same subject three years later.[557] With *Creative Cooking*, which sold relatively well, also came appearances on radio and television shows, at least in California.[558] He managed to make something of a name for himself in the culinary world. In a review of the second cookbook, for instance, the reviewer emphasized the chapter on salad dressing, which she called "in a larger sense a truly original contribution to the art of cuisine."[559]

At this time he was also nominated for election to the Board of Overseers of Harvard College, a highly prestigious body of that venerable institution. Since both TR and FDR had been elected earlier, recognition would in many ways have put NR on a par with his namesakes, but he knew that he had little chance of being elected. He mainly attributed this to his having been "out of circulation so long."[560] He did not get the position.[561]

He also wrote the introduction to Admiral Horthy's memoirs, published in the United States in 1956 (the book had appeared in Hungarian and German three years earlier). In it he praised the former regent of Hungary almost to the point of creating a four-page hagiography. He characterized Horthy as "a typical sea-dog," whose "integrity and courage were outstanding, as was his devotion to

---

[556] Nicholas Roosevelt to Allen W. Dulles, December 16, 1952, Box 5, Dulles, Allen, Nicholas Roosevelt Papers.
[557] Nicholas Roosevelt, *Creative Cooking* (New York: Harper and & Brothers, 1956); *Good Cooking* (New York: Harper & Brothers, 1959). Nicholas Roosevelt to Harold Phelps Stokes, February 8, 1957, Folder 89, Roosevelt, Nicholas, 1932, 1953, 1957, n.d. Box 3, Series I. Correspondence, Harold Phelps Stokes Papers, Yale Archives.
[558] Nicholas Roosevelt to Arthur Krock, October 30, 1956, Roosevelt, Nicholas, 1923, 1932, 1942–1970, Box 52, Series 2: Correspondence, 1916–1974, Arthur Krock Papers.
[559] Mary Frost Mabon, "The Salad Master," *Sports Illustrated* 11, no. 4, (July 27, 1959): 40.
[560] Nicholas Roosevelt to Arthur Hays Sulzberger, January 12, 1955, Arthur Hays Sulzberger Papers.
[561] On the Board's history, see, https://www.harvard.edu/about/leadership-and-governance/board-of-overseers/; https://en.wikipedia.org/wiki/Harvard_Board_of_Overseers; https://snaccooperative.org/view/84889135, all three accessed September 15, 2022.

duty" and "was a symbol of sanity, order and stability in an unstable, disordered and sick Europe."[562] As to the role of Hungary during World War II, that is, having joined the German camp, Roosevelt attributed it to the sheer force of history and did not blame Horthy: when "Horthy appeared to go along with Hitler, it was because he was faced with force which neither resistance nor appeasement could curb."[563] He also emphasized that Horthy clearly saw the Bolshevist menace that later materialized in the wake of World War II. However, he was painfully silent on Horthy's responsibility when it came to the Holocaust. Still acting as regent during the German occupation in 1944, Horthy did nothing to stop the collection and deportation of the Hungarian Jews, except in Budapest. This apologetic tone was strikingly similar to that in the memoir of another former American minister to Hungary, John F. Montgomery, whose recollections of his eight years in Hungary between 1933 and 1941 was titled *Hungary, the Unwilling Satellite*.[564]

NR penned the Horthy introduction the same year that the Hungarian Revolution against the Soviet Union took place in October. The tragically heroic and short-lived freedom fight was welcome news in the West for its sheer momentum and was taken as proof that the peoples of Eastern Europe were very much against the oppressive communist political system that had been forced on them. NR proved to be a realist in his assessment at a point, October 30, when it still looked that there was a chance the revolution might succeed in the face of terrible odds. He expressed his hope that it would be so, but he feared "that adequate preparations had not been made, and that, in consequence, the uprising is premature."[565] The Hungarian Revolution was crushed in a matter of days by the Soviet army, but it showed both the deep-seated cracks within the Soviet system and that the people in the eastern half of Europe wished to work out their own destinies.

The Soviet intervention and brutal suppression of the Hungarians only stoked NR's anti-Communism, which was long standing. He reacted accordingly eighteen months after the Hungarian resistance was crushed. At a lecture he labeled communism "as one of the greatest forces of evil in the world, and as one of the greatest delusions." He believed with his whole heart that the American system of individualism and the various freedoms it provided would shield the younger generations of Americans from "the quackery of communism." But the challenge was still formidable, and it was essential for present and future U.S. governments "to take the

---

[562] Nicholas Horthy, *Memoirs* (Safety Harbor, FL: Simon Publications, 2000), 5, 7.
[563] Ibid., 7.
[564] John Flournoy Montgomery, *Hungary: The Unwilling Satellite* (New York: DevinAdair Company, 1947).
[565] Nicholas Roosevelt to Arthur Krock, October 30, 1956.

lead in the preservation of the free world and of democracy."[566] In addition to the Soviet question, he lectured on this occasion about technological innovations, various ideas such as those of Darwin or Marx, the state of sexual freedom, and better living standards in the last hundred years. Then he offered a few forecasts: life would become easier, the United States would have to take on a bigger role in the international arena, after the end of the Cold War there would be a great economic crisis, a larger government, and he thought that people in general must be better informed.

NR was not satisfied with American foreign policy at the time either. Not necessarily with respect to the American no-show in Hungarian affairs, because despite the rhetoric of liberation of the captive nations, this was not a realistic mode of action for the United States. Rather he disagreed with the steps taken in the Middle East. Although in the case of the Suez Canal crisis, the United States was on the right side of history, two years later this was questionable. As a way of showing commitment and credibility, Eisenhower sent the marines to Lebanon in July 1958 in the midst of a civil war there, and the forces managed to stifle the regional turmoil for a while.[567] NR was of the opinion that the Eisenhower administration had blundered and had alienated the Arab world. Not only was it not wise politics to intervene in others' domestic troubles, he thought, but by hurting local nationalistic forces under the cover of fighting international communism, America had "still further lost moral stature (of which we had none to spare) and have made it plain to the world that our foreign policy is impulsive, unthought [sic] out and inconsistent."[568] But this was a mild reaction compared to his dissatisfaction a year earlier when he vented his anger on John Foster Dulles, the secretary of state. He found fault with the unbending and belligerent style of Dulles, which seemed to produce no results in the international arena but instead seemed to sow even more bitter seeds of discontent. "A long truce would then be easier to attain," he wrote, "in a world which knows that rightness is not the exclusive monopoly of one man alone, and that cooperation comes through agreement, and no through the imposition of one man's didactic—and often mistaken—ideas."[569]

In 1960, during the presidential campaign, one of John F. Kennedy's advisors, journalist and historian Allan Nevins, suggested that the future president send his new book, *The Strategy of Peace*, to NR. Roosevelt, for his part, was "impressed with

---

[566] The quotes are from "A Look towards the Year 2000—The Shape of Things to Come," April 21, 1958, File: Mss – Lectures – Monterey College Address, Box 63, Nicholas Roosevelt Papers.
[567] Probably the best scholarly work on the Lebanon Crisis is Douglas Little, "His Finest Hour? Eisenhower, Lebanon, and the 1958 Middle East Crisis," *Diplomatic History* 20, no. 1, (Winter 1996): 27–54.
[568] Nicholas Roosevelt to Arthur Hays Sulzberger, July 25, 1958, Arthur Hays Sulzberger Papers.
[569] Nicholas Roosevelt to Harold Phelps Stokes, February 8, 1957.

the simplicity and clarity of your presentation," and hinted at wanting to vote for Kennedy despite the latter being a Democrat.[570] NR may not have been the only Republican changing party lines that November, and the razor-thin election results gave a Kennedy victory.

Still, the foreign policy of the United States did not change much if at all, so Roosevelt remained dissatisfied with Washington, but this was the least of his concerns in 1961. At the end of June that year, his wife of twenty-five years, Tirzah, died of a sudden brain hemorrhage at the age of fifty-six. There is scant evidence of his feelings and thoughts about her death, but this must have been a huge blow. At the age of sixty-eight, he suddenly found himself totally alone.

His main activity remained pursuing his hobbies: cooking, activism in conservation, and writing. In this latter category he produced one final volume concerning American history that studied the past on a very personal level—his reminiscences of his surrogate father, titled *Theodore Roosevelt: The Man as I Knew Him*. The former president's legacy had always loomed large in NR's life. Now that he was growing older, he looked back with yearning to his younger years and his first and greatest hero.

Theodore Roosevelt was at the center of attention all his life, and with his passing, his colorful personality and tumultuous pre-, post-White House years and return to politics in 1912 all gave ample fodder for historical scrutiny. Few in American history have had more books written about them than the 26th president. NR was not an accomplished historian, but he studied it, had been a good journalist, and had the personal knowledge of TR that others did not possess. This was enough to warrant a volume that was supposed to present the former president from a different angle. Ferdinand Cowle Iglehart had written a book on TR with the very same title in 1919—*Theodore Roosevelt. The Man as I Knew Him*. NR's title may have been a reference to that volume either as homage or as a challenge.[571] In either case, it bears remembering that NR was only twenty-six years old when TR passed away, and during World War I he was mainly in Europe, therefore the bulk of his memories came from his childhood or teenage years. And he crafted the book as such: a personal reminiscence.[572]

The book gave detailed accounts of his various contacts with Theodore Roosevelt and the emphasis was always on the personal. He devoted ample space

---

[570] J. F. Kennedy to Nicholas Roosevelt, June 23, 1960, and Nicholas Roosevelt to J. F. Kennedy, July 6, 1960, File: Kennedy, John F., Box 8, Nicholas Roosevelt Papers.
[571] Ferdinand Cowle Iglehart, *Theodore Roosevelt: The Man as I Knew Him* (New York: The Christian Herald, 1919).
[572] Nicholas Roosevelt, *Theodore Roosevelt*.

"We're not trying to escape from people, just unnecessary people," says Nicholas Roosevelt, (kin to Theodore Roosevelt). At 77, a writer, he can look back over busy years including those spent as ambassador to Hungary, and as a newspaper executive. But he treasures the present calm of his sunny garden on California's Big Sur, see here on May 9, 1969. (AP Photo/George Brich)

to his childhood when TR acted in his father's stead, TR's family members, various aspects of TR's presidency, the 1912 campaign, the former president's views concerning World War I—altogether loud praise for his beloved Teddy. Interestingly— or perhaps naturally—he used the book as an exercise in self-congratulating as well. He peppered it with sentences praising his own keen observations as if to prove that he was a worthy disciple of TR. As he put it more emphatically in a private letter to a colleague, "As I look back over the record I see that I was brash, impudent and over-cocky, but that I was an exceptionally alert observer and a good evaluator."[573] The reviews typically agreed that the book offered little fresh understanding on Theodore Roosevelt, since most of what was presented has been based on already available material. Naturally, the own diary excerpts and letters did offer a fresh look, but the consensus was that the TR-bias was somewhat too strong.[574]

---

[573] Nicholas Roosevelt to Arthur Krock, April 9, 1967, Folder: Roosevelt, Nicholas, 1923, 1932, 1942–1970, Box 52, Series 2: Correspondence, 1916–1974, Arthur Krock Papers.
[574] John Braeman, "Theodore Roosevelt: The Man as I Knew Him. By Nicholas Roosevelt," *The Journal of American History*, 54, no. 3 (Dec. 1967): 693–94; Armarius, "Potpourri," *The North American Review*, 252, no. 4 (Jul. 1967): 41.

Back in July 1913, NR was party to TR's trip to Arizona, just a year prior to the territory becoming the newest member state. Obviously, that large region was sparsely populated and offered fertile territory for TR's interest in the natural wonders of the landscape, because despite the prevailing desert in the southwest of the state, to the north there are high mountains, plateaus, the Colorado River, and, of course, the Grand Canyon. Teddy Roosevelt wrote a three-part article on the trip that appeared in *The Outlook* magazine in October 1913.[575] Next to the descriptions of wildlife, adventure, anthropology, and an assortment of the melting pot ideas, the articles were an outcry for governmental protection of the land and the natural resources, flora and fauna on it. TR was the first president who was active in setting aside national parks under governmental supervision in order to preserve them for future generations, and he also created executive authority to found national monuments. Based on the articles in *The Outlook*, it is clear that early on NR had had a taste of this terrain and had acquired "a practical and working familiarity with ranch life, with the round-up, and with travelling through the desert and on the mountains."[576]

He also devoted a chapter in his book on TR to this Arizona adventure.[577] He recaptured some of the more interesting and exciting moments of the tour, like his shooting a mountain lion, or trekking dangerous paths in the Grand Canyon. NR used many of his original diary entries to tell his perspective on the story, therefore they should be read together with TR's articles on the trip. His diary pages and occasional parts of letters are interesting but really do not add much to the story as it was introduced by TR in 1913.

In many ways inspired by his experiences alongside TR, in his more mature years NR became an active member of the conservationist movement in the United States and beyond. He played a part in the Save the Redwoods League and also served on California's recreation commission. As a culmination of these efforts, his final book was titled *Conservation: Now or Never*.[578] He argued for more set-asides of forests so wildlife in general, but rare and endangered species in particular, could be protected to a greater degree. Although a reviewer found some parts of the book

---

[575] Theodore Roosevelt, "A Cougar Hunt on the Rim of the Grand Canyon," *The Outlook* 105 (October 4, 1913): 259–66; "Across the Navajo Desert," *The Outlook* 105 (October 11, 1913): 309–317; "The Hopi Snake Dance," *The Outlook* 105 (October 18, 1913): 365–73.

[576] Theodore Roosevelt, "A Cougar Hunt on the Rim of the Grand Canyon," 259.

[577] Nicholas Roosevelt, *Theodore Roosevelt*, 110–25.

[578] Nicholas Roosevelt, *Conservation: Now or Never*, (New York: Dodd, Mead & Company, 1970). Already at the launch of the book on TR, the publisher had approached him to write this volume. Nicholas Roosevelt to Arthur Krock, April 9, 1967.

"a rather skimpy rehash of oft-published historical material," the author proposed "that we seek the course of idealism above materialism, ecology and esthetics above economic profitability."[579]

Conclusions

With this last book, Nicholas Roosevelt's active career practically came to a finish, although he lived until 1982. In interpreting his long and colorful career it is important to state that he witnessed history many times at first hand, he published widely and had influential contacts in the U.S. government. Still, it is impossible to measure whether his reports, articles, and letters had any discernible influence on the decision makers of American domestic and foreign policy. In any event, he was a reliable chronicler of the momentous decades of the first half of the twentieth century.

Although NR was fairly successful and had an interesting and eventful career, he could never step out of the intellectual and historical shadow of Theodore Roosevelt—nor did he want to. He genuinely believed that the package he got from the former president provided good service on his path to whatever profession he would pursue. On the other hand, his oversized ego and ambition propelled him to reach higher than his allocated abilities allowed. Despite his pedigree and skills, he could never really fill TR's shoes. And although on the personal level he liked his distant relative FDR, NR could never overcome what he saw as the New Deal's deleterious effect on the American system and society. He wanted to serve but also wanted recognition, and he never received it to the extent he felt was his due. One has the feeling that he spent the better part of his adult life vindicating his perception that he was right and had seen things coming that others could not perceive.

These frustrations notwithstanding, he still managed—due to circumstances and his own skill—to find the niche where he would fit: journalism and second-rank government service; the former at major newspapers and magazines, the latter as minister to Hungary and in a mid-level job at the OWI. After all, he belonged to that thin layer of upper-class Americans who believed in service as a duty. Either in the form of governmental commission or educating the public through writing or other forms of communication, NR was convinced that he served his country in the best American civic tradition. Even his feud with FDR and the New Deal

---

[579] Michael Frome, "*Conservation: Now or Never*. By Nicholas Roosevelt," *Forest History Newsletter* 14, no. 3 (October 1970): 35.

must be evaluated in this light. His was not a petty partisan or personally motivated and vindictive attack on the president's policies. His biting criticisms were made in the name of calling attention to what he perceived as an assault on the traditional American system, and he only wished to educate the populace and open the eyes of those whom his voice reached.

Also, as he aptly titled his memoir, he was witness to history and to enormous changes within the United States and the world at large. At the time of his birth, the population of the country was 63 million; when he died, it had grown to about 230 million. From an overwhelmingly white, Anglo-Saxon, Protestant country in the early 1890s, at the time of his death in 1982 a clear trend showed movement toward a more multiracial and multicultural society. When NR was born, the first cars had just started to roll; when he passed, cars were everywhere and supersonic Concordes flew between Europe and America in under four hours, and the world was on the cusp of the Internet. When he entered Harvard, 2,265 people were enrolled; by the early 1980s, this number had tripled and the student body was no longer all-white and affluent and many minority groups were represented. The United States army was a scant 40,000 soldiers, it had only started to flex its muscles in the Western Hemisphere, and followed the Washingtonian tradition of staying away from Europe or European alliances. In sharp contrast, by the 1980s it was the second largest military but the most advanced and sophisticated in the world. America was the unquestioned leader of the western world and the principal member of many international organizations—economic, military, and cultural alike. When NR was growing up, the American government was a limited body of politicians that focused on few issues. Then, commencing in earnest with the New Deal, by the time of Ronald Reagan's administration it had grown into a huge bureaucratic organization with almost three million employees. Over NR's lifespan, the United States changed almost breathtakingly in every dimension. He was a chronicler of some of those changes for about half a century. His perspectives on domestic and foreign policy enrich our knowledge of twentieth century America.

APPENDIX

1. *Account of the Republican National Convention at Chicago, June 1912, compiled from notes taken on the spot by Nicholas Roosevelt.* **Typescript, after 1912. MS Am 2915. Houghton Library, Harvard University, Cambridge, Mass.**

Excerpt

The Convention was scheduled at 11:00, but Charlie dragged me off in time to arrive there at 10, and we had to wait around, one at one end, and the other at the opposite end of the hall until 12:00 o'clock.

It was finally opened, and they then proceeded with the reading of the minority reports and the majority reports of the Credentials Committee. In every case, the gentleman from Indiana, Mr. Watson, moved that the case be laid upon the table. After the California contest had been laid aside on a vote of 542 to 529, in spite of a cracking good though rather radical speech by Johnson, and a denunciation of the President of the United States by Heney, it became evident that we could expect no justice from the hands of the Convention, which promptly assumed more a farcical attitude than ever. The feeling, after this case was with us throughout the whole day, and towards evening it became a hooting riot. Even a football game didn't approach this for gaiety and boisterousness. Whenever Root or a Taft man rose to speak, someone would give a couple of toots on a shrill whistle, and all the Roosevelt delegates would slowly commence chugging, getting faster and faster all the time. You could hear this choo-choo-choo noise so vividly that several times I thought I saw a steamroller bearing down the hall.

During one of the pauses, when there had been lull after much cheering, a delegate climbed upon his chair and yelled out at the top of his lungs, "Mr. Chairman, I wish to call a point of order!" So Root banged and banged with his gavel for about five minutes, and at last got the whole hall quiet. Whereupon the man rose, and called out: "Mr. Chairman, I wish to call this point of order. The steamroller is exceeding its speed limit." Mr. Root actually had the sense of humor to admit that the point was well taken.

Of all days of the Convention, this was perhaps the wildest, as regards noise and hooting. During another pause, a delegate jumped up and said: "Mr. Chairman, I move that during this recess we hear from Messrs. Crane and Penrose on party regularity!"

If a Taft man so much as mentioned the "people" or the fact that Taft stood for Government of, for and by the people, the galleries would hoot and boo with vigor. If nothing else was going on, the New Jersey delegation would get up en masse, and give vent to the following:

> "..........................Who are we?
> We are the delegates from New Jersey.
> Are we in it? Just you wait.
> We'll give Teddy twenty-eight straight!"

This would generally be followed by a cheer led by old Albert Bushnell Hart of Harvard:

"Massachusetts eighteen, Massachusetts eighteen, Massachusetts eighteen! Roosevelt, first, last and all the time!"

West Virginia and California would follow, and then someone would start a "We want Teddy! We want Teddy!" which would be taken up all over the house for a while.

Towards seven o'clock, as Root began to speak, someone called out "All aboard!" blew a whistle and commenced chugging with the result that the whole place went wild. Finally a man took the platform to defend some Taft case, and leaning way forward started to speak. Suddenly a man from Massachusetts called out in a very severe tone "Stand up straight!" and so startled the speaker that he did suddenly straighten up. Of course the whole place went wild again, and Root had to adjourn the session. It was just as well, for the steamroller was working at enough of a pace to crush the Republican Party.

That night, as usual, there was a delegates' meeting. I attended it without giving lunch or dinner.

Gov. Fort opened it, saying he was for us, come what may. He had first voted in 64 for Lincoln, but now he would vote for Roosevelt. He hated the change, but he felt that the time had come, and we must do it. He cautioned us against the divided house, which would surely fall, and advised concerted action.

While he was speaking, Cousin Theodore was brought in amid far greater applause than the delegates had ever before accorded him. He was in a most cheerful mood and made by the far the best and most amusing speech I have yet heard from him.

"We are now facing a great question," he began, "a great question not only in the history of the United States, but also in the history of popular government.... Primaries are idle if they can be overturned by the National Committee..." He pronounced the conduct of Messrs. Barnes, Penrose, et al, criminal enough to land them in jail if only they were small men. No ward politicians combining for the sole purpose of overthrowing by illegal methods the choice of the majority of the people would remain unconvicted [sic].

"They (Barnes and the rest) are trying to cheat the people out of their choice of the highest gift the people can offer to any man.... A number of technically honest men have assisted leaders more strictly technical to commit these outrages, thinking we would protest and then lie down and let them do what they want.... Why, Barnes and Penrose think it a compliment to have it said of them how 'raw' their actions have been. Mr. Barnes enjoys nothing better than seeing his man lie down and stay there.... But we'll not lie down.... I won't submit to be swindled out of the people's victory by the politicians."

He declared that they stole all that they thought was necessary to secure the majority for them. This sentiment I heard confirmed by a delegate from Illinois who asserted that McKinley had told him that would be the case way back in March— But as Cousin Theodore said—"If a man steal a pair of horses from you, do you expect to be satisfied if he brings you back one and says he has no use for it!"

"You remember that perfectly delicious phrase of the gentleman on the Credentials Committee which I quoted to you last night—that of course the acts of the National Committee were supreme over state legislation."

He then thanked them for all they had done, and advised them to go slow, saying that for his part he wouldn't tell his plans till the morrow, because, as we used to say out in the short grass country, it used to be a mark of sagacity not to say what you were going to do, till you did it.

When he had been hurried away, Henry Allen of Kansas took the floor. He said he was glad to see that men who had left the Convention Hall after the steamroller had been exceeding its speed limit, could still fight. He reminded them that they were here for the principles.

"Payne," he said, "had pleaded with us in the name of the Republican Party to preserve it after T. R. had handed it over to him and Taft with a full Republican Congress—and they had destroyed it, lost their hold in the House, and eighteen Republican Governors—and yet he pleaded with us to save the party when he had destroyed it."

(I might mention here that Payne's speech was hooted and that he himself looked like a white haired chickenfooted beer-barrel—the boy orator, they called him).

Well,—Allen said we must go in an orderly way. We will not bolt, but we will sit silent and will not approve, and later we will submit our case to the people.

James Garfield, a clean looking, forceful young person of the finest type gave us a straight talk about as follows:

"Getting out was of course a very serious proposition. But we must fight on because they are ignoble men who have not at heart the principles for which we fight. We fight because the control of the Republican party has passed into the hands of a few people who use it for personal or corporate interest. It is they who have been untrue to the principles of the Republican Party.

It is for us to say we will have no part in the making of a platform or nomination with those contested men still seated. The Convention is itself a revolution by an oligarchy run by men not representing the people of their own States. We have now gone beyond the limit and we must stop. We must band together, for we have no easy job before us and have to fight the special interest."

He then stopped, reached down for a paper handed to him and exclaimed—"Now this is interesting—very interesting—Here is a statement made two years ago by Mr. Root about Penrose and his servants"—that they were a "criminal set masquerading under the banner of the Republican Party." And Root is now practically the servant of Barnes and Penrose.

Johnson was then loudly called for, and took the floor with less of his fighting spirit. He appeared tired, and was quiet and almost sentimental—a great contrast to his former speeches—but sincere as ever.

He said:

"Such a move means more than a desire to bolt or to nominate an individual. It is going forward in this country not only to make it politically but industrially free…. The people in a great moral question decide in the right, and they must have the power of expression. We bring back to the people the gifts that have been stolen for personal and corporate interest."

As far as he himself was concerned, the end had come when they decided against the California question. If the National Committee can nullify that, they can nullify any State legislation. They nullified a right of California ratified by all the courts of the United States.

"The time has now come when the delegates must take their choice, not only because the Convention has been stolen, but because it was a question of the rule of all the people or of just a few."

Tomorrow is your day for determination! No one need come, but he hoped all those who are wide eyed would help to form an American party for all humanity!

When Johnson was through, the crowd began to pour in, although it was already after midnight. Senator Poindexter started to make a speech, but owing to the fact that the public was present, I know he would not say anything of such extreme interest, and as I hadn't had any food since breakfast, I gladly accepted Regis Post's invitation to have a little supper. We went to the executive offices and collected Teddy Douglas, Tyree, Mr. Carmann and a few others, and went down to have some refreshments. Mr. Post and I left them to get something in the line of more substantial food. We sat down at a table in silence, and suddenly he looked up, took a coin out of his pocket, and casually remarked, "I'll match you to see who gets a paper to find out about the Harvard Yale race!" We had forgotten that Yale and Harvard existed!

He lost the toss, and on his return, brought with him a Mr. Batcheldor, delegate from Vermont, and former Rough Rider, who joined us for a good little supper, and discussed plans and the situation in general.

As usual, it was three o'clock before we even began to get to bed. So ended the day before last of the Convention. And all the leaders were absolutely happy!

I sat in the Coliseum from 9:00 A.M. till 9:00 P.M. of the last session and for the first time since it began, things failed to have such an absorbing interest. All day they hooter and whistled and choo-chooed, and when Henry Allen of Kansas said he had an announcement to read from Theodore Roosevelt, there was cheering for twenty minutes. His message was a denunciation of the Convention, and a request that his men would not vote on any business of the Convention. 109 did. 344 did not.

In the middle of the afternoon, I took another seat. I got into conversation with some men beside me, and it was soon evident by their extreme bitterness that they were for LaFollette. Of all hard-feeling I have yet been able to find, there is none that can approach that of LaFollette and his followers against Cousin Theodore. My neighbor began attacking T. R. in a most disgraceful fashion, to which I made mild replies. At last he began saying that he was a liar and a thief, and that he had sent his henchmen into Wisconsin to work for LaFollette and then turned them over to himself.

"Is that right!" said I.

"It certainly is!"...and he then proceeded in bitter terms to accuse him of sending Garfield in there to steal votes from LaFollette.

"I don't think that happened, did it!" said I with true meekness.

Whereupon he snapped out: "I suppose you think you know what you're talking about, don't you?" and turned away in semi-disgust.

"Why I don't know?," said I.

"Well you don't!" he exclaimed as if to terminate the conversation.

So I tapped him gently on the arm, and turned my hat inside up, pointing to it as I tapped.

"Just look here," said I, and he read in large capitals, "Nicholas Roosevelt" and below it "don't swipe." He let out an exclamation of rage, and for twenty-five minutes didn't speak a word.

Finally the balloting began to take place, and then occurred the disgraceful episode of Root and the two Massachusetts delegates. I have it recorded in my diary as follows:

"Root's action about the two Massachusetts delegates looks equal to the worst steamroller tactics ever employed by Barnes or others. A roll call had been held for Northern Carolina, with the result of one for Taft, two for Roosevelt and twenty-two not voting. When it came to Massachusetts the secretary called out '18 for Taft, 18 present but not voting.' Whereupon Root came forward and said that a roll call was demanded.

The first man to answer was a Taft man. The second (Fosdick, I believe) rose and said, 'Present, but I refuse to vote!'

Everyone cheered, and Root banged for order. When he got it, he came to the front of the platform, shaking his gavel, and called out: 'You have been sent here by your State to vote. If you refuse to do your duty your alternate will be called upon.'

In an instant there was a riot. The whole house rose and protested and fists were angrily shaken in the Massachusetts delegation. Finally the police were called, and when all was quiet again, Root caused the roll to be called. When Fosdick's name was read again, he cried out:

'No man on God's earth can make me vote in this Convention!' Whereupon Root called his alternate. Two alternates in all cast their vote for Taft, thereby adding two more to his list.

When this was announced, there was such a howl that Root came forward and said that hereafter the alternates would not be called upon. That was his parting shot. He knew that through the confusion in the Massachusetts law the alternates at large were for Taft. Six of them, however, refused to vote, and he only gained two. But he certainly showed his coldblooded nerve when he said that hereafter alternates would not be called upon.

The final vote was Taft 561, not voting 344, Roosevelt 109, LaFollette 52, Cummins 17, absent 9, and Hughes 2."

These 344 delegates who had refused to vote, met that evening, with 78 contested delegates, and nominated Cousin Theodore for President of the United States on the now Progressive ticket. This was all in Orchestra Hall, which, unfortunately, I did not reach till shortly before he himself arrived. When I came out of the Convention Hall, I fell in with a man whom I had seen round headquarters, and who wanted me to have supper with him. So we went off, and as Col. Lyons was eating in the same place I didn't think I'd miss anything if I waited till he left.

When it was announced at the regular Convention that Taft had been nominated the cheering lasted for scarcely a minute. I left as soon as it was over, and going first to the hotel met a band bearing a great banner of Taft, marching down Michigan Avenue. There was literally not a single cheer or even a hand clap as it went by. This shows how strongly the people felt for our good old "man of straw."

It took me a long time to get into the Orchestra Hall meeting, as I knew no one except the same doorkeeper who tried to keep me out of other meetings. At last Linden Bates and his father came along, and I got in with them.

The house went wild on Cousin Theodore's arrival, and everyone cheered and howled and yelled, and the organ played ragtime, and everyone was delighted. He finally managed to still the cheering, and as he was about to speak, old Prof. Hart got up and led his "Massachusetts eighteen" yell, which of course was followed by New Jersey's "twenty-eight straight" and started things off again.

It appears that the nomination had been partially tendered to him by this mass of delegates, but it is true that they never really nominated him. He made a speech of acceptance, all the same, which I quote from my diary:

"He was glad that Convention formed in theft had gone out in theft.

'A snapper up of unconsidered trifles'—Root—saw a chance for theft that has been overlooked (the two Massachusetts delegates).... He accepted the nomination on two conditions—first, that the contest be not carried along the old party lines, and that the delegates go home and find out the sentiment of their people; and second, that they should feel entirely free to substitute any man in his place if they deemed it better for the movement. In such a case, he would give him his heartiest support.

'The platform will do away with sectionalism—it must appeal to North and South, East and West, and wherever the Republican Party is true to its founders, he hopes it will win.

'The late Convention was organized in cynical defiance of the people's wishes.... No community is truly civilized when there is a difference between stealing a purse and stealing an office.

'The great principles are that the people can rule and that they must do so with a spirit of justice to all.'"

There was a great deal of cheering when it was all over, and it was arranged to meet in the morning.

My diary reads:

"Everything taken together, I am terribly sorry about it all, and I hate to see Cousin Theodore in such a position. Of course he has handed the Republican Party a terrible slap, but I don't like it, and his attitude puzzles me a little. We have left Hadley and Benson and Borah, the first of whom would have been a great moral aid. Johnson stays to fight, as well as Stubbs and Bass, and of course, lots of others, including Flynn. But we've got a terrific fight against Republicans, Democrats, Bosses, Interests and Newspapers."

I failed to realize at the time, that it was impossible for him to accept a nomination at the hands of a Convention he had denounced as so flagrantly dishonest. But in spite of that, the Republican Party died hard, and I hated to see it go. For some unknown reason, it caused numerous pangs. I had to wait till the next day before I could really feel cheerful about it. But everyone was delighted, and people everywhere were still for "Teddy." We heard that night under our windows cries of "Poor Taft, Poor Taft!" And yet he had just been renominated! It shows how strongly the people of Chicago felt that Taft had honestly been nominated and that he was the choice of the people.

That finished the proceedings of the Convention and gave the papers something to be bitter for another four months.

2. *A History of a Few Weeks. Being an Account of Experience in Austria and Hungary during the Armistice.* by Nicholas Roosevelt, Captain, 322d Infantry, Member of the Austrian Field Party, American Commission to Negotiate Peace, 1919.

Box 18, Nicholas Roosevelt Papers

Chapter VIII. Austrian Politics.

To follow the newspapers intelligently, it was necessary to know the various editors and their policies. In doing this Dr. Lippe of the Neue Freie Presse was a great help. He arranged for meetings, and supplied information freely in order to elucidate points that were not clear.

The foremost newspaper in Vienna at the time was the Arbeiter Zeitung. Dr. Friedrich Adler, a socialist, convicted of murder, was formerly editor, and during the old regime the paper was heavily censored. With the collapse of the Empire, it sprang into place as the leading socialist organ, and on the death of Dr. Adler, was taken over by Friedrich Austerlitz. Dr. Otto Bauer, the Foreign Minister, was an editor of the paper, and it was generally considered to be the medium of expression for his personal views, even though he no longer could devote much time to it.

Next in influence (though for a generation—until the end of the war—it had had no equal) was the Neue Freie Presse, a paper having a position in Central Europe corresponding with that of the London Times.

The Fremden Blatt, formerly the official organ of the Imperial and Royal Foreign Office, was dying a natural death, not having the support of the Republic. In March it ceased to exist, and became the Neue Tag, under which title it was rapidly becoming the best and most interesting paper in Vienna.

January 22.
The last few days I have spent in interviewing different newspaper men in connection with the general internal situation. I saw first of all Benedict of the Neue Freie Presse, a most interesting Jew, large, fat, square-headed, but with the nose and mouth of the race. He spoke excellent English, but interlarded his conversation with 'aber' and 'also' in true German style. The man was well informed—very well informed—and spoke with vigor but with moderation. He answered all the questions I put to him with great clearness; went on at length to give me details about what he considered the important things at present. His interview is elsewhere.

While unprepossessing, he has the intellectual qualities of his race, and besides that, a genuine familiarity with the questions of this part of the world.

Wickham Steed in his most interesting book "The Hapsburg Monarchy," which the Imperial Government would not allow to be sold within the Empire—a book which Mr. Coolidge, who is probably more familiar with conditions in the old Empire than any other American, characterized as the best work of its kind written about Austria—Steed, in speaking of Dr. Benedict, says that it used to be told in Vienna that next to Dr. Benedict, Kaiser Franz Joseph was the most influential man in Austria.

The interview, written up the next morning, follows:

"Dr. Benedict started out by stating that Austria's main object for the present must be to live through the crisis which has been brought about owing to her complete defeat. He stated that she was entirely helpless and was so dependent on the other nations which formerly made up the Austro-Hungarian monarchy that she was unable to continue her economic existence unless pressure was brought to bear from the outside on them, and especially on the Czecho-Slovak state, to resume their commercial intercourse with Austria. He stated that within the present boundaries of German Austria the necessary raw materials were not to be found, and that Austria had depended principally on Bohemia and, in part, on Hungary for grain and other foodstuffs. Later in the conversation he came back to this question, which he considers the most vital one of the moment, and said that in his opinion the only possible solution was an immediate economic union with the Czecho-Slovak state, Hungary and Serbia in a Zollverein. To accomplish this, pressure from the outside would be necessary. He added that such a union could not possibly be a political one, inasmuch as both the Magyars and the Czechs were of too intolerant and too aggressive a disposition. Under the old monarchy their co-existence was possible in view of the strongly centralized power; but the unwillingness, especially of the Czechs, to observe moderation—he added that this was not a new development on their part—made their political existence together impossible. He took it for granted that German Austria would eventually unite with Germany, but he did not feel that this would take place immediately. Before such a movement could be seriously considered, it was necessary that the question of the expense of the war and of the national debt of the monarchy be adjusted and be fairly divided between the different portions of the old empire. And above all, it is necessary that the German Austrian state be enabled to get the necessary food and materials so as to be able to live anyway until the next harvest without facing starvation and economic ruin, with the consequent terrible danger of the spread of Bolshevism.

"In speaking of the present political situation Dr. Benedict said that there were three main political groups—the Bürgerliche Demokraten, the Christliche Sozialen and the Sozial Demokraten. The relative strength of these parties in the coming election he estimated to be about as follows: Bürgerliche Demokraten 15%; Christliche Sozialen 45%; Sozial Demokraten 40%. He added that in his opinion between 80 and 85 per cent of the people will vote in this coming election. The suffrage is without any restrictions for both men and women above the age of 20. What is called a preferential form of ballot will be used."

"He considered the Christliche Sozial party as probably the strongest individual group, owing to the great extent to which the Church was back of it. Even though the Church had perhaps lost some of its influence with the downfall of the monarchy, yet it was rapidly regaining it, and was strong in the rural districts and through its influence over the women. The Church naturally gathered to itself certain of the oldest conservative forces."

"The Sozial Demokraten were also very strong, as they represented the mass of the radical opinion. From an intellectual point of view, they are followers of the Marx theories. The practical side of this is shown in an accentuation of the class feeling between the employer and the employee and (from the point of view of the employer) a desire to do as little work as possible. In spite of these radical tendencies, there is no taint of Bolshevism in this party. As far as any political group can be said to be at present back of the union with German the Sozial Demokraten are the most important, and are in favor of such a union chiefly because they feel that with the triumph of social democracy in Germany they will get additional prestige and power when Austria becomes a portion of the German republic."

"The Bürgliche [sic] Demokraten party, to which apparently the majority of 'respectable' people belong, is weak owing to a lack of organization. He says that it is essentially of the middle classes of Vienna. As such it is opposed to radical measures, and has the support of the financial interests. He expects this party to hold the balance of power in the coming parliament."

"The duty of the coming parliament, which will be elected for a period of two years, is to reorganize the government of the new republic. Dr. Benedict considers that the average class of candidates who have so far presented themselves did not represent the best forces in the country. The more intellectual classes and the financial group and other of the more conservative forces are not well represented."

In the course of his talk about the internal political conditions, Dr. Benedict referred constantly to the external situation, and especially to the economic conditions. He casually assumed that England had started the war for her own selfish economic purpose; added that form such a point of view it had not been successful for England, and that owing to her tremendous losses in men and material and to the very heavy debt which she has incurred, that she had permanently lost her economic prestige, and that America would be virtually forced to take over the role of the principal economic power in the world. He expected to see the financial center shift from London to New York; and consequently that in the coming years America and not England would hold the balance of power. In view of this condition he claimed that it was of the greatest importance to America that Germany should not be crushed economically to such a point that she was unable to resist the Bolshevik peril from the East. It was generally thought, he said, that the state of education in Germany and the general soberness of the German people would be a sufficient barrier against Bolshevism, but facts up to the present showed that this was not so. He mentioned that his correspondent in Berlin had informed him in a private letter that the A. E. G. of Berlin, which employs in the neighborhood of 40,000 people, and had been famous for the excellent care it took of its employees, had been one of the successful fields of Bolshevik propaganda, and that the majority of the workingmen there had gone over to the Bolshevist side. As far as the intellectuals were concerned, many of them, too, were subject to the contagious influence of Bolshevism—especially students and persons of intellectual development with small financial resources. He added that Rosa Luxemburg was the daughter of a professor of philosophy, well known for his conservative tendencies. He had himself seen here in Vienna the children of university professors and other cultured persons won over by Bolshevik propaganda. If Germany was disorganized and economically crushed to the extent that she was unable to resist this propaganda, it would soon spread to the rest of Europe. What probably would be necessary, in his opinion, was an alliance of England, Franc and America with Germany in order successfully to avoid the Slav peril.

As far as Bolshevik activities here in Vienna were concerned, they were of slight importance up to the present, but he, like everyone else, fears that if unemployment and the bad food conditions continue long enough, the Russian agents, who are known to be working under the protection of the Russian Red Cross, will be able to cause serious trouble. He added that the office of the Neue Freie Presse was captured by the Bolsheviki on the 11th of November, and that it was only with the greatest difficulty that he got rid of them. As it was, they informed him that the Neue Freie Presse would hereafter be published as "The Red Flag," and they even obliged him to get out two numbers, one of which he was able to show me. This was merely a sheet—an announcement signed by the two Bolshevist leaders. This is about the only case of riotous action that he knows of.

I asked him to what extent he considered the newspapers an influence in the present election. He answered that before the war newspapers were not very widely read in Austria, but that the habit has become an important one, and that even though the fighting has stopped, a great many more people read them now than before. The majority subscribe to papers and read only one or two in their homes. All those persons, however, who frequent the coffeehouses read a great number of different papers. The circulation of the Neue Freie Presse was over 100,000 and its number of readers even greater. As far as the Arbeiter Zeitung was concerned, he estimated it at 60,000.

January 22.
Then I saw Austerlitz. He is more of a German—I imagine somewhat of the type of the Germans who left the fatherland in '48. A socialist—radically inclined, but none the less extremely intelligent and very well informed, too. He is a more aggressive personality, but he had not a trace of the Prussian to him. His most striking characteristic was his eyes, which had a peculiar vivid sparkle, behind the usual more or less thick glasses. He, too, was one of these square-faced large-necked men. I don't think he was too keen to talk, but he got away with it all right, and gave me a favorable impression of the forces leading the socialist wing here—of which he himself is one of the most influential members. He gave me an amusing description of old Franz Joseph, who had made possible the holding together of the monarchy in recent years owing to the prestige that he had gathered about his person, and owing to the fact that he had reigned so long that there were few people living who had been born before he was Emperor, and that the people had a sort of respect for the very fact that this man had been Emperor before their fathers even were born. The Emperor Charles he described as a pleasant, but perfectly colorless man, who anyway had never expected to be Emperor, and was not specially anxious to have the job. And as for the Bolsheviki—he scorned them. They were not a danger here, nor in Germany. The fight for the new order was sufficiently satisfyingly represented to the proletariat by the program of the German and Austrian Social Democrats, who were in favor of thoroughly socialist methods. The more radical Bolshevist movement was the direct result of conditions in Russia, where political freedom had not existed anywhere near to the extent it had West of that country, and that the people there didn't understand the new freedom, and wanted to abuse it. As a matter of fact, the actual Bolsheviki, as he had been informed, were going right around the circle and getting as bad as the old imperialists. There was no room for that kind of a wild, unstable force in these countries. "And what, after all, is Bolshevism?" he

said. "It is nothing but the program of the Socialists in a more active and intolerant form. People call Bolshevism almost any kind of movement against the old established order." He estimated that in the coming elections the Sozial Demokraten would have about 40%, the Christliche Sozialen about 40%, and the Bürgerliche Demokraten about 20%. The last named partly he considered as of little importance, and he expected that the Social Democrats would exercise the guiding influence in the coming political life of Austria. One of the fundamental principles for which they stood was a union with the Sozial Demokratik forces of Germany. The idea of a revival of the old union with Hungary, the Czecho-Slovak state, and the Yugo-Slavs was out of the question, as the German element would be swamped by the Slavs.

The next party I saw was one Dr. Friedrich Funder, editor of the Reichspost, and described to me as the mouthpiece of his Eminence, the Prince Cardinal Archbishop of Vienna, Dr. Piffl. Funder was a black-frocked, pale-faced, bearded, smooth-looking gentleman, who came out for the old monarchy, and all the forces of reaction.

His paper is the principal supporter of the Christliche Sozial party, and he told me that they expect to have the majority in the coming elections, through a coalition with the Bürgerliche Demokrat group. His estimate was that the Sozial Demokraten would have about 40%, the Christliche Sozialen about 40 to 45%, and the Bürgerliche Demokraten the rest. He spoke of the question of an alliance with Germany as the most important political question of the present. His party was opposed to such an alliance chiefly because they were anxious that the old Austrian nation and the old Austrian ideals should not be lost, and they fear that in such an alliance the North German element would predominate. If they were sure that the South German people would have the upper hand, they would favor joining in with them. He explained that the reason that the German Centrum Party was in favor if the union was because it would largely strengthen the Catholic influence in Germany, and would also help in the fight against Bolshevism, which the Church has always strongly opposed. It is more to the interests of the German Catholic Party, therefore, that to the Austrian.

He looked forward to the reestablishment sooner or later of the old Austro-Hungarian nation. He considered the present republic as merely a stage in the revolution—"a crisis" he called it. He would not specify what form such a revived nation would take, but implied that it must be a monarchy or at least a highly centralized autocratic republic. Many people, he said, who favored a restoration of the monarchy were not actually in favor of Hapsburgs. Some had even seriously brought forward the proposition of the Hohenzollerns. This was particularly in evidence in the work done by representatives of the German Alt Deutsch Party. He claimed that these people founded "The Mittag," a noonday paper of large circulation, backed by 8 million crowns of Germany money and furnished with paper from Germany. An active propaganda was carried out against the Hapsburgs by this paper in the hope that with their downfall the power of the Hohenzollerns might extend over German Austria.

As far as the party as a whole was concerned, it would go in favor of a monarchy if the republic or the present form of government lost its popularity or did not prove successful. If, however, the sentiment remained strongly in favor of a republic, he did not feel that they were able to make a definite fight against the socialist forces. A coalition of some sort was inevitable in the immediate future.

In speaking of the Bolshevik influence, Dr. Funder said that the good old conservatism of the Austrian countryman had been undermined by the war. Not only had the Bolsheviki on the Russian front flooded the lines with propaganda against the Emperor and the Kaiser, and in favor of liberty, but the men had had much spare time on their hands, and had taken to reading the newspapers, and so gotten strange ideas in their heads; and that worse still, they were in the trenches for many days, with nothing to do but to think, and that in consequence evil influences rapidly made themselves felt. This might possibly affect the old hold of the Church.

Chapter XV. Budapest for the First Time.

Before leaving Paris we had been told that our trip would last about six weeks. With the passing of that period and no prospect in sight of the termination of the mission, many of us were becoming restless.

No man better fitted for his position than Mr. Coolidge could have been found in the United States. He combined great historical knowledge with a shrewd political sense, and he knew intimately the details of the Austro-Hungarian question. His languages made it possible for him to mix on an equal footing with all nationalities, and to the study of conditions he brought a highly-trained mind sharpened in the school of experience. And yet, curiously enough, he was not an easy chief. Lacking executive ability, being extremely cautious in the formulating of a decision, and having most of the traditional characteristics of the professor, he never would actively approve or disapprove a given piece of work. It was therefore almost impossible for us to know whether we were doing what would be of use to him or merely wasting our own time, his time, and the time of the Government.

Naturally this did not assuage our unrest. Storey, who had been head of the Budapest Mission, was the only one in a sufficiently independent position to take active measures, and he returned to Paris towards the 25th of February. Goodwin was left in Budapest, much against his will, as he also was keen to return. Davis was planning to leave early in March, and Campagnoli talked of nothing but the day of his departure.

I too was getting restless. I had but little work, and all of it could be done equally well or better by some other member of the staff. It had boiled down to keeping a close eye for all news, and trying to gauge public opinion on the questions of the day.

I therefore decided to resign. What happened was written up two days later: February 27.

"Tuesday I sprang my trap. Going to A.C.C., I said causally:

'Have you any objection if I engage a berth to Paris on the 13th?'

'What for?'

'Because it is about time I rejoin my regiment.'

He hemmed and backed around, and said he didn't like to see his organization broken up, etc., and paddled about noncommittally but in general disapprovingly. I pointed out that there was nothing left to do that others couldn't do better, and that I had already once gotten out of the diplomatic service, and had come on this job as my health wouldn't allow me to be with my division, etc. No decision. Then, yesterday A.M. before breakfast, he called me aside.

'I have been thinking of sending you to Bucharest to get the Roumanian side of things. Storey has just been through Transylvania, and you might see what they have to say in Roumania.'

As a servant of the Government my first thought was 'We have a Legation there;' my second 'The Roumanians have probably flooded Paris with this dope.' I mentioned both. They rolled off his back. And then I saw it. The little boy should be appeased with a piece of candy! And after that he must be good and promise not to shock papa's nerves anymore.'"

It was characteristic of Mr. Coolidge. He could not make up his mind to let me go because he feared he might perhaps need me. So he sent me off on this trip with the expectation that on my return I would be satisfied to stay on.

Budapest, February 27.

"There was nothing else to do but go. I packed up, consulted Storey at length on Transylvania, was told by the railroad people I probably couldn't get a place on the Orient Express; cursed my luck that an abscess in my nose should pain me like a toothache and make me look like a rum-hound with a scarlet nose; laughed with Davis about it; slept soundly last night; worried my head off, lest I couldn't get a place on the train this A.M.; went to the station, got on; looked as if I owned a whole compartment; saw others thrown off; and finally breathed a sigh of relief when the train pulled out.

And here I am in Budapest.

Instead of the journey being like crossing Siberia in a stage-coach full of Jewish immigrants, as the trip used to be, it was an easy seven-hour run, very comfortable, in a wagon-lit car, with diner, and my first real meal in months. Levin (one of our Couriers) and one Hughes, of the Standard Oil, and I ride together. As the plains of Hungary were as flat and as dull as Illinois, we talked of everything from the Jews to the army. Incidentally, at Pressburg the train was boarded by Czech soldiers, who rode for almost an hour—evidently through the territory claimed as Czech by them and indignantly denied by Hungarians, who say it is Hungarian, and the Austrians who say it is German. The motto of these fellows is 'What's mine is mine, what's yours is mine, what's his is mine.'

One of the navy men met me at the station, and we grabbed an ancient hack and came to the Ritz, or 'Duna Palota,' as it is called. The hall was filled with toasters, as in Madrid, so I went up and got clean, and soon Goodwin came in with Ferguson. Goodwin, like all the rest of us, was keen to break away, and wanted all possible gossip about [a] chance to do so. I'm afraid they're not big. He just got back from Temesvar and Arad—he was studying the Banat question—and we hardly got through the more common things before we had finished dinner and Turkish coffee and it was 9 P.M. and he had a report to finish, and I this entry to make.

So enough said for the present."

My mission was to make a study of the Transylvanian question, stopping first to hear what the Hungarians had to say about it, and then going to Bucarest [sic] to learn the Roumanain side. To this latter, I was to devote particular attention, as all our previous reports had been based on Magyar sources, and Mr. Coolidge was anxious to have the Roumanian point of view. The work was to be supplementary to an investigation made on the spot by Storey, who had visited Transylvania in the early part of February.

Claimed by both countries, Transylvania also demanded the right of complete autonomy and independence for itself. Geographically and economically the region forms a part of the Hungarian system, but ethnically it is divided into a patchwork of racial settlements. The towns are largely Magyar or Saxon in population and the country mostly Roumanian, with the exception of the Szekler settlement in the extreme Eastern portion.

The Szeklers are a tribe of the Magyars who moved into the region in the 11th century—shortly after the various Magyar tribes had spread out and were settling on the Hungarian plains. They went into Transylvania as a frontier colony. And as such they have maintained a certain spirit of independence for centuries. All reports show them to be simple, industrious, active people, not very highly developed, but intensely patriotic about their own locality. Contrasted with the Roumanians they are a more vigorous, healthy and intelligent race.

Goodwin, as I said, was in charge of our mission to Hungary. He told me the names of the various persons he thought I ought to see, and then sent for Zerkowitz.

Zerkowitz is a Hungarian Jew. He accompanied Count Apponyi (in some minor capacity) to America in 1907 and had lived there for some eight or ten years, being at first a miner in Pennsylvania, and later having some connection with the Immigration Authorities at Ellis Island. At present he was head of the Danube Navigation Co., and had been charged by the Karolyi Government to be of assistance to the American Mission. He accompanied Storey and Goodwin as interpreter, and did many minor things for them, such as telephoning, making appointments, etc., and by his knowledge of Budapest combined with an almost American energy and quickness rendered himself invaluable. Middle-aged, rather distinguished looking in a non-Hebraic way, and always well dressed, he resembled a successful banker, though he was somewhat superlative in his courteousness, and there was about him just a suggestion of something foreign, and almost Oriental.

As manager of the Hungarian propaganda bureau he at once drew up a list of the people I ought to see and made appointments with them. From that moment on, including the hectic days of the Bolshevik outbreak, he never failed to make himself useful, and to be extremely courteous.

He arranged for me to see the Prime Minister, Berenky [*sic*]; Count Albert Apponyi, former Prime Minister and leader of the Conservative forces—a pan-German of the extreme type and in a way the Hungarian counter part of Tirpitz; the former Minister of Nationalities Jaszy; Count Paul Teleki, a prominent geographer and the directing mind back of the Hungarian propaganda bureau; and the President of the Republic, Count Karolyi.

February 28.

"A remarkable day. Breakfast at 9, and then to the French Consulate to get accommodations for the train to Bucarest [sic], and as soon as back, off with Zerkowitz (Goodwin's Hungarian aide) to see the Prime Minister. His name is Berenky. He is a large, stout, dark man, who received me in French, and talked with me for about twenty minutes, with nothing special to the point to say, and giving me the impression of being somewhat colorless. Perhaps the language was a bar to him—but I wasn't impressed. We talked scatteringly of Transylvania. I asked him about its being made an Independent State—about a proposed neutral zone—both good leads. And he played up poorly.

From his palace—one of the big palaces on the hill formerly, I think, the Royal Chancellery, and opposite the Royal Palace—we went to see Apponyi. He, too, is living on the hill now, in an old house with a little courtyard and a small arcade. We went down a simple narrow corridor on the ground floor, hung with photos of banquets to [honor] him in America. The last door on the left was open. I was ushered in by a butler in plain clothes. Behind a big desk in a small simple room with a low ceiling, he sat writing, with his upstanding gray hair, and long square gray beard, bent somewhat over his desk. He looked up, put down his pen, got up, took me by both hands, and said, 'First of all I want to express to you my sympathy on the death of your father.' I started to say something, and he at once saw he had made a mistake, and said, 'Ah, then you are not his son!' I said 'No,' and by this time we had gotten seated, and I told him how I remembered distinctly his having been to Oyster Bay years ago, and how I always associated him with that visit. I then explained my mission, and soon he got started going. He gave me statistics about the Roumanians in Transylvania, and slams at their mismanagement.

He played up unceasingly the theme of an individual Hungary. He said that if Hungary was robbed and despoiled, she would never rest content until, after uniting herself to Germany, the 'oppressed' Central Powers had gotten their revenge. And it wouldn't take long. They would concentrate all their energy and all their hate on the destruction of European Peace until they got back their former possessions. He then launched into economic reasons—the waters, the productions, coal, etc., and I was treated to a dose of 'Hungary uber alles,' to all of which I listened peaceably and with great interest, until he started in a little cynically about Wilson's Fourteen Points, and finally said that if Wilson failed, and Hungary was dismembered in contradiction with all principles of justice, that all the members of all these outraged nationalities (in America) would unite to make him and his party pay. The blood rose up in the back of my neck, and I pitched right in. 'If they do that there'll be trouble' I said. 'If they try to make a fuss like the Germans did, they will pay for it and they will regret it. There is one thing this war has taught Americans—that you can't be an American and an Irishman, and American and an Englishman, at the same time. Col. Roosevelt was absolutely right when he came out so vigorously for an all-American point of view. If these people try that kind of nonsense they'll get into trouble.' And he at once tried to backwater a bit, but came back that it might be done as a matter of internal politics. So I pitched in again, for I was mad, and after we had talked on a bit more, I thought it was best to leave. He is an interesting old scoundrel—very intelligent, perfectly unrepentant, and a thorough Chauvinist. Were I to stay here longer, I should like very much to see more of him. He stands for the highest product of the old regime in Hungary, and was, I suppose, one of the leading men in Europe, although he is now almost seventy-five. His hair stands up straight on top of a high, narrow forehead, and his nose is like a great beak, and his beard long and trimmed off squarely, giving his head an appearance of great length.

From Apponyi's I came back to the Hotel, and we had lunch with Count Teleki. He is a smallish man, with a lined face, rather cloudy blue eyes, and a black moustache. His claim to fame lies in his being a geographer. At first he didn't appeal to me so much, but after lunch I got him up in the office before a gigantic map of Hungary, and I told him I was going to ask him forty questions. So I pointed in, and I have rarely spent a more interesting two hours. Here was a man who knew exactly what I wanted to know, and I could turn the tap on or off at will, and switch him to those things which I wanted to know more about. We started on the ethnic origin of the Magyars, Szeklers, and Roumanians, and he described to me their different relationship, their probable route of approach, their time of arrival, the nature of their existence, their subsequent tribal wars, and gave me a mass of information that filled up many gaps in my scant knowledge of Hungarian affairs. And as my interest is almost greater in the ethnic than in the purely historical, and this was a racial expert, I got almost everything I wanted to know. It was like applying a suction pump to him, and I gave no quarter, pulling him back relentlessly to the points that I was keen about, and holding him to my chosen themes. As we stood there before this gigantic map, I thought, in one of the brief lulls, of what Goodwin and I were saying last night—how incredible it was that we, who two years ago were following our own peaceful existences, should find ourselves deep in the problem of dismembering an empire, and should seriously give the consideration of our immature judgments to the passionate arguments made by ardent Hungarians nationalists that they will never stand for the dismemberment of their country. There is something so characteristically American about it—something so fresh, so ingenuous, so youthful, about our coming, young, and previously unconscious of the existence of Hungary (or Austria) and here learn from the leading men of the country what we need to learn, and having complete access to any and all persons of knowledge and ability and power, of all classes—to lend a willing ear and apply American commonsense, untrammeled by tradition."

There is no point in going into the details of this fascinating talk. They can be found in books; and all I was doing was filling up my background, and satiating my curiosity. When at last he had to break away, he begged me to come to lunch on Sunday, and promised to send me all manner of dope, and said he would on that day fill me up with all further information I wanted.

This was 3:30. At that moment a delegation from the Hungarian Federation of Labor called. Goodwin asked me to interpret, so I translated that they begged us to personally investigate the outrages committed upon Hungarian workers in the occupied regions by the new national states. He said he knew we couldn't do much, but it would be satisfying to the workers here if they even knew we had taken the matter under consideration. The spokesman was one of the Hungarian delegates to the International Socialists Conference at Berne. He and his friends that he brought were all plain, simple, healthy looking people. In American I should have put them down for railroad engineers or some such.

Budapest, March 1.
"In the morning, yesterday, Jaszy, former Minister of Nationalities, called on me. He was unamenable [sic] to mental control, and refuse to stick to the subject about which I sought information, and instead held forth in the usual style."

March 2.
"In the evening we went to the Opera—The Magic Flute. Excessively dull. Following it Zerkowitz took us around to an Artists' Club, where there was a dinner in our honor, and later a concert, followed by dancing. At our table were a number of painters et al, including Halmi, Bilinski, Tolni, et al, and our dinner was delayed and interrupted by the constant arrival of new members, including the Italian Mission; and as the table was too small, as more came some would get up and leave. It was most informal. There followed a good concert, and then dancing. It was an interesting gathering—perhaps the majority of the most noted Hungarian artists, authors, musicians, and full of gaiety and enthusiasm. These people have much spirit, and at the same time have an appearance of energy that is almost American. And it seems to me, as I thought—the intelligent Hungarian is a fine animal. But the others (?).

The hardest thing, however, seems to be to persuade people that one isn't an Ambassador Extraordinary, and that one's ideals lean towards modesty and retirement rather than towards banquets and receptions, and that one isn't at all what one is made out to be."

March 6.
"On the morning of the 2nd, another example of the unrepentant sinners. Apponyi called, together with one Szecheny and another Count, to deliver an address on the part of one of the nationalities, praying that they be not removed from the free, generous, liberal, for-1000-years-famed-for-its-lack-of-oppression-rule of the Magyars, and delivered under the tyrannical yoke of another and therefore barbarous people. The old sinner sat on the sofa, erect, unrepentant, ferocious, and laid down the law in menacing language, ending up with the threat that if Wilson failed to prevent the dismemberment of Hungary, the Magyars would never cease to cause trouble to their neighbors until they had won back their native land in toto. Szecheny, a handsome, proud looking old devil, with a white beard and a monocle, sat back in his chair and gazed at the ceiling, except once, when he cast at Goodwin and myself a withering glance of disdain. When they got up, I spent about five minutes walking up and down the room muttering 'Damn scoundrels! Damned unrepentant sinners!' and swearing. They are the pan-Germans, and Apponyi is the Ludendorff or Bethmann Holwig of Hungary. D----d old scoundrel!

I lunched with Telecki—a very wise man—to meet one Baron Bent—or some such, and later a Prof. S, both specialists on History, and who handed me out much interesting stuff, but all in the same old vein. Telecki's wife is very good-looking, and their house really homelike in our sense."

Chapter XIX. Bucharest

Bucharest, March 6.
"God save us, what a Country!
I came nearer to murder tonight than I have in months. After the Chief of Staff of Roumania had implied to me that Americans in Hungary had been carrying on to an extent almost of doing espionage for Hungary, two numbskulls from Transylvania told me six times the same thing, and six times I explained it to them; and when they told me the seventh, I lost my temper and told them I didn't see why they persisted in thinking I was lying to them. I wanted to crack their heads together and was wildly exasperated with this infernal Oriental indirection. The d--- roundheads

were all het up because Storey had seen the Hungarians in Transylvania. I told them we already knew the sentiments of the Roumanians and Saxons there, and for that reason we wanted to see the sentiments of those whom we didn't know. Why see the Roumanians when we knew how they felt? D----d Oriental Scoundrels!

Apparently honesty is not the best policy here—and talk! Great grief, what a line they gave me! Try as I would to pin them down to brass tacks, they kept going over the same old stuff, and in a manner so dull that I was driven to despair. George would stop for breath and Henry would commence, and when Henry was winded George would start. Any question I would ask would be answered by a long story aside from the point—and as a rule I couldn't even open my mouth. During the dinner the wife as well as Henry talked to me, both at the same time, on different subjects. The husband looked like a fat Jew pig, with a fat, flabby snout—and he is one of Roumania's biggest cheeses. It even had very little of the musical comic. Too horribly humdrum. Too hopelessly devoid of any point of view larger than a pinhead—and may the devil take those persons who use three hours to say what can be said in three minutes.

The Minister at least was simple and went right ahead and worked while the goats gossiped, and he at least didn't try to sling bull. But to h--- with all propagandists, bores, and slingers of bull! When I get to Hades I hope it may be my job to tend the fires over which these three classes roast."

This rather warm entry was the first one I wrote in Roumania. I was so mad at the time, and so disgusted with the country that every detail of the room in which I wrote stands out vividly in my mind. I was in the Hotel Capca, on the top floor, at a table in the center of the room. The tablecloth was red and white. Opposite me stood a shabby washstand. The window was open at my left—a little low window— and an iron bedstead stood in the corner, covered with a red and pink spread.

I never lost this disgust for the people and their ways.

In the filthy hotel where Morgan and I had been billeted I managed to get breakfast for the price of 15 lei, or about $1.50. For this money I had a little pot of vile coffee, some goat's milk and two bad eggs. I ate by the open window looking into the back yard. It was full of tin cans and garbage, and rich odors were wafted up to me. As soon as I was through I went in search of new quarters, and was finally taken in temporarily by the Red Cross while I sought out some decent place to stay.

"The next morning (after our arrival) to the legation to say 'howdy' to Vopicka. He wasn't up, so we went to the Inter-Allied Mission for visas and reservations. The French run the whole thing—control all incomings and outgoings of Roumania— and as French officialdom in Roumania is no better than the same in France, it took all morning."

Bucharest, March 12.

When I got back to the Legation I found old Vopicka, and I must say I was attracted to him from the first. I have rarely met a man with a more open, hearty, friendly disposition. Born a Czech, he became a successful Chicago brewer and then a ward politician. He was appointed Minister to Bulgaria, Roumania, and Serbia in 1913, and I remember that on his way out he got in Dutch by stopping at Prague and making a strongly ant-Austrian public address. He speaks several Slavic tongues, German, and French; is apparently ignorant and uneducated but with great charm, a warm heart, and an open, frank, kind nature. And, as far as I can see, he is the hero of Roumania. Everyone knows him, and during the two hours I dined with him at the Elysee people were all the time coming up to him and greeting him with great cheer and heartiness. I can well see how this can appeal to these people.

A.C.C. told me a story about him which I checked up and believe to be true. Shortly after he appeared in Bulgaria for the first time, he attended a session of the Bulgarian Parliament at which the King and Queen were present. Some of the deputies got up and attacked the King with such violence that the Queen broke down and left, weeping. Vopicka rushed to a telephone and called up the Palace to ask if he could see the Queen at once. He was told 'No' but jumped into his auto and went there. At the door he was again refused, but went right in and found the Queen still all worked up. So he proceeded to tell her that what the deputies had said was nothing—that she's never heard what the delegates to an American State Legislature said, and that his Bulgarian attack was nothing in comparison. And he stayed there an hour or more and left her quieted and cheered up, and his lifelong friend.

Well, old Vopicka asked me to dine, and so I went off to see Col. Yates, the Military Attache, whom I found to be pretty well up on the job and well informed. He laid out a plan of campaign, and I then went about getting a place to sleep that wasn't a hog-style. The Red Cross came to our rescue and put us up for that night in an extra room they had, and I arranged that I should take Krasnahan's room at Capca. Krasnahan is an Armenian American, working for Col. Yates on Bolshevism, et al.

That night I dined with the Minister and got him to tell me all about himself, etc., and prepared the way for his taking me to see everyone.

So the next (Wednesday) afternoon he took me to see Gen. Berthelot. Berthelot is in charge of the Roumanian army operations—a large, fat, cheerful, black-headed Frenchman, who was quite ready to unburden his soul, and said that he had told the Roumanians that just because the Hungarians had oppressed in the past was no reason for the Roumanians doing it now. He favored complete autonomy, and the creation of a neutral zone. Storey had thought he was strongly pro-Roumanian, but I wasn't struck that way. I think his attitude was perfectly French. He sent for his Chief of Staff and told him to direct G. L. to place all material on Transylvania at my disposal. So the Chief of Staff took me to the French H.Q. and introduced me to Commandant Paulier, Chief of Intelligence, a very pleasant, well-informed man. He got the dossiers—Hungarian and Roumanian Complaints—and as neither concerned me I thanked him and explained that was none of my business, and finally I got him talking. He said that I would soon find out that I was no longer in Europe—and that the Orient and the West would never meet. He spoke of the lowness of ideals, morals, and Government; the poorness of the officers; the corruption, etc.; and I later had the opportunity to confirm a good many of his impressions. He said he thought an International Police was essential along the border, and he told me that of all the complaints received there were none from the Czeklers [sic].

I dined that evening with Yates at the Elysee, and we talked of War Department red tape, of the Bolshevists, of the Roumanians, for the soldiers of which he had a great admiration, etc., and had a good time.

Incidentally, the night before, after dining with Vopicka, I met Morgan at Maxims—a regular Parisian cabaret joint with very bad music, bad wines, many French and Roumanian Officers and low females—that resembled such a joint anywhere, except that you had a feeling that no matter what happened the Police would never interfere, nor the management. As they have a law that no one can be on the streets between one and six A.M., it prolongs Café life into the day, so I cleared out before one A.M.

On Thursday morning, which was the 6th, Yates took me around to see Gen. Prezan, the Roumanian Chief of Staff. He is an elderly, gray-headed man, and he at once launched into an attack on Storey, and sending for his Chief of Staff read a report on him, implying that Storey was a Hungarian spy. As it happened, Storey, as usual, had been a d---- f--- and had ignored the fact that Transylvania was a military zone of Occupation; had come there unannounced by Yates or Vopicka, and wanted to bring in two Hungarians. The Roumanians being low anyway, discovered in Storey a spy, and as he sought information of the number and distribution of the Roumanian troops, which in no way concerned him, and being put off tried to get the same dope from the Prefect, they were convinced they had unearthed the real thing. Prezan's attitude, and the ingenuity of their proof that Storey was the paid agent of the Hungarian Government, had something of the musical comedy stuff. And so again I had to apologize for and explain Storey. Yeates was indignant, and the fact is that Storey is simply an idiot.

This action of Storey's was the same to which I referred in the entry at the head of this Chapter. From the more detailed report which I made to Mr. Coolidge it can be seen how they happened to get the impression that he was working for the Hungarians.

The report follows:

"When I called on the Rumanain Chief of Staff, Gen. Prezan, he was indignant over a report sent him by the officer who had accompanied Storey through Transylvania. The General read most of this report to Col. Yates and myself. It was, in brief, as follows:

Mr. Storey had arrived at the Rumanian line of occupation accompanied by the Hungarians whom he wished to take across the border with him. The territory was in the hands of Rumanian troops of occupation operating with their center at Bucharest, where the American Government had military and diplomatic representatives. Mr. Storey was in no way accredited by these representatives. Addressing himself to the military commander he asked permission for himself, an unknown unaccredited American accompanied by two Hungarians to make as inspection of the zone of occupation. The military commander, deeming that he could not grant this permission without authority from Bucharest, put off Storey. Storey then went to Dr. Maniu, the head of the civilian Transylvanian government, and Dr. Maniu then requested that he be allowed to make his proposed trip, the Hungarians being in the meantime left out. The military government acceded. Storey then in an interview with the military commander asked for particulars about the strength and distribution of the Rumanian forces. This he was not given. And when later he had an interview with the Prefect of the region he asked the same questions of the Prefect. Later on during his tour he visited the towns which were only Hungarian; he talked almost exclusively with Hungarians; and at Koloszvar [sic] he was closeted for two hours with a certain Hungarian of English origin suspected of being one of the strong anti-Rumanian agitators. The people with whom he spoke among Rumanian officials have the impression that he was distinctly pro-Hungarian.

It was quite evident that Mr. Storey should have entered the zone of occupation only with the knowledge and consent of our representatives in Rumania. I told Gen. Prezan as much, and added that as far as his demanding military information was concerned, I knew that it was merely in order to fill out his studies of the whole situation. It is easily understood, however, that a civilian arriving accompanied by two enemy subjects, showing great curiosity about military matters, can easily be a subject of suspicion. As far as Storey's conversations with Hungarians were concerned, I pointed out that we were particularly anxious to know the sentiments of the Hungarians there; and that as regards the apparently pro-Hungarian leanings of Mr. Storey, he had access to nothing but Hungarian propaganda during the last six weeks, and it was with full knowledge of this fact that I had been sent to Rumanians to hear what the Rumanians had to say.

In the course of the conversation Gen. Prezan implied that Storey was in the pay of the Hungarians. In talking with other Rumanians I found this same highminded sentiment; and this opinion coupled with their terrible fear that Storey had not seen the thing through Rumanian eyes was indirectly the most obvious sign of the weakness of the Rumanian cause and of the extravagance of their attitude."

The visit had been made for the purpose of ascertaining the sentiment of the inhabitants of Transylvania, and it was to get supplementary information about this same question that I had come to Bucarest [sic].

Storey had clearly made a serious blunder by not proceeding about the thing in a proper manner, through our Legation in Bucarest [sic]. For after all, the zone was a military zone of occupation, and as yet only an armistice was in force between the two belligerents. Such a situation naturally required proper authorization for a visit.

"In the afternoon the Chief of Staff, Antonescu, received me, and showed me the wild Roumanian claims, and said 'statistics' were now in the press supporting them. It is easy to print statistics today. So I asked him what they would do if they didn't get them. 'Roumania has an honor! Roumania has an army!' was the answer, and he added that as far as his personal idea was concerned, as long as there were two men in the world there would be war.

He is a youngish-looking individual, intelligent, but not particularly impressive mentally.

In the afternoon of Thursday the Minister took me round to call on Princess Mavrocordato. She, like most other Roumanian 'Princely' houses, belongs to the descendants of the Greek Phanariots. She was fat, dull, ugly, and covered with perfume, and the company present was about the same.

What a place! And what people! To outward appearances it is a mixture of Albuquerque, New Mexico, and Ellis Island. If course the strange costumes are interesting—brigands in sheepskin coats and fur hats; highly embroidered vests and clothes; barefooted women; oxen-drawn carts; carriages with Russian garbed drivers, and Western American tinsel. But the rest ------!!"

That same evening I went with Vopicka to have dinner with the acting Prime Minister, Constantinescu. He was at the head of the Government during the absence of Bratianu, at the moment Chief of the Roumanian Delegation to the Pars Conference. The delegates from Transylvania Pop, and Popovici, were there, as well as the one from Bessarabia, and it was the effect of this evening that was reflected in the entry of March 6th at the head of this Chapter. It was Pop and Popovici that I wanted to murder. It was Pop and Popovici who told me straight out six times that Storey was in the pay of the Hungarians. And it was Pop and Popovici who refused to be pinned down to brass tacks and kept going over the same old stuff in such a dull manner that I wanted to crack their heads together. "George" was Pop, and "Henry" was Popovici, and when "George" stopped breath "Henry" would start in, and vice versa.

The "wife" was the wife of the Acting Prime Minister—a dull woman who spoke German. And "the husband who looked like a fat Jew pig with a fat, flabby snout" was the Acting Prime Minister. But he was apparently simple, and I understand was more or less efficient.

The Prime Minister's brother, Gen. Constantinescu, was also at the dinner, and he asked me to his house later. He at least was a gentleman.

March 13.
"On Friday, which was the 7th, Col. Yates took me around to see Gen Vaitoianu, Minister of War. He struck me as a man well above the average Roumanian—intelligent, quiet, and not so extravagant in his assertions. Of course he spoke for the whole Roumanian claims, but I don't think he expected to get them. Col. Yates pointed out that if they got the Serbian portion of the Banat the Roumanians would be opposite Belgrade.

'They must move their Capital,' said Vaitoianu.

'How would you like it if they told you you must move your Capital?' asked Yates.

'Not at all. We wouldn't do it.'

'That's what they say, and that's why they demand the tete de pont of the Banat.'

'If they need such a tete de pont, we had better ask for one for Bucarest [sic],' said the General, and pointed to a part on the south of the Danube.'"

It was this question of the Banat as well as the extreme claims for Transylvania that appeared to me to be so unreasonable in the Roumanians. The Banat was one of the richest agricultural districts of Hungary, and was inhabited by Roumanians, Serbians, Hungarians and Germans scattered about like a patchwork quilt, except in the western and southwestern part, which was almost exclusively Serb. The Roumanians claimed the whole thing. In Transylvania they claimed to the River Theiss as a line very much beyond even the most extreme pro-Roumanian ethnic claim. They showed a desire to grab everything in sight.

But to return to the interview with Gen. Vaitoianu:

"He then went on to talk about various possible boundaries, and especially in the Dobroudja region. Nothing of special note came up, except his claim for the Roumanians in the region of Timok. An intelligent man I should say he is half-German.

I had lunch with the Polish-American correspondent of the Chicago Tribune, and a Roumanian Socialist newspaper man by the name of Cores—an intelligent, sensible man, who told me much about the Bolsheviki and Russia. When I asked him whether the Roumanians expected to get all the Banat he said, 'No; why should they? All we want is the eastern part.' And he cranked up the disinterestedness of the Americans and their help to Roumania, and the need of American capital, and particularly of American technical ability in the development of Roumania's natural resources. He was agin' [sic] the French.

In the afternoon I called upon Jorga, the leading Roumanian Historian, and, I should say, a man of breadth of vision. I was sorry to have only a very short time to see him, for he has made a special study about the crusaders. He furnished me with maps and pamphlets (Roumanian Propaganda) and also some maps which the Peace Conference wanted. I was to go, after seeing Jorga, to the Princess Cantacouzene's with the Minister, but his car didn't show up, so there was nothing doing until dinner that evening, when we went to Gen. Constantinescu's. The house was full of perfume, and the reception room hung with rugs and furnished in Oriental style. The two daughters of the house were dressed in Roumanian peasant costume—magnificent, rich, heavy embroidery, in simple pattern and high colors. Having very black hair and very white faces, there was a distinctly Oriental appearance to them—although they spoke French and English, discoursed of the theatre and wines in Paris, and one was a Red Cross nurse.

Saturday was notable chiefly for my visit to Madame Prezan, who is the wife of the Chief of Staff and Lady-in-waiting to the Queen. To outward appearances she was a sensible European, and talked first of her relief work in a good way. Then she switched, and ran the French into the ground, and told me she knew that Col. Vix (in Budapest) had been bought by the Hungarians. I wanted to brain her, but I merely told her politely I was incredulous, and she insisted on her point. From a woman in her position I considered it outrageous, and it appears it is an indication of the attitude of the people towards the world in general—that all are bought with ease."

It might not have been so bad had she not been so insistent. Knowing the French higher officers, it was obvious that this particular thing was the last thing in the world of which one of them could be accused. And furthermore, knowing Col. Vix, and knowing much about him, it was even more obvious to me that this story was merely a malicious lie. Coming from the wife of the Chief of Staff of the Roumanian army it was peculiarly nauseating. What she said about the French in Bucharest was on the same plane.

"I lunched Saturday, March 8th, at the French Officers' mess, with Commandant Paullion. There was Commandant Cartier, who had just arrived from Paris, bound for Constantinople, and who spoke much of Russia. He is Chief of the Intelligence Section of the General Staff of the Allied Armies in the Orient.

In the evening, dinner with Vopicka—rather a lot of champagne, and the old boy very talkative and really very nice. A most likable old scout.

And early the next morning to the station, and on the Orient Express, where I talked much with the Serbian Minister to Roumania, who had a Charlie Chaplin way of shoving his hat over his eye, etc., while he informed the ingenuous young American about Serbia, Hungary, Bulgaria and Roumania, and said that the Germans' greatest error was in the peace of Bret Litovsk—that had they there refused to demand indemnities, territories, etc., they would have had the moral support of the world, and crushed the spirit of the Allies and prevented America from coming in.

Otherwise nothing of special interest to relate. The Hungarian plains were flat, rich, and middle-western looking, and made the old Minister declaim about the 'beauties' of this 'garden country.'

At Vienna, to find the world still turning around, although even in the ten days' absence I was completely out of touch with the situation, so rapidly do things move. I spent Tuesday dictating my report on Transylvania, and Wednesday tried to take up a few loose ends, and then decided I had better get back to the 322nd [regiment]. Thursday night we dined with von Pflugl, who pulled off another Tyrolese Forever dinner, which was attended almost exclusively by members of the Christian Socialist party, and was supposed to convert us to a more flourishing Tyrol—an excellent meal. I sat next to a little old Tyrolese priest, with white hair and a face like a boy; I wanted to take him and put him in a garden and hear him talk. He was a former Reichstag member from Brixen. And Hoffinger was there, just back from Berlin with wild tales of 80,000 Government troops fighting 80,000 Spartacists in Berlin while he was there—artillery, minenwerfers, etc., and a real live war in progress again. I couldn't help feeling that I wished it were perhaps as true as he said it was. I asked him about Brockdorff Rantzau. 'A moderate man,' he said. And so it went."

Chapter XXX. Going Before the Commissioners

While I was still working over the report, Dulles announced sententiously:

"You will go before the commissioners tomorrow at ten o'clock."

It was said with the same touch of reverence with which the chief introducer of Ambassadors announces an audience with His Majesty.

I returned to my labors.

A little while later, after receiving a telephone message, Dulles announced:

"The Commissioners will not meet tomorrow morning. You and Mr. Coolidge will go before the Commissioners at 2:30 tomorrow afternoon."

This appointment remained unchanged, and ten minutes before the hour we were in the antechamber waiting. William Bullitt, fresh from Russia, entered the Commissioners' room just as we arrived.

"He has the President's ear," someone whispered in an awed tone. "He's just back from Lenin."

In a few minutes he came out.

"The Commissioners will see you now," said Chris Herter, recording secretary.

We entered and were introduced. The "Commissioners" were Lansing, Bliss and White. Their function was evidently similar to that of a Vice-President.

"Do you wish to deal with Austria or Hungary first?" said Herter to Mr. Lansing.

Lansing referred the question to Mr. Coolidge.

"Perhaps Hungary first," he suggested. "Capt. Roosevelt has just come from there and can give the latest news."

"All right."

"Capt. Roosevelt, will you tell us about Hungary?" said the Secretary.

I had the feeling of taking a college examination, the first question being "Tell all you know about Hungary."

I gave a brief sketch of what had happened. Mr. Lansing and Gen. Bliss threw in a question here and there.

Finally:

"Well, Captain, what is your solution?" asked Mr. Lansing.

I bristled at the term "solution."

"It seems to me, Sir, that that's for Paris to decide," said I. "I can only give you the solution suggested by the British and Italians—military intervention; the British Representative told me, as I was leaving, to tell them in Paris that 10,000 men would do the trick."

"We've had experience," said the Secretary to Gen. Bliss, "with sending small forces for intervention. Look at Russia."

"Yes," said the General. "It isn't worth sending troops unless you send enough. But…"

"Isn't there any other way out?" Mr. Lansing asked.

"Well, Sir, all I can say is that whatever you do, it must be done immediately. The one thing that is fatal is delay. Think of the possible effect on the Germans!"

"Yes, that's right," Mr. White broke in. "Capt. Roosevelt is quite right. We mustn't overlook the possible effect on the Germans."

"What it comes down to, Sir," said I, turning to Mr. Lansing, "is that the Hungarians have told the Conference to go to the Devil, and now add, 'What are you going to do about it?'"

"Yes, that's right," said Mr. White again, nodding his head.

"Whatever is done," I repeated, "it must be done promptly. Of course I don't know much about conditions, but it strikes me that unless immediate action is taken, the danger of the Germans profiting by the example is great."

"When was the President to take this question up with the French?" said Gen. Bliss, who was beginning to appreciate the need of action.

"At three o'clock," Lansing answered.

We all looked at our watches. It was about a quarter before three.

"Well, can't we get word to him not to take it up until I can see him?" asked the General.

Lansing hesitated.

"I wonder if I can't get him on the telephone," said Bliss; and he had Herter put in a call for the President's house.

We talked a little more—chiefly Bliss and Lansing, while Herter tried to get Mr. Wilson on the telephone. The subject was obviously unfamiliar to them, and I thought of Goodwin's account of going before the Commissioners when he returned from Budapest a few days previously and they sent for a Cram's atlas and had him show them where's where in Hungary.

When our ten minutes were up Mr. Lansing announced he had to leave. So we all rose, and Gen. Bliss said he would get hold of the President and impress on him the need of prompt action. We shook hands, and Mr. Coolidge and I then went to his room.

The only notes I made at that time referred to this meeting and also to dining with Mr. White that night, when Gen. Bliss also was present. They were written up in Vienna as follows on April 5th:

" 'A,' 'E,' 'I,' 'O,' 'U,' are the five vowels in the alphabet. 'A' is obstinate, self-willed, provincial and hardheaded to an appalling degree. Frank Simonds said of 'A' that practically everyone has his form of insanity, and 'A's' was the League of Nations.

'E' is quiet, unobtrusive, intelligent and able. But I think 'E' with his greater understanding cannot prevail over the obstinacy of 'A.'

Henry Adams characterized 'I' to me as 'a first class clerk.' More need not be said.

'O' is an ancient, and living in the America of the 70's. Goodwin calls him 'Gaga.'

'U' flourished in the last-half of the 19th Century, and knows well the German words to the hymn 'Rock of Ages.' He has admirable manners, and when he stands up the weight of his body is so great it makes him very bow-legged. But 'U' at least has heard of Europe.

The rest of the alphabet very according to phonetic rules—labials, hard, soft, etc.

But the letter 'A' dominates the whole thing. I had not expected to see it so, for I had thought that 'E' in his knowingness would be able to prevail. Frank Simonds painted a picture so gloomy that even my pessimism became optimism in comparison. He claims local political motives alone are dominating 'A' and that he will listen to absolutely no one. It has come down to bargaining between 'A,' the bullfrog, the big Wop, and the Beefeater, each fighting for his own political skin; the other things thrown to the dogs.

As far as I can make out, the same close harmony between 'E' and 'A' no longer exists, although 'E' stands well above the others in council. 'I,' 'O' and 'U' are dummies—figureheads—and also fatheads. G's tale of going before them was heart-rendering. They sent for an old Cram's atlas to locate a certain country in Europe, and asked the questions I would expect some of the doughboys to ask. They showed a previous knowledge of the problem that would fill a hummingbird's egg!"

"A" was of course Wilson, "E" was House, "I" Lansing, "O" Bliss, and "U" White.

As far as I can see, one man alone, Gen. Bliss, had a definite, clear-cut policy. This was to have nothing to do with Europe. He was strongly in favor of our washing our hands of the whole business and pulling out for good. It rather appalled me at first, as it sounded almost impossible to do so without losing everything we had gained in the way of prestige and influence. But I later saw he was right.

"All the Americans are good for," he said to me at dinner that night at Mr. White's, "is to settle a quarrel between two lumbermen on the Wabash."

It summed up his opinion of our ability as peace makers.

He nearly bowled me over a few minutes later when he said of the Entente policy in Hungary respecting the Vix note and the violation of the armistice which it provided, that this was only comparable to the rape of Belgium by the Germans.

This was said at a dinner party—there were some eight persons present, including the Butler Wrights, the Grafton Minots, Mr. White and myself. It showed a lack of true understanding of the situation or else a carelessness of speech, which was disillusioning.

His statement that he had investigated the matter of the passing of the Vix decision by the Supreme Council in Paris and had found that it had been railroaded through without coming to the attention of the American and British representatives was equally depressing. But he failed to state that he had been the American Representative at the Supreme Council meeting, and he gave none of the details mentioned by Day.

What it really amounted to was that we had allowed such a thing to be slipped over in blissful ignorance. And if it happened this time, why not again?

Mr. White struck me as being strongly anti-French. He ridiculed lightly their various innocent schemes to get us to guarantee the German debt, and spoke of them as difficult to get along with.

The diary continues, apropos of things in general at Paris:

"I had thought we would have learned, after fourteen months of letter writing to the Kaiser about the Lusitania, the true value of words. But Woodrow Wilson still persists in this ingenuous conception that a phrase, a mere group of fine-sounding words, an academic expression of pious and highly commendable hope, a well-worded, moralistic rhetorical sentence expressing the laudable sentiment that this world, this world of worlds, must be made an inspiring place for our children (and our children's children) to live in; that this verbal patent medicine will purge Europe of her ills overnight, and introduce the reign of brotherly love. A sentence, a fine-sounding paragraph, written in most perfect English, will destroy the hatred of centuries—will change the racial jealousies of a thousand years' standing, will fill empty stomachs and clothe shivering bodies. There is something rather wonderful in this highhanded scorn for the 'practical' things of life; but one is every now and then tempted to wonder whether purely material things and even traditions don't have an occasional influence on humanity.

And the pity of it, the truly awful pity, is that the ship is being driven with increasing speed upon the reef of ruin, and that if it is wrecked, not only will it be his doing, but it will give a blow to idealism as a force in history which may set us back thousands of years.

WORDS, WORDS, WORDS!"

APPENDIX

3. Nicholas Roosevelt, *The Philippines. A Treasure and a Problem*, New York: J. H. Sears & Company, Inc., 1926.

Chapter XV. Bearing A Thankless Burden

When the Philippine Islands were ceded to the United States by Spain under the terms of the Treaty of Paris, it was our right to hold and develop them primarily for the benefit of our own people. To have done so would have been in accordance with the usual customs of nations and with the recognized principles of international law. Instead, we announced to the world that we would hold the Philippines in trust and administer them for the benefit of the Filipino peoples. This was a new departure in the practice of nations—an adventure in international altruism.

Throughout the past twenty-five years, our original declaration has been consistently adhered to. Most of the Presidents and high officials in the American Government, beginning with McKinley, have stressed the idea of trusteeship. Its complete realization is as much the object of American effort now as when the policy was first announced.

One aspect of this situation has, however, been neglected. This is, that we agreed to hold the

Islands in trust, not for a small class of professional political agitators; not for the descendants of Spanish and Chinese mestizos; not for the Tagalogs; not for any other single group; but for the benefit of all of the people in all the Islands. In other words, our duties as trustees are to Moros and Igórots as well as to the Christian Filipinos; to the Malays of various strains as well as to those with Spanish and Chinese blood in their veins; to the ignorant peasants in the remote districts as well as to the "ilustrados" in Manila; to the farmers as well as to the politicians.

In discussing the obligations which we have thus assumed as trustee, Vice-Governor E. A. Gilmore, who, before coming to the Islands, was Professor and Acting Dean of the University of Wisconsin Law School, recently made the following pertinent comment:

"Being an obligation voluntarily assumed, it is a right and duty of the trustee to determine the terms and conditions upon which the trust will be executed and the time and manner for its termination or modification. There has been, however, during all these years a persistent demand on the part of a certain number of the beneficiaries of the trust, that it should be terminated or that the powers of the trustee should be turned over to these claimants. Invoking a political principle of representative government familiar to the people of the United States and applicable to the conditions prevailing there, these claimants have purported to speak in behalf of all the beneficiaries of the trust.

Even assuming that this small group voices the sentiments of all the beneficiaries, the question still remains for the trustee to decide whether it will be for the benefit of all to terminate or modify the trust. As in the case of ordinary trusts known to the law and the courts, there is constant danger of a premature termination or modification, as a result of the persistence of a small number of the beneficiaries. A study of the course of events during the past twenty-five years, discloses that the principal difficulty with which the trustee of the Philippines has had to contend is the preservation of the powers of the trustee sufficiently long or under sufficiently proper conditions to give reasonable assurances of the realization of the object for which the trust was created.

The great danger in the present situation is to be found in the assumption that the social, economic and political development in the Islands has proceeded to a point where the general political principles, safely applicable elsewhere, can be relied upon to justify a modification of the trust or a relinquishment or restriction of the powers of the trustee."

In other words, it is our duty as trustee to resist the demands of one group of beneficiaries that the trust be broken in their behalf. We must execute the trust for the benefit of all the beneficiaries, and we—not the beneficiaries—must decide when the trust can be terminated.

So much for the legalistic interpretation of our relation to the Filipino peoples. The extent to which we have yet discharged our obligations as trustee—either to the politicians or to the dumb and illiterate electorate—has been described in the foregoing chapters. It may not be amiss to summarize again our promises and our performances.

When we went into the Philippines we promised to establish order. This we have done. For the last two decades the Filipinos have enjoyed uninterrupted peace. This order, however, rests on one thing alone—the might of the United States. General Wood's apt phrase has already been quoted, to the effect that stability under the flag must not be taken to indicate stability when that flag is withdrawn. In the opinion of Americans competent to judge conditions in the Islands, the withdrawal of the United States in the near future would be followed by serious disorders and, ultimately, by civil war.

We promised to install schools and to break the wall of illiteracy. Owing to the differences in dialect we agreed to make English the medium of instruction and the lingua franca. To-day there are about 6400 school buildings in the Philippines of which nearly two-thirds are temporary structures. There are 27,305 teachers, and about 1,000,000 pupils. Most of the teachers have had only a rudimentary education. The pupils average less than three years in school and during this time they learn about the equivalent of the first grade in the primary schools in America. The principal stress has been on academic and political rather than on practical education. About a million Filipinos know a little English, but the language which they use—even in the schools—is a mere caricature of English as spoken in the United States and Great Britain.

We promised to clean up the public health of the Islands. We have checked the virulent epidemics, but have only begun work on the economically destructive minor ailments which are sapping the vitality of the Filipino peoples. Ninety per cent of the Islanders still suffer from intestinal parasites. Neither the officials nor the people are yet sufficiently health-conscious to prevent the recurrence of epidemics as soon as American supervision is relaxed.

We agreed to defend them from outside aggression. This is only possible so long as we remain in the Islands.

We undertook to help them develop their economic resources. The Islands, rich as the Indies, can be made under diligent supervision to yield rubber, camphor, quinine and spices, to the profit of natives and foreigners. Those crops which at present are raised for export can be so increased by scientific agricultural methods that the annual output will far exceed that of today and the Filipino peoples will be proportionately wealthier. As yet practically nothing has been done to modernize agricultural practices. Only 12½ per cent of the land is under cultivation. The communications system which we established is still far from complete.

We told the world that we would prepare the Filipinos for self-government so that they could play their part as an independent nation in the Pacific. We have given them the outward forms of democracy and virtually complete autonomy. They have shown that they have not mastered even the rudiments of democracy—unless a passion for political intrigue can be considered a capacity for independence.

Finally, we have announced that we were going to give them the benefit of our modern civilization, and that as our "little brown brothers" they would become the bearers of American ideals in the East. A few thousand Filipinos know and understand something of American civilization. Most of the "ilustrados," in so far as they have any cultural leanings, prefer the civilization of Spain to that of America. Spanish, not English, is the language of the better classes. The rank and file have no idea of what America is or stands for. If they know anything of American civilization, it is a strange game called baseball, which their children have brought back from the schools. The majority of them live as they did before America took over the Islands—though perhaps more healthily and happily.

In brief, our promises to the Filipino peoples have not yet been redeemed. Our duty as trustee is only half discharged. To withdraw from the Islands now or in the near future would be a betrayal of the great mass of the Filipino peoples, and a stain on the fair name and integrity of the American nation. It would be a tacit admission of our inability to govern another people either to their or our advantage. Finally, it would unloose the forces of war and revolution throughout Asia.

How, under the circumstances, there can be any serious talk of immediate independence, either among Filipinos or Americans, passes understanding. We have set our hand to the plow and cannot turn back. The question should not be "Shall we unhitch the team and pretend that the field is ready for harvest?" but "What can we do to hasten the plowing and harrowing so that the seeds of self-government may grow in a properly prepared soil?" The task of creating a nation out of peoples as backward and divergent in language as the Filipinos is necessarily very long. "First the blade, then the ear, then the full corn in the ear." It is not a question of a few years, but of a few generations. Americans who have studied the problem closely—and this includes men who know the Filipinos intimately from long association and from actual experience in administration—say that at least three generations must pass before the people will be sufficiently advanced to enable them to stand by themselves.

As there is little chance of the Philippines being cast adrift immediately the great danger is that the sentimentality of the American people and the ignorance of their politicians will lead to a continuation of half measures. Filipinos, Americans, Spaniards, all foreigners in the Philippines, are agreed that the greatest single obstacle to the development of the Islands is the lack of a clear-cut statement of policy by the American Government. "Anything is better than the present uncertainty," is the way Filipinos of all parties phrased it. The continuation of this uncertainty will be almost inevitable if our government seeks to compromise with the Filipino politicians and grant them further power without making possible the efficient administration of the government by competent Americans.

America's duty is clear—to administer the trust for all the Filipinos until they are sufficiently advanced to look after themselves. We have done too much sentimentalizing about the Islands; we have cherished too many illusions. The time is at hand to examine the record coldly; to accept the obvious conclusion that independence is out of the question for two or three generations at least; and to shoulder our burden courageously, carrying through the thankless task to completion. This means to govern the Philippines efficiently, to create a colonial service which will enlist competent men in the lower positions—men of the type who went to the Islands in the days of Cameron Forbes, ready to sacrifice their lives, if need be, in order to serve their country by helping to lead the Filipinos to the light. Such men would flock to the Philippines tomorrow, if they knew that America was prepared to carry the white man's burden with dignity and that the government would support them effectively. We still have the chance to show that we can create a system of colonial government that is at the same time competent, and considerate; that we can be tolerant without being weak; that we can develop the economic resources of the Islands with profit to the natives as well as to ourselves. Only then, will it be worth the while of men of General Wood's caliber to make the sacrifice required of those who govern the Philippines.

Our first quarter of a century in the Philippines has been an experiment in misapplied altruism. The second quarter should be an era of efficiency. The third quarter will probably be a time of transition, and the last will see the birth of a business partnership. Today, at the beginning of the second quarter, we are blamed by the world for having played with fire and failed to learn our lesson. Instead of gratitude we have the resentment of the politicians. In our own eyes, we stand convicted of having failed to complete what we set out to do and of having permitted ignorance and impractical idealism to blind us to our failure.

It is no easy task, this which we have so long hoped to evade. We have trifled with the white man's burden during the past twenty-five years, half believing that by closing our eyes and loudly insisting that no such burden existed, we could dodge our Responsibility. Our ignorance has been used to bolster theories, and we have applied panaceas without diagnosing conditions. We have taken full credit for achievements that are still only half completed, and have even prided ourselves on one of the most fatuous and naive political blunders of modern history, the assumption that in seventeen years a conglomeration of twelve million illiterate peoples, but little advanced from their primitive barbarism, speaking many different dialects and living on hundreds of remote islands, could be prepared for a modern democratic form of government.

We owe it to ourselves, therefore, as well as to the great masses of the Filipino peoples, to recognize our mistakes and to make good our promises. This means "going the whole hog" and giving future governors sufficient powers to govern the Philippines efficiently. It means investing more money in the Islands: establishing a series of agricultural schools and farm stations, and inaugurating a widespread campaign to introduce modern agricultural methods; developing roads and interisland communications to such a point that the peoples of the remote islands can ship their produce with regularity; clearing virgin lands, and establishing plantations of rubber, coconuts, sugar and other tropical products. Much money will have to be spent on the education system and the children kept in school long enough to obtain the rudiments of a practical education. This will necessitate importing at least enough American teachers to give experienced American instruction to the Filipino men and women who will teach in the Islands. In short, the people—all the people, and not only a small class of Chinese and Spanish half-castes—will have to be prepared for self-government.

This formidable undertaking will require patience, tact, and ability. There are few men in America to-day equipped for proconsular work. The understanding of colonial problems is rare among us. Not one American in fifty has any conception of our responsibilities in the Philippines, or of what we have done and have left undone there. Not one in a thousand realizes the danger to the world peace of giving the Filipinos independence under present conditions. It follows, therefore, that an extensive educational campaign will have to be conducted in America, if our people are to realize that the Philippine problem is one of the most difficult which we have ever had to face, and that its solution requires long years of unrelenting supervision. There are no "lightly proffered laurels" in carrying the white man's burden.

The first step should be to study the colonial system of the other powers in the Far East. This will demand greater humbleness than we have been inclined to show in the past, but it should be more than recompensed by our subsequent pride in work better done. The lessons of the Dutch will probably prove the most valuable to us as so many of their problems in the Netherlands East Indies have been like ours in the Philippines. Their system is by no means perfect. From it, however, we can learn much of value—what not to do as well as what to do. Congress, therefore, should provide for a commission of experts to visit Java, India, Ceylon, the Straits Settlements, French Indo-China and the Philippines to study colonial administration with a view to recommending a more efficient form of government than that which we now have in the Philippines. This would take the place of the proposed biennial visit to the Islands of a committee of Senators and Representatives—a plan that would afford unlimited opportunity for delaying decisions and would give the Filipino politicians a new method of trying to deprive the American Governor-General of the support of the home government.

The next step is for the American people to make it clear that they have no intention of relinquishing the Islands for at least two or three generations. This will end the agitation by the politicians and will afford time to begin the economic development of the Islands, so profitable to the Filipinos and so useful to us. We have made a success of big business in America. Only by applying to the utmost our capacity for organization can we cope with the infinite handicaps of a tropical people and climate, and wring prosperity out of inertia.

Not the political, but the economic and educational factors are fundamental. The task is to develop the latent wealth of the Philippines so that the Filipinos will have that sound economic foundation on which alone a self-sustaining state can meet world competition.

Relieving the Filipino peoples of the burden of ill health so that they can better compete with their fellows, and carrying through with thoroughness a campaign of education that will prepare the people to look after their own affairs are prerequisites to merely political problems. In considering possible new forms of relationship between the United States and the Philippines, that one should be chosen which holds the greatest promise of hastening these preparatory processes.

The Filipino politicians have consistently pretended that we do not intend to give them the greatest amount of autonomy that they can capably bear. They know, however, that we have nothing to gain by exercising political control over local affairs. In fact, over the entire Insular Government we need only sufficient power to check unwise, inefficient or corrupt practices and to halt sinister efforts to block the progressive development of the Filipinos toward self-sufficiency. American supervision must be complete enough to be constructive, but more than this is unnecessary. There neither is nor ever has been any desire to "exploit" the Philippines. In the relation between the United States and the Philippines during the quarter of a century of American occupation the Filipinos have been immeasurably the gainers. We need not expect gratitude from them, but we must insist on a frank recognition, at least on the part of the politicos, that the existing obligations are mutual. To date the Filipinos have singularly failed to give that share of cooperation which is their part of the bargain.

In all discussions of the Philippines it must be to me in mind that the Islands, as pointed out in Chapter VI, cannot be taken out of their geographical framework. Our Philippine policy will have its repercussion throughout Asia. It will be watched in India and China. It will affect even the great world of Islam that stretches from Mindanao to Morocco. As the well-known Swedish historian, Rudolf Kjellen, quaintly phrased it, the United States is a sort of "geographical Janus" with one face toward Europe and the other toward Asia. During the last fifty years only the eyes and ears of the Atlantic face have been open. Now at last we are beginning to look across the Pacific. Whatever our attitude toward Europe and the League of Nations we cannot remain aloof from Asia. We are, in fact, an Asiatic power, and developments in Eastern Asia are of great concern to us. It will not be long before our national prosperity will be affected by any serious interference with our trade with China and the tropical East. As our surplus of exportable merchandise increases, our commerce with Asia will assume greater importance. The late James J. Hill foresaw this more than thirty years ago, and in building his railroads in the Northwest had in mind the ultimate transportation of the products of Asia across the continent. It may not be possible to do as some of the American business men in the Philippines want, and establish a great *entrepot* in Manila, making that the port of distribution for American products throughout Asia. The distance from the Pacific Coast to Manila is so much greater than to Shanghai that freight rates are a serious handicap. But Manila may well become the port of transshipment for our equatorial trade. It is and will surely remain the base of our naval power on which rests our prestige. The late Theodore Roosevelt always insisted that the 20th century would be the century of the Pacific. He might have added that the Philippines are our key to the Pacific.

History shows that the golden age of a nation and its period of most flourishing overseas commerce have usually coincided. Greece, Rome, Venice, Spain, Holland, England—all reached their greatest cultural heights at the time of the development of their great foreign trade. Even in our own history the New England that produced Emerson, Thoreau, Channing, Prescott, Motley and Parkman, was the New England of the China trade and clipper ships.

As it was in the last century so it may be again, and with the development of the United States as a great maritime and naval power we may see a cultural renaissance such as that which took place in England during her period of great overseas expansion.

If we decide to make the Philippines a model of efficient colonial administration, and to develop the vast resources of the Islands to the profit of all concerned, we shall earn the respect of the world. Failure, through sentimentality, to change the governmental system of half-measures created by the Jones Law will cause the story of our political relations with the Philippines to pass into history as a chronicle of misguided good intentions. If we withdraw before our task is done, it will be recorded to our shame, and throughout the East we shall have the reproaches of the Europeans and the scorn of the Asiatics. Our Philippine policy is not a domestic but an international issue. It affects all of Eastern Asia as well as ourselves and the Filipinos, by what we do there we shall be judged throughout the world.

A great treasure is in our hands—but a great problem.

4. Box 59 Dispatches from Hungary 1930–1933, Nicholas Roosevelt Papers

As indicated in my telegram No. 20 of July 5, 5 p.m., a serious crisis in Hungary's financial affairs has been averted—at least temporarily—and arrangements have finally been made looking toward the reorganization of Hungary's finances. At the same time sufficient short-term credits are being provided so as to prevent a collapse of the Hungarian currency and to make it possible for the Government to carry on for a number of months in the face of the present acute economic depression.

The Department is aware from previous despatches [sic] that for months the financial position of the Government has become constantly weaker and that the Government has attempted to hide the true facts and has done nothing to try to avert financial disaster. The situation was bad enough in the middle of May. The announcement at that time that the Austrian Creditanstalt had collapsed was followed by constantly increasing withdrawals of short-term credits from Hungarian banks. These banks were thus forced to call on the Hungarian National Bank for support in order to obtain funds to repay demands which they would otherwise have been unable to meet. The position of the National Bank, as reported in my telegram No. 15 of June 25, 3 p.m., and despatch [sic] No. 122 of June 29, had become steadily worse since February. These extra demands for assistance from various Hungarian banking organizations not only exhausted the reserve of foreign exchange which the National Bank held but also placed such a strain on that institution's credit that it had secretly to turn for help to the Bank of International Settlements.

On June 30, I had a long talk with one of the directors if the National Bank who is most active in its affairs, Dr. Bela Schober, and found him frankly afraid for the fate of his institution. He told me that instead of a hundred million pengös of short-term credits having been withdrawn from Hungarian banks by foreign creditors the sum had by that day reached 130 million pengös. He pointed out that the gold reserves were severely depleted and that, despite the credit of 15 million dollars secretly obtained from the Bank of International Settlements, the continued demands on the National Bank were placing it under a desperate strain.

On July 4, Dr. René Charron, who, like Mr. Royall Tyler, had been one of Mr. Jeremiah Smith, Junior's, principal assistants in the control of Hungary's finances, told me that during the previous week he had been in constant conferences with the directors of the National Bank, with Count Bethlen and with various private bankers in Budapest. The position of the National Bank, he said, had become so desperate that unless drastic measures were taken immediately it would be impossible to prevent the inflation of the currency and the collapse of the bank with serious consequences for Hungary. He told me, as I reported in my telegram of July 5, that he had informed the Prime Minister on July 2 that unless something were done by July 4 it would be impossible to stave off the calamity. I asked him if Count Bethlen appeared to have grasped at last the seriousness of the situation and Mr. Charron replied that there was no longer any doubt that he understood it. He said, furthermore, that he was satisfied that Count Bethlen would now push through the necessary reforms.

Mr. Charron, while ostensibly representing the firm of Lee Higginson and Co., in reality came to Budapest to study Hungary's finances for the Bank of International Settlements and the Bank of England. He appears to have been authorized by the B. I. S. to conduct negotiations in its name, and succeeded on July 4 in making an agreement between the Prime Minister, a group of Hungarian banks headed by the Commercial Bank, and the Bank of International Settlements, apparently representing various central banks in Europe. A translation of this agreement, which must be considered as secret, is attached hereto as Annex I and formed the basis of my telegram No. 20. It provides that the Government shall put through Parliament, when it convenes on July 18, a law granting full powers to the Prime Minister, or his agents, to effect the administrative and fiscal reform necessary for a reestablishment of a budgetary equilibrium. The powers thus granted are to run at least for the current fiscal year. Similar powers were granted to the Prime Minister's office during the reorganization of Hungary's finance under the control of Mr. Smith.

The local banks, headed by the Commercial Bank, agree for their part to arrange for the placing of 25 million dollars of 18 month treasury certificates of which 20% is to be taken up in Hungary by these banks and the balance placed abroad through their intermediary. This provision is important because it places Hungary in the position of participating in her own rehabilitation. At the same time it is calculated to reestablish confidence on the part of foreign leaders owing to the fact that the principal agent for the bank is Mr. Philipp Weiss, President of the Commercial Bank, who is regarded throughout Europe as the ablest banker in Hungary. His institution is known to be one of the soundest and most conservative banks on the Continent. It should be noted that Paragraph 3 of the Annex specifically provides that the Hungarian Government will guarantee the contributions made by the Hungarian banks. Mr. Charron warned me that this provision would at no time be made public. It should be noted as it suggests on a very small scale that the Hungarian Government in an emergency is not unwilling to follow a course somewhat like that which the Austrian Government followed with respect to the Creditanstalt.

While not included in the attached copy of the agreement, Mr. Charron informed me that the Bank of International Settlements on its part would advance 10 million dollars to the Hungarian National Bank. This is an addition to the 15 million dollars already secretly advanced. I understand that these 10 million dollars will form part of the 25 million dollars of short-term credits which is provided for in the above-mentioned agreement. Inasmuch as the Hungarian banks agree to take 5 million dollars, it means that only 10 million dollars are left to be raised abroad. The Hungarian newspapers of yesterday (July 6) carried the report that the negotiations for this credit of 25 million dollars had been completed. I have no definite information that this is so, but I feel certain that the money will be obtained shortly.

This arrangement is of course only of temporary value serving the purpose of enabling the Government to exist financially during the next six months. It is not without significance that in a printed statement, Mr. Philipp Weiss, President of the Commercial Bank and the principal spokesman for the bankers in this arrangement, implies that the sum of 25 million dollars may not be adequate and adds that further discussions are being held on this point.

As indicated in my telegram No. 20, Mr. Charron estimates that a minimum of 70 million dollars in long-term loans is needed in order to enable the Government to make a clean start financially. It will be noted that Dr. Schober of the National Bank expressed his opinion to me last week that 50 million dollars might suffice. This sum would be used not only to cover the fiscal deficit but also to refund the outstanding short-term obligations.

It is interesting to note that the statement of Mr. Philipp Weiss, already referred to, lays principal emphasis on the good security that can be furnished by Hungary for a long-term loan. He points out that the revenues set aside to cover the service of the League of Nations Reconstruction Loan are seven times greater than the sum actually needed for interest and amortization. From this he deduces that there is ample security for the flotation of a new long-term loan of from 100 to 200 million dollars. In my opinion Dr. Weiss' views on this subject should be taken with reserve. He is obviously talking for home consumption, as the general financial position of the Hungarian State does not warrant the assumption that the budget can carry an extra 40 to 80 million pengös a year which would be the service charge on a loan such as he mentions.

The possibility of floating such a loan will depend largely on the ability and energy with which the Prime Minister undertakes the necessary administrative reforms to cut expenses and increase revenues within the next few months. Unless he acts promptly, fearlessly and drastically another crisis may again occur.

Respectfully yours,
N. Roosevelt to Henry L. Stimson, No. 128, July 7, 1931.

Enclosure.
1. The Hungarian Government agrees to put through Parliament, as soon as that body convenes, a law granting the Government full powers during a definite period in order to carry out a program of administrative and fiscal reform having as its object the reestablishment, as soon as possible, of budgetary equilibrium, both by effecting economy in expenses and by increasing receipts. This law, granting full powers to the Government, should remain in force at least until the end of the current fiscal year.

2. The Government will confide to a syndicate of local banks the task of preparing for the placing, as soon as possible, of (1) millions of Treasury certificates, payable in (2) months, to be taken up in part (3) by local banks and the remainder by foreign banks both, if possible, payable in foreign currency. This operation is designed to furnish the Government with the necessary operating funds now lacking, as well as to replenish the National Bank's supply of foreign currency.

3. The Hungarian Government will charge the Commercial Bank of Pest, as soon as the Treasury certificates are issued, to communicate with local financial institutions and with the principal short-term foreign creditors with a view to preventing the possible danger of further precipitate withdrawals of foreign capital. These local banks, which will be charged with this operation, will agree to contribute the means at their disposal, each one of them individually determining the amount of its contribution; it being understood that the Hungarian Government will guarantee these contributions thus made available to the market.

Note: £8,000,000 (1)
   18 months (2)
   20% (3)

Above figures were given to the Minister verbally by Mr. Charron, and were later publicly confirmed.

CONFIDENTIAL.
MEMORANDUM ON SAFEGUARDING INVESTORS (without date, sometime after May 1932).

APPENDIX

Criticism of American bankers for floating loans now in default has elicited partisan explanations that have done little to answer three fundamental questions affecting the interest of American investors in foreign securities:

1, What part, if any, of the losses incurred by American investors in foreign securities might have been avoided?

2, What can be done to salvage as much as possible for the bondholders?

3, What can be done to prevent reckless lending in the future?

Reasons for Defaults.

Unfortunately, the bankers and brokers of America share their fellow-countrymen's ignorance of foreign affairs. Their lack of comprehension of the interplay of foreign financial and political conditions and the reaction of international politics and international finance does not, however, exonerate them from blame in connection with unsound loans to foreign governments and enterprises—loans too often made under the stress of competition and without adequate study of the true nature of the issues involved. American officials abroad can bear witness to the superficiality of the investigations made by most of the representatives of American financial business houses wishing to place loans in Europe and South America. So also can Mr. S. Parker Gilbert, who, as Agent General of Reparations in Germany, issued repeated warnings against the unsound nature of many of the loans being advanced by American and other bankers to Germany. But the issuing houses ignored his advice. In Germany and elsewhere they competed for the privilege (and the commissions) of lending, deaf to the warnings of persons on the spot who knew local conditions better than did their agents.

It is only fair to the bankers and brokers, however, to recognize that mistakes of ignorance and judgment are not alone responsible for the present low levels at which so many foreign securities are selling. Defaults and temporary suspensions of payment in part or in full are due to all manner of causes, amongst which figure largely the drop in world prices, the excessive trade restrictions imposed since the credit crisis of 1929, the abandonment of the gold standard, the obstacles resulting from the so-called "transfer problem," the basic insolvency of some countries due to inherent poverty or excessive borrowing, and the effects of bad faith on the part of individual debtors. Nothing is gained by attempting to assign the major portion of the blame to any one of these causes, but unless and until they are all recognized it is impossible to form a fair estimate of the probable capacity to pay off the different debtors.

Only a few instances are necessary to clarify this. In certain countries of Central Europe, for example, defaults have occurred due to the difficulty of obtaining foreign exchange to effect payments. In other words, the ultimate debtor is solvent but circumstances prevent him from transferring payments. In other countries debtors have used the world economic depression as an excuse to bring pressure on their creditors with the purpose of avoiding or reducing their just obligations. Some loans are in default for the simple reason that they were essentially unsound when floated. In still other cases payments in foreign currency could probably be made if trade returned to the 1930 level.

Need for a Salvaging Organization.
Without attempting to assess all the causes of default, it is pertinent to consider what can be done to minimize the losses of American investors who bought foreign securities that have since defaulted. Unfortunately, the bankers and brokers have been less interested in salvaging the long-term debts which they "passed on" to the public than in seeking to save what they can of the short-term credits which they advanced directly out of their own funds. Hence but little concerted effort has been made to deal with this problem. In England, where the "international bankers" made mistakes a century ago that closely paralleled those of our own bankers since the World War, a bondholder protective association was formed for the purpose of endeavoring to recoup as much as possible of the enormous volume of defaulted foreign bonds in possession of British investors. An idea of the work of this committee may be judged from the fact that in the course of its existence it has arranged settlements on defaults totaling the staggering sum of more than $5,000,000,000.

So long as American investors are not represented by such an organization whereas the English and other foreign investors are so represented, the Americans will find it harder to obtain fair treatment than will foreign claimants. Furthermore, so long as the American investors are disunited, it is difficult to invoke diplomatic protection in their behalf. As a rule rival national interests are seeking privileges for their own creditors at the expense of other foreign claimants. Hence the player of the lone hand finds the cards stacked against him, and his ignorance of basic conditions further handicaps him. He lacks the strength that comes from union, and is often checked by the activities of other American creditors working by themselves. If American interests are to be best served they must be represented by delegates empowered to speak for all creditors, carrying the prestige of a group that is well organized and powerful.

A plea for the formation of an American bondholders' protective association was made by Mr. Allen W. Dulles in an article in "FOREIGN AFFAIRS" for April 1932, entitled "The Protection of American Foreign Bondholders." The function of such an organization would be to coordinate and supplement work already being done along these lines by such organizations as the Institute of International Finance and the Foreign Securities Committee of the Investment Bankers Association, not to mention other periodic groups working to protect the holders of certain specific issues of foreign bonds. This organization need not be elaborate nor costly, and should be comprised of a council representing various investment issuing houses, together with a small permanent personnel. Its function would be to obtain and distribute information about financial and economic conditions in foreign countries in which American investors are interested, and to represent the bondholders in negotiations with foreign governments and individual creditors whenever this could be effectively done—either at international conferences or in direct negotiations with the debtor governments or individuals. In other words this association would serve as the central agency for performing in the interest of bondholders such services as American bankers initiated in connection with Mexico after the defaults of recent years. It would be empowered to recommend to the investors to make settlements at less than face value if this should appear desirable, or to participate in refunding operations or take any other action which local circumstances dictate.

Special Knowledge and Technique Required.
Such representatives, if they are to avoid repeating the mistakes of individual American creditors seeking settlements with their debtors during the last eighteen months, must recognize that the debtors in no two countries suffer from the same handicaps. The negotiations of the "standstill agreements" respecting the short-term debts of Austria and Hungary, for example, were delayed and complicated by the persistent belief of the New York bankers that the basic conditions in these countries were the same as in Germany. Hence they sought to apply the terms of the German settlement to Austria and Hungary. As a matter of fact, in Germany the problem of paying foreign creditors was intimately involved with international political questions such as reparations. Basically the country was able to produce and, despite momentary troubles, to obtain a big enough favorable balance of payments to be able to resume remittances to its creditors. In Czechoslovakia the volume of foreign debts was very small and the producing capacity of the country remained large, but transfer restrictions were imposed as a precautionary measure. In Austria the transfer restrictions were due to the essentially unbalanced economic life of the

country which made a large excess of imports over exports inevitable, without adequate compensation in the form of invisible items. In Hungary the troubles were due to reckless and excessive borrowing by a basically impoverished country, which, like all of the Eastern European States, suffered severely from the agricultural crisis. In Rumania the problem was largely budgetary, and hence political, due in no small degree to the misappropriation of public funds. In Yugoslavia political questions, both internal and external, aggravated the weakness of the Government's financial position.

Future Lending Must Be Supervised.
These local differences concern not only creditors whose bonds are now in default, but also present and future creditors of all classes. It is not enough, therefore, merely to salvage. The interests of present foreign bondholders will need protection when new credits are again offered abroad so that there will not be a repetition of the policy of reckless lending which did so much to bring about the present world crisis.

A precedent for such work exists in the second Chinese consortium which was formed by groups of bankers from the principal creditor countries for the purpose of preventing unwise lending to China and for safeguarding the interests of loans already placed in that country. While the parallel is not absolute, the principle involved is the same, namely, that a committee should be formed in each of the principal creditor countries which should designate a member to sit on an international board for the purpose of supervising new loans to European and Latin American countries and at the same time to protect investments already made. The difficulties in the way of the creation of such a group may prove insurmountable. French financial policy in particular is so intertwined with French political ambitions that France may be unwilling to "play the game." Nevertheless, even if the group were to consist only of English, American and Dutch investment bankers, it could do much to check unwise lending.

American investors, so long unprotected, would gain from the existence of an American group authorized to examine and express an opinion—if not to pass judgment—on all new foreign loans offered in the American market. By serving as a clearing house of information about conditions in foreign countries and their foreign debts such a committee could do for long-term securities what Mr. Montague Norman recently regretted had not been done by the American and British banks that advanced short-term credits to Germany and other Central European countries—enable the lenders to know how much money their rivals and associate were advancing abroad and so avoid the multiplication of loans to individual concerns or governments to such an extent as to threaten the ultimate solvency of the borrower and to invite disaster for all lenders alike.

Unfortunately, American bankers and investment houses not only resent restrictions on their freedom of action but are also hesitant about cooperating with their fellow-bankers and brokers, even when such cooperation is clearly in their own interests. This renders difficult the formation even of an American group. At the same time it emphasizes the need for such a group, as the experiences of the last fifteen years of foreign financing shows only too clearly the evils of competition instead of cooperation in foreign lending and the inevitable losses due to what might be termed "blind loans"—that is to say advances, either short-term or long-term, made without full knowledge of the debtors' other commitments. To mention two cases in point, it is inconceivable that American bankers would have extended as large credits to the Austrian Creditanstalt as they did had they been fully aware of that institution's other borrowings from abroad. Likewise, if American borrowings and investment brokers had been aware of the rapidity with which Hungary was accumulating an enormous debt—the country having since the war amassed a per capita debt that is almost half again as great as that of Germany—they would surely not have continued to put money into Hungary. Had there been such as organization as is now proposed it could have helped check this reckless lending and so have prevented ultimate losses for American bondholders.

Salvaging and Supervising Closely Related.
Inasmuch as the work of helping to recoup the losses incurred through the foreign bonds already in default touches in many ways the work of preventing future unwise lending, the permanent staff on the bondholders protective association could at the same time serve as the permanent staff of the consortium group. There might be advantages in having a separate board or council of directors for the two groups, even though each would be selected largely from members of the same issuing banks or brokerage houses. But their function would overlap, and much of the information which they would obtain would be of value to both groups.

The exact details of the organization of these groups can only be determined after extensive study. But unless American bankers and brokers are willing to adopt some such cooperative measures as these they will not have profited from the lessons of post-war financing. To paraphrase the famous saying of Benjamin Franklin, either they must work together or they will fail separately—and with them will suffer most of their clients—future as well as past.

5. Nicholas Roosevelt, "Franklin Delano Roosevelt," *The American Mercury* 39, no. 155 (November 1936): 329–331.

Those who know him best say that he is politically astute but not politically wise—that he is smart but not deep. He reacts to public opinion with extraordinary sensitiveness, but he never stops to think things through. Although his ability to collect information is excellent, his mental processes are essentially shallow. New labels catch his fancy readily—especially when they glitter with vote-winning possibilities. He has the easy optimism of the sheltered rich; hence he hails the most impractical schemes as plausible. Benevolence is one of his dominant traits; but it is the benevolence of the patrician who feels that he can best help his people because he knows what they should have. He complacently promises anything to anyone, regardless of his inability to make good on most of his promises. Above all he is an opportunist, ready to change his destination and his principles with every new wind.

This chameleon-like quality has made it possible for Franklin Delano Roosevelt to pose as a great Liberal at the same time that he is fostering reactionary activities. Because he does not think things through, he is unaware that the New Deal is basically paternalistic. No doubt he sincerely believes he is a plumed Progressive. Yet he is, in fact, the unconscious leader of world reaction in America today.

In this the President is running true to form. Few public men have ever had greater sensitiveness to currents of popular thought—and reaction is the order of the day. In Europe it has triumphed everywhere outside of Great Britain, Scandinavia, Holland, and Switzerland, thanks to the advocates of one or other of the many forms of paternalism. Popular government has been thrown out the window. The rights of the individual to freedom of thought and freedom of expression—and often even freedom of initiative—have been crushed. It was inevitable that these currents of reaction should drift across the Atlantic. The responsive Mr. Roosevelt—his extraordinary antennae atingle—sensed the changes in the air. His advisers brought him reactionary proposals dressed in attractive labels of new Liberalism. Because these proposals seemed to have popular appeal, he embraced them, insisting shrewdly that they were parts of a "New Deal." This was good politics. But because his mind is mercurial rather than profound, he confused novelty of labels with fresh ideas.

Mr. Roosevelt, of course, would deny vigorously that he has placed himself at the head of the forces of reaction, but the record is there to prove it. And some of his enemies believe that the record of the New Deal is a reflection of his own personality. Because he is vindictive when people have turned against him, and because he cannot tolerate men of true ability, they say that he has the instincts of a dictator.

He has, it is true, the supreme self-confidence which is essential for the success of a Caesar, a Mussolini, or a Hitler. He also enjoys power for its own sake. But he lacks the ruthlessness, the constancy of purpose and the fanatical determination to achieve a specific end, which seem to be characteristic of the true dictator.

Instead, he is eager to make people happy and comfortable. It has even been said of him that his ideal of the More Abundant Life is a butler in every home.

But in his readiness to accept measures that strengthen his powers, Mr. Roosevelt, as in so many other matters, seems unaware of the implications of his acts. He, who may not wish to be a dictator, nevertheless has lent himself to the creation of new machinery of government which, in the hands of a less benevolent ruler, might well be used to set up a Fascist State. He has sought to control the nation's industries and agriculture. He has prepared the way for government control of credit. He has made a rubber stamp of Congress and has established government by decree. All these things tend towards paternalism—and away from the American system.

To Mr. Roosevelt, the Constitution is apparently an out-moded document, drafted in the horse-and-buggy days. He believes that the powers of the Supreme Court can constrict too effectively the Presidential initiative. He feels that the Constitution is too rigid and old-fashioned to be workable. This is in sharp contrast with his characterization of the Constitution in 1930 as "the most marvelously elastic compilation of rules of government ever written." And here again the apparent contradiction is traceable to the conflicting elements in Mr. Roosevelt's character. In 1930 he sincerely believed what he said about the Constitution; in fact, he was an ardent advocate of States' Rights and an opponent of strengthening the national government. But by 1935, the Constitution had thwarted him. His reaction was like that of a spoiled child checked by a power which it cannot circumvent.

So angry was he when the Supreme Court ruled out the NRA that he, ordinarily good-natured in his public relations, followed the extraordinary procedure of summoning the press and for an hour and a half indulging in a bitter attack on all that the decision implied as a check on social progress. He spoke in the name of Liberalism, but he failed to see that in this instance it was the Constitution which had protected the cause of Liberalism and that he himself had been the advocate of reaction in the guise of paternalism. He seemed unaware that it was against just such policies as his that the framers of the Constitution had deliberately guarded, and that they had done so because they realized that Liberalism needed special protection from the tendencies of government to augment its own powers.

Mr. Roosevelt and the New Dealers now insist that they never even contemplated any change in the Constitution—let alone any change in the American form of government. This is all very well for campaign purposes. It is even conceivable that Mr. Roosevelt himself—prior to the Supreme Court's invalidation of the NRA—did not realize that any change in government was even implied in the New Deal. Mr. Roosevelt, as already explained, rarely looks below the surface of the waters. But the facts speak plainly.

The whole concept of the New Deal is that a paternalistic federal government shall look after its people. There is no question that so long as Mr. Roosevelt is President, government will be benevolent as well as paternalistic. Benevolence, as has been already explained, is one of his outstanding traits. But a paternalistic government, however benevolent, is nevertheless reactionary. It is the antithesis of the American system. When, incidentally, a paternalistic government is not benevolent, it becomes the Germany of Hitler or the Russia of Stalin.

We are, thank Heaven, still far removed from this possibility. But if the reactionary forces which Mr. Roosevelt has done so much to strengthen are successful in putting him back into office, true Liberalism will have a desperate fight to survive. Mr. Roosevelt's very affability and warmheartedness will be dangerous because they will help him continue to delude people into regarding him as a Liberal. For some strange reason, Liberals are usually supposed to be kindly, benevolent, charming people, and reactionaries sour, selfish, and sinister. Mr. Roosevelt has all the "front" of the perfect Liberal. This makes him all the more useful to those reactionaries who, in the name of a New Deal and a More Abundant Life, are following in America the course that has destroyed democratic Liberalism in Europe. Mr. Roosevelt has identified himself with the reactionaries. This is why true progressives now oppose him.

6. Nicholas Roosevelt, "Partners for Peace," November 27, 1941, Folder: Lectures—Mills College 1941, Box 59, Nicholas Roosevelt Papers.

A famous French economist, author and lecturer, Professor Andre Siegfried, wrote a book fifteen years ago which was translated into English under the title "America Comes of Age." The United States has, indeed, come of age, but in international affairs it still tends to conduct itself with complacent irresponsibility.

I realize that in saying this I am treading on a controversy which has torn the country wide open. But we cannot see clearly where we are going unless we are prepared to meet controversial issues frankly. This does not mean to meet them with such slogans as "interventionist" and "isolationist." These are epithets rather than descriptions of policy. So intolerantly have they been abused that they arouse emotional responses, whereas the record should be examined in cold reason.

The record shows beyond question that no nation can bury its head in the sand and say smugly: "What happens elsewhere does not concern us." In these days of universal radio and stratoplanes, when it takes an airplane less than seven hours to fly from Canada to England, and when men have dropped bombs in Berlin one afternoon and lunched in San Francisco the next noon, it is folly to pretend that any nation can exist in security, regardless of what goes on elsewhere in the world. To think that it can do so is to dream rather than to reason—to indulge in that most futile of all fanciful pastimes—thinking how nice it would be if the world were made of green cheese, or how pleasant it would be if only we had a million dollars. "If only"—those words are the gateway to self-delusion. They furnish an escape from reality, and invite an evasion of the truth. The truth is that we are in the midst of one of the greatest world crises of all time. We cannot ignore it. We cannot avoid its consequences. We cannot pretend that its outcome is of no concern to those of us in this room. It is of overwhelming concern, and I venture to predict that it will directly affect the lives of each one of us.

I know how hard it is for many of you to believe this. In July of 1914 I had just graduated from Harvard and had been appointed assistant to Professor Edward Channing in the American history department. I was engaged in research in the Federalist period of our history, studying manuscript material in the library of the Connecticut Historical Society at Hartford. Each day I spent reading original letters in the handwriting of Alexander Hamilton, George Cabot, Fisher Ames, Rufus King and other members of the Federalist party. And each afternoon, as I passed the office of the Hartford Courant, I glanced at the summarized bulletins in the window. On July 31st these read: "Germany presents Russia with Ultimatum." On

August 3rd they read: "Germany invades Belgium." I glanced at them with a certain amount of curiosity, and hurried on to the home of the cousins with whom I was staying in Farmington. In the morning I returned to my dusty volumes of early American letters, as indifferent to the news from Europe as if it were news from Mars. Little did I realize that as a by-product of the acts of Germans whose names I did not even know, I should find myself within three months in war-torn France, and within three years an officer in the A.E.F.—I, who knew nothing of war, never dreamed of being a soldier, and who, had someone told me that an American expeditionary force would soon be sent to Europe, would have been utterly incredulous. Ever since then the World War has profoundly influenced my life. Can anyone pretend that its resumption two years ago—for that is just what happened—it was resumed—will not continue to affect my life—and yours?

I use the word "resumption" advisedly. With our fondness for labels we have fallen into the custom of speaking of "World War I" and "World War II." This is as misleading as is the accepting of an arbitrary date, such as 1914, or 1814, or 1939 as the boundary beyond which we cease to trace causes and origins. Periods in history do not have a clearly defined beginning or end. They form part of an endless chain of events.

Let me be specific. We have repeatedly heard that this war is the result of a thing called "Hitlerism" and that this "Hitlerism" is something new in the world. It began to take shape, we are told, when Hitler came to power in 1933.

This is a superficial point of view. What Hitler did was to give new life to a German policy which had been in the process of formation for more than two generations. You will find most of Hitler's ideas about the domination of Europe and the world by the master German race set forth by such German writers as Friedrich Naumann and Paul Rohrback a generation ago. These ideas were part of the thinking of the German high command before the outbreak of the war in 1914. They were held by hundreds of thousands of Germans even in the days of Germany's greatest weakness in 1922 and '23. They were repeated to me by Germans within six weeks after the armistice of 1918 when I was a member of a delegation sent to Vienna by the American Commission to Negotiate Peace. The point of view of the Germans with whom I spoke was that Germany had not lost the war, but that events had made it expedient for the Germans to stop fighting for the present. "This is only an interruption," one of them explained to me. "When the time comes we shall take up the fight again and push on to victory."

Hitler injected into these ideas of Pan-Germanisn his own fanaticism. To put them into effect he resorted to absolutism of the baldest kind. In so doing he set back the hands of the clock to those early days before parliamentarianism or political liberalism had become forces in the world. The kind of dictatorship that he established was not new. It was old—as old as ancient Rome, or ancient Persia, or Babylonia. He simply streamlined what the ancients called tyranny. His success is a matter of history.

The genius of Hitler lies not in the originality of his thinking—for it is in no sense original—but in his application of a very simple principle: "One at a time." The more classical expression of this doctrine is "Divide and conquer." It is one of the oldest and soundest strategies. If you have two enemies, drive a wedge between them. If you are fighting only one, and you can weaken him at home, do so. Once Hitler convinced himself that the great nations of the world would not join together to prevent international highway robbery his course was clear. He began where opposition and reaction was likely to be least—by sending his troops into the Rhineland, from which, under the terms of the Versailles treaty, they were excluded. I have talked with well informed Germans about this. They are agreed that the German troops had orders to withdraw immediately if they met with any resistance from the French and British. But the leaders of these two countries were divided about taking a "strong" stand. Hitler correctly deduced that they were afraid to risk a showdown.

His next move was to occupy a territory which he and others passionately insisted was German Austria. When, again, the allies did nothing but bluster, he knew he was the master of Europe. Next he took the German sections of Czechoslovakia. Then the rest of that country. Then the formerly German territories of Danzig and Polish East Prussia. In every case the British and French expressed their indignation but did nothing either to help their friends and allies or to save themselves. Both nations deluded themselves that they could buy safety by appeasement. Each successive mouthful whetted Hitler's appetite and increased his scorn for his enemies.

Doubtless Hitler thought that Poland, also, would be sacrificed by the British and French in the hope of peace. But it wasn't. Too late, they saw that only force would halt him. This did not change his tactics. It only modified them. He annihilated Poland, and paused for breath preparatory to resuming his policy of one at a time. In April 1940, without warning, he took, in quick succession, Denmark and Norway. Another pause. A month later it was the Low Countries—Holland and Belgium. Still another pause. Then France. A long pause. Then Rumania. Then Hungary. Then Bulgaria. (These three by threat and blackmail, rather than by military occupation. They have given him full military cooperation.) Then Yugoslavia. Then Greece. Then Russia.

With each successive step he announced positively and definitely that he was satisfied—that he wanted nothing further. Let me quote his very words to you:

On May 21, 1935, he said: "Germany neither intends nor wishes to interfere in the internal affairs of Austria, to annex Austria or to conclude an anschluss [sic]."

Yet on March 12, 1938, Germany annexed Austria.

With regard to Czechoslovakia he said, right after the Munich settlement, on September 26, 1938: "We have assured all our immediate neighbors of the integrity of their territory as far as Germany is concerned. That is no hollow phrase; it is our sacred will.... The Sudetenland is the last territorial claim which I have to make in Europe.... I have assured Mr. Chamberlain, and I emphasize it now, that when this problem is solved Germany has no other territorial problems in Europe."

Yet in October, 1938, Germany occupied the Sudetenland and on March 14, 1939, occupied the rest of Czechoslovakia.

About Poland he said, on May 21, 1935: "Germany has concluded a non-aggression pact with Poland which is more than a valuable contribution to European peace, and she will adhere to it unconditionally." And, again, on September 26, 1938: "We are all determined, and also convinced, that our agreement (with Poland) will bring about lasting and continuous pacification.... We are two peoples. They shall live."

Yet on September 1, 1939, Germany invaded Poland.

With respect to the Low Countries he declared on September 26, 1938: "The new Reich has endeavored to continue the traditional friendship with Holland.... Immediately after I had taken over the government I tried to establish friendly relations with Belgium." And on October 6, 1939, he added: We have given guarantees for the states in the west."

Yet on May 10, 1940, Germany invaded Holland and Belgium.

But the list is not yet complete. On June 1, 1939, he said: "I believe in this all the more since a solidly founded and trustful relationship of Germany toward Yugoslavia—now that through historic events we have become neighbors with common borders established for all time—will not only secure a permanent peace between our two peoples and countries but beyond that will provide an element of calm for our jittery continent."

Yet on April 6, 1941, Germany invaded Yugoslavia.

As for Russia—here are the terms from the non-aggression pact between Germany and Russia which Hitler signed on August 24, 1939: "The German Reich government and the Union of the Soviet Socialist Republics ... have decided the following:

Article I

"The two contracting parties obligate themselves to refrain from every act of force, every aggressive action and every attack against one another, including any single action or that taken in conjunction with other powers."

Yet on June 22, 1941, Germany invaded Russia.

Nobody questions that Great Britain is next on the list. If she goes, the United States will be alone in the new world—alone to face the most powerful, the most ruthless and the most successful military machine mankind has ever seen. And do not delude yourselves into thinking that Hitler would permit us to go our own way. We would be, as I have already pointed out, public enemy number one for the simple reason that we would be the only power in the world that could interfere with his plans and ambitions.

As a matter of fact, Hitler has already been using within the United States the very same tactics that have been so successful elsewhere. His agents, playing on the Americans' hatred of war, have been skillfully dividing the American people. They have sought to stir up racial jealousies among the foreign born. They figure that by encouraging the opposition to the President's foreign policy they can paralyze his actions, and that by fostering strikes in American defense industries they can weaken the affectiveness [sic] of the American defense effort. Make no mistake about it. Every serious embarrassment to the President's conduct of foreign policy, every strike, every increase in internal discord in the United States, plays into Hitler's hands.

The lesson is so plain that I marvel that there are still Americans who fail to understand it. Whether or not we want war has nothing to do with it. Hitler's other victims made the same mistakes. They refused to believe that Hitler was willing to fight, and continued, until actually invaded, to hope that he was merely bluffing. By their failure to get together in time to take joint action to stop him, they became his successive victims.

If, in August of 1939, the world had believed that Hitler would attack one nation after another—neutrals included—the reaction to his initial moves would have been different. So also, if it had been made clear beyond any possible doubt to Hitler that he would face the united opposition of Great Britain, France, Holland, Belgium, Poland, Russia and the United States, it is inconceivable that he would have attempted to make war. Yet because each nation said complacently, as incident followed incident, "This is no concern of ours," these steps became in very truth their nemesis. They delivered themselves into the hands of their enemy through their own blindness and folly.

The success of Hitler's method can be traced to events which occurred even before he came to power. The starting point was the decision of Japan in September 1931, to tear up the Nine Power Treaty signed at Washington in 1922 and to occupy Manchuria. This treaty, you will remember, was drawn up for the express purpose of insuring the political and territorial integrity of China. We knew, in 1922—I saw "we" because I was present at most of the Washington conference—that Japan was eager to annex Manchuria. The treaty in which Japan pledged her word not to dismember China was part of a series of agreements, some of which made substantial concessions to Japan. It was the hope of all but the Japanese delegates to the Washington conference that these treaties would preserve the peace in the Pacific for many decades.

But in 1931, as I pointed out in my discussion of the challenge of the world revolution, Great Britain was passing through the worst economic crisis in its history. The Japanese leaders decided that the British would be so preoccupied that they would not bother to protest if Japan took that occasion to seize Manchuria. Accordingly, on the pretext that a Japanese railway guard had been murdered outside of Mukden, they proceeded to occupy this great province of China. The American Secretary of State, anxious to prevent the dismemberment of China and to preserve the treaty structure of the Washington Conference, called on the British Minister of Foreign Affairs to join in demanding that Japan cease such aggression. Unfortunately, Sir John Simon, the British Foreign Minister, replied that he was very sorry, but the British government did not feel that the Manchurian incident was its funeral. Sir John, of course, used more elegant language. But that was the substance of his reply.

That was the beginning of the rise of the era of brute force. It was the signal to Japan to go ahead and conquer China. The Japanese said to themselves that if the British would not join with the Americans there would be no effective opposition to their aggression. The rest is history. China is still trying to throw out the Japanese, and they continue to spread out and seize more Chinese territory. It could have been prevented if only the British and the Americans had worked together. But the British were too busy with their own problems to care about what was happening in remote Manchuria.

The failure of the powers to halt Japan in Manchuria paved the way for Italy's conquest of Ethiopia, and led directly to Hitler's aggression in Europe. The smaller nations with aggressive tendencies made up their minds that the larger nations would not join hands in stopping them. They guessed right. The ultimate result was the disastrous war which is now raging throughout the world.

This leads to the question—What caused this war?

It has been the fashion, as you know, to echo Hitler's denunciations of the Versailles treaty, and to say that the terms of this document made the present war inevitable. It has been described as virtually enslaving the German people after robbing them of their means of livelihood. I had a part—a very small part—in the making of the last peace—not as a negotiator, but merely as an observer studying and reporting on conditions in, and on the demands of, the small countries in Eastern Europe. I have since lived several years in that part of the world. And this much I can say—that although serious mistakes were made in the peace settlements, and injustices were done, the treaties helped millions of people realize long suppressed desires for nationhood. It freed Poles, Czechs, Croats and other peoples from alien domination, even though in the process, it brought smaller number of other nationalities under foreign yoke. The Germans suffered—of course—and had to pay an indemnity. But what they lost was as nothing compared to the systematic looting of an entire continent which they have carried out during the present war. They have stripped the conquered countries of their machinery and their animals. They have robbed them of their foods. They have even stolen the babies' blankets. Nothing—absolutely nothing—that was done to Germany at Versailles approaches in injustice or cruelty what Germany already has done to its present victims. Incidentally, compared to the treaty of Brest Litovsk which the Germans imposed on Russian in 1917 [*sic*], the Versailles treaty was kind and gentle.

Wars are not caused by peace treaties. They are caused by the greed and lust for power of certain nations. As a matter of fact, in retrospect, the greatest mistake of the Versailles treaty was not that it treated Germany too harshly, but that it failed to make adequate provisions to prevent Germany from rearming and starting the war anew.

I cannot sufficiently emphasize the fact that the present war is merely a resumption of Germany's policy before the last war. Hitler, as I have already explained, has given a new twist to the old policies. He has substituted a dictatorship for the Kaiser. He has carried the idea of the "Herren Volk"—the idea that Germans are the master race—to the logical conclusion that the function of "inferior" races is to serve the German masters. Thus he is organizing the conquered countries as Germany's vassals. He has expanded the old German ideal of "a place in the sun" into creating a great world empire to replace the British Empire. But the fundamentals are the same: Germany is destined by the Almighty to conquer the world and rule by force of arms.

Many people have expressed the belief that if Germany is defeated the Germans will abandon their passion for war. Why should they? The history of the Prussians is a history of wars. For generations the Germans people have been taught to glorify war. We cannot take the risk that the leopard will change its spots. We have to make sure that Germany will never be able to start another war with any prospect of victory. Do you realize that three times within the memory of my good mother, who is now in her eighty-fourth year, Germany has started a major war? Are we to permit a fourth war within another quarter century? That, it seems to me, is intolerable.

How, then, prevent it?

As I see it, there is only one way in which it can be done. This is for the strongest nations in the world to get together after this war and to enter into an iron-clad compact that they will use the full strength of their naval, military, air and economic forces against any nation anywhere which seeks to disturb the peace, or which uses force to try to take away from another nation something which it wants.

There must be, in other words, an international police force. This force must consist of the strong, rather than of the many. It must be prepared to act anywhere, at a moment's notice.

Who would make up this force?

Obviously the United States and the British Commonwealth of Nations, because they would be the strongest powers left in the world.

As a matter of fact, the combination of Great Britain and the United States would outweigh any power anywhere. Common sense would, of course, demand that these two nations would take steps to disarm Germany and to prevent any nation from attempting to rearm. It would be folly to base a peace on an international force and then permit one or more of the disarmed nations to do as Germany did after Versailles and build up sufficient armament to defy the international police force. As well, in civil life, permit paroled criminals to obtain all the guns that they need in order to resume a career of crime. If there is to be an international police force the use of arms must be strictly limited to that body. No merely national armed force can be permitted to exist other than the local police forces of each community and nation.

I realize that many objections can be raised to such a proposal. The most obvious is that it would, in effect, "freeze" the boundaries and the political arrangements that may be made when peace is re-established, and that if mistakes are made and injustices are incorporated into these treaties, there will be no redress. I can imagine the fervid denunciation by some new Hitler, saying that this system would fit the bonds of slavery on the German people for all time.

But these objections are easily answered. The agreement to use the armed force of the United States and Great Britain to preserve the peace does not mean that non-military means of settling disputed questions and of reconciling conflicting claims and aspirations would be banned. Quite the contrary—the establishment of the international police force would be made with the express understanding that it would be used only to prevent war, and that disputes arising between nations would be settled by peaceful means. The purpose would be not to rivet a static political condition upon the world, but to make a new war impossible.

Because this distinction is all-important, let me elaborate it. The objective is to prevent a new world war. An international police force would furnish the machinery for insuring peace. It would *not* mean that the United States and Great Britain would tell each nation what it must do and would then force the nations to comply. It would *not* mean that the two policing powers would impose their will upon the world. All that they would do would be to say: "If you resort to force, we will use our combined forces against you." They would leave the settlement of international rivalries to diplomatic means, or to arbitration or adjudication or negotiation.

There is no reason why either the United States and Great Britain should take part as a principal in such proceedings, any more than the army or the police force of the United States takes part in the deliberations of our own courts or of arbitral bodies. In fact, the plan calls for leaving to the various nations of the world the fullest possible control over their own affairs. Only if a nation sought to build up its army or navy or air forces would the police powers intervene internally.

The further objection is likely to be made both here and abroad that, inasmuch as such an international police force would be composed of Americans and British, it would not operate to prevent aggressive acts by either of those nations. Agreed. But it is necessary to use such means as are at hand and to look at the world as it is. If you will examine the history of these two countries you will see that in the last fifty years they have moved away from aggression and expansion towards the policy of live and let live. The British have made the dominions virtually completely independent. Ireland has remained neutral during the war to date. The Americans have withdrawn from Cuba and have promised the Philippines their independence. They have dropped the policy of interference in the internal affairs of weak neighbors in this hemisphere. Neither the United States nor Great Britain covets the territory of any other nation. No two powerful nations can be said to be more disinterested.

It must not be forgotten that neither of these nations built up its present armaments to assist in policies of expansion. They had nothing to gain by war and much to lose. Their prime interest was in the prevention of war. Germany, in contrast, built for war and wanted war. It was only when Great Britain and the United States failed to halt aggression, as in Manchuria in 1931, and later in Ethiopia, and then in Austria, that they endangered world peace. It was not because of their armed forces that the world war started, but because they failed to pool their armed forces in order to preserve the peace. The cooperation of these two powers in the future for the preservation of peace would be little more than a new affirmation of the great strength that they possess. Another war would be for them disastrous. Hence their entire interest would be concentrated not on making war but on preserving peace.

Obviously the exercise of such power would place upon them the moral obligation of restraint. They would, of course, have the opportunity of abusing their strength. But I think that all but a comparatively small number of persons who have inherited family or racial grievances against the England of the 16th and 17th centuries, or against the United States of the early 19th century, would agree that these nations are unlikely to misuse their trust. Neither people is warlike. Neither covets more territory.

From the American point of view there are, of course, specific objections. It will be said, for example, that by participating in joint action we should be, in effect, underwriting the British Empire and making ourselves responsible for its quarrels and ambitions.

It is obviously undesirable for the United States to commit itself to the underwriting of the British Empire. But this can be avoided by making it plain that the obligations to use the armed forces jointly does not apply to any quarrel within the territory of either nation. That is to say, if Ireland or India were to revolt against Great Britain, there would be no obligation of the Americans to help the British put down the revolt. By the same token if the Philippines were to revolt against the United States, there would be no obligation of the British to intervene in aid of the United States. If, however, Japan were to attack the Philippines, Great Britain would be obliged to fight by the side of the United States. It should be expressly noted that the police power would only be called into active use in the event that a nation prepared for war or threatened war. It would not impose on the United States or Great Britain the obligation of intervening in the internal affairs of other nations.

Americans are sure to ask: "Wouldn't this mean that we might have to send our boys to die in foreign lands?"

I answer: "Yes, of course, such a possibility exists, but the likelihood of their having to go would be small indeed."

The reason for this is comparatively simple—that if a would-be aggressor nation knew for a certainty that the entire might of the United States and the British

Commonwealth of Nations would be turned against it if it attacked a neighbor, it would not dare to make the attack.

But the mere organizations of an international police force is not enough. We must establish the foundations of a new international order. The economic basis of this new order is unrestricted trade—the freest possible movement of goods of all kinds between nations. Ever since the last war more and more obstacles have been placed in the way of international commerce. In Europe the motivating reason has been the mistaken doctrine of military necessity. The nations of the continent have sought to make themselves economically self-sufficient in order to be stronger in war. This has led to such foolish things as the growing of wheat in window boxes in the Austria Tyrol when the plains of Hungary one hundred miles away were overflowing with the finest wheat in the world. It led Germany to attempt to increase its own big population to such a point that it could not get along without lard and bacon from Iowa. The result was that the German people went without enough fats and the farmers of Iowa went broke because they could not sell their surplus of lard and bacon.

The United States is by no means free from blame for obstructing the flow of international trade. For years, wedded to the doctrine of high tariffs, it decided in the midst of the great world depression to increase the tariff rates on a large number of articles. This was the Smoot-Hawley tariff which so many of us had hoped that President Hoover would veto in 1930.

Any attempt to lower the trade barriers will, of course, present great difficulties. Nowhere will the opposition be more vocal than here in the United States. But inasmuch as the great economic task which all nations face when this war is over will be to repair the ravages of war and to replace the countless goods of all kinds that have been destroyed, the common objective must be to stimulate production everywhere. This means that there must be ready access to supplies of raw materials and ready markets for the products of different nations. While a certain amount of protection will probably prove unavoidable and may well be desirable, the objective should be to reduce all tariffs gradually.

A precedent exists which may point the way. This is the so-called Ouchy agreement between the Netherlands and Belgium in 1929 [*sic*] under the terms of which the two governments undertook to lower their tariffs by a fixed percentage each year. It is obvious that if each tariff were to be reduced five per cent each year, in twenty years all tariffs would be reduced to zero.

I am aware that such a proposal runs counter to a century of protectionism in this country. I realize that it would also present many practical complications. But

I link it with a proposal for an international police force because some sort of organized effort to facilitate the freer interchange of goods is indispensible [sic] if the nations which lack certain essentials are to be enabled to obtain them on reasonable terms. It is folly to try to perpetuate economic nationalism—and a high tariff is one of the chief bulwarks of economic nationalism—in the light of the many indications that such a policy has been so disastrous.

In addition to facilitating the exchange of goods of all kinds, which, as I have pointed out, is the essential economic basis of a new international order, it is highly desirable that the political basis of a new order be laid in Europe. If the nations of Europe could devise some sort of machinery for adjusting their quarrels without resort to war, it would do much to check those sources of friction which in the past have so often grown into excuses for war.

The example of Switzerland and in the United States suggests the possibility of establishing a federal union in Europe. The essence of federalism implies leaving to each unit the largest possible amount of freedom in all local matters, delegating to a superior authority the power to deal with matters affecting the common interest. Switzerland elaborated such a system long ago. Here in America the states that formed the union retained full powers to run their own affairs, but empowered the new federal government to deal with such questions as defense, international relations, common currency and finance and other similar problems.

The British Commonwealth of Nations has evolved in the same direction. There the crown is the unifying force. But the various dominions—Ireland, Australia, New Zealand, Canada—run their own internal affairs without interference from London. They benefit from cooperation, but escape the disadvantages of control imposed by distant rule.

Why can not Europe do the same? Why may it not be possible for the various nations of Europe, while preserving their complete internal independence, to unite in matters of currency, commerce and transportation, and to create machinery for settling disputes between states amicably? Certainly if they have the assurance that in the event of attempted aggression by one of them, the full might of the United States and the British Commonwealth of Nations would be used against the aggressor, the fear of war would largely disappear—and it is this fear of war which has done so much to paralyze European thinking and to force European states to spend their wealth on defense.

If a European federal union is formed it should be confined to the nations of that continent. There is no need for American participation in such a superstate. But it may well be objected that cooperation in reducing tariff barriers and participation in an international police force would involve distinct departures from America's traditional policy of aloofness from European affairs.

This policy is so sound that it cannot and must not be lightly discarded. It has its roots in the hope and belief that we can avoid the mistakes of Europe. It assumes that the best way of doing this is to keep out of Europe's quarrels. Nowhere has this ideal been more clearly stated that in George Washington's oft-quoted words in his "Farewell Address." Europe, he said, "had a set of primary interests which to us have none or a very remote relation. Hence she must be engaged in frequent controversies, the causes of which are essentially foreign to our concerns. Hence, therefore, it must be unwise in us to implicate ourselves by artificial ties in the ordinary vicissitudes of her politics or the ordinary combinations and collisions of her friendships or enmities."

But it is essential to note that the important word in this passage is "ordinary." It was against the *ordinary* quarrels of Europe that [President] Washington warned us. The very fact that he used the word *"ordinary"* implies that he recognized that *extraordinary* conditions might arise. There have been, since he fathered these words, three major wars—the Napoleonic wars, the first World War, and the present conflict. Our war of 1812 was a side issue of the Napoleonic conflict. We were drawn in largely because Great Britain attempted to keep our shipping off the seas. It is not amiss to point out that it was Germany's attempt to do the same in 1917 that finally brought us unto the first world war. We are already deeply engaged in the present conflict.

It is no disrespect to the memory of George Washington to say that even if there were no implication in his Farewell Address that there might come extraordinary occasions when we might find it expedient to join with other nations, the very fact that it is so much to our interest to make it impossible for another war to break out, warrants a departure from the policy of no alliance which we have followed for so many decades. And let me remind you that not even the avoidance of alliances has kept us out of past wars.

We have tried almost every device for preventing war except such a partnership for peace such as I have outlined. We have sought to secure peace by isolation, peace by diplomatic correspondence, peace by treaties outlawing war, peace by limiting armaments, peace by petitions, peace by prayers, peace by abstention, peace by renunciation, peace by appeasement. They have all failed. This is because none of them took account of the fact that peace did not depend on our own wishes but on the aggressive acts of war-like nations. It was not the unwarlike nations like China or the Netherlands or ourselves that had to be held in check, but those countries which, like Germany and Japan, looked upon war as the most useful instrument of national policy. These nations cared nothing for arbitration or petitions, or renunciation—so long as they did not have to arbitrate, or renounce anything themselves. Their only interest in disarmament was to see their intended victims disarmed. As I said on an earlier occasion, Germany had been preaching war, praising war, and waging war for half a century. Japan has been practicing war during this same period. The only thing that can ever stop such nations is the actual evidence that armed forces so vastly superior to their own will be used against them that they cannot possibly win.

This much is sure—that unless the United States is willing to take its share of responsibility for world peace another war cannot be prevented. The tradition of war is so deeply ingrained in so many nations, and they are so convinced that they can achieve their ambitions by war, that it will be difficult indeed to induce them to abandon war as an instrument of national policy. The history of Europe since its early dawn is a history of war. The influence of this tradition cannot be lessened by rationalizing about the futility of war today. Nor can it be softened by inveighing against hate and preaching brotherly love among the nations. What good does it do to tell a Dutchman or a Belgian or a Norwegian, whose home has been destroyed and whose children have died of starvation as a result of Germany's invasion, that he ought not to harbor hatred against Germany?

The problem, therefore, boils down to devising the means of preventing any country from going to war. If we accept the premise that nations will continue to contemplate war—and it is unrealistic to assume that they will do otherwise—and if we accept the further premise that it is to our interest and that of all the world to avoid another war at all costs, we cannot escape the conclusion that the United States has a direct stake in the means of preventing another war. If we accept this conclusion we are led to the next logical step, which is that it is futile, cowardly and irresponsible on the part of the United States to take the position that while it does not want another war to start, it is unwilling to do anything which might commit it to using its armed forces outside of the limits of continental United States. That is very much like saying you will only fight a fire in your own house.

Either peace is worth paying for or it is not. Certainly it cannot be insured without sacrifice. If we are prepared to sit back and say: "We are fed up with wars; Let the rest of the world fight if it wants to; it's not our funeral," then what I have urged is of no avail. If we do that we make clear to the world that we refuse to learn from events. One of the verses in the Book of Proverbs warns that "Though thou shouldest bray a fool in a mortar among wheat with a pestle, yet will not his foolishness depart from him."

Many persons have praised a hands-off policy as "isolation." It is no such thing. It may be non-intervention, but as isolation it is a delusion, because it assumes that a mere wish can prevent unpleasant things from effecting [*sic*] us. As well say that the lightning will never strike, or a hurricane or earthquake engulf us, because we do not want to have them do so. Even when isolation is rationalized by being phrased in the military term of "defense" it is still unreal, because we cannot, merely by building up our defenses, isolate ourselves against world forces. In fact, isolation is even more dangerous when phrased as "defense," because it gives a false sense of security. France had its Maginot Line. England had its navy and the Channel. Because each deluded itself that this was enough to keep it safe—that is, because each was thinking only in terms of the defensive—it could not avert war. The defensive is, in reality, a policy of inaction. It is a policy of weakness and incompetence—a policy of waiting for the blow to fall, hoping that something will turn up to avert it.

If we assume that because we have the Atlantic Ocean on one side and the Pacific on the other we can continue indifferent to what happens in Europe or Asia we shall be deluding ourselves as completely as did the French and British. Let us not think in terms of a possible attack on our own country. That is just what the French and British did. Let us, instead, look beyond mere defense against assault to the larger and more fundamental problem of preventing war from starting anywhere. This means that we must take our responsibility courageously. We have the clear lesson of what happens when nations fail to do so. France and Great Britain were bound by self-interest as well as by various commitments to maintain the territorial integrity of Austria. Yet when Hitler made it plain that he was going to annex Austria, neither power was willing to face its responsibility. Both nations had helped create Czechoslovakia. Yet they sacrificed that country on the altar of appeasement. This unwillingness to meet their responsibility encouraged Hitler to fresh aggressions. How tragically futile, in retrospect, is Mr. Chamberlain's phrase on his return from Munich in the spring of 1939: "Peace in our time." Those who knew Central Europe knew that the Munich settlement meant war. As a matter of fact, they knew that there would be war from the moment that Mr. Anthony Eden resigned as Foreign Secretary immediately following personal attacks on him made in public by Hitler and Mussolini. England and France were evading their responsibilities a year before the Munich agreement. In so doing they were making war sure.

It is an old saying that only the strong can be free. I should like to add to this that only the strong can help the weak to be free. If we believe in freedom for others as for ourselves, if we desire peace through the world, then we who are strong must take our share of the responsibility to keep war from other nations. I am not suggesting that we should impose our will, or our form of government, or our ideals, on the rest of the world. I am not referring to such projects as spreading four—or ten—or fifty—freedoms throughout the globe. I am referring only to a single objective—the prevention of the outbreak of another war, be it small or large. I maintain that we should be prepared to become partners for peace and to this end I, for one, would gladly see us make whatever sacrifices may be necessary. If it means risking sending our boys to the ends of the world I am for it—provided only that we do it with every ounce of strength that is in us, and without fear or falter. If it means pooling our armed forces with the British, I am for it—provided that we do not evade our responsibilities or refuse to take our full share of the burden. We cannot have peace without doing our part to maintain it—and peace we must have if we and the rest of the world are to survive.

Bibliography

Primary Sources
Adolph S. Ochs Papers, New York Times Company Records, New York, U.S.A.
Allen W. Dulles Papers, Digital Files.
Arthur Hays Sulzberger Papers, New York Times Company Records, New York, U.S.A.
New York Times Company Records, New York, U.S.A.
Bank of England Archive, London, UK.
Department of Rare Books and Special Collections, Princeton University Library, Princeton, NJ, U.S.A.
Franklin D. Roosevelt Library, Hyde Park, NY, U.S.A.
Houghton Library, Harvard University, Cambridge, MA, U.S.A.
National Archives and Records Administration (NARA). Washington, D. C., U.S.A.
Manuscript and Archives, Yale University Library, New Haven, CT, U.S.A.
Massachusetts Historical Society, Boston, MA, U.S.A.
Seeley G. Mudd Manuscript Library, Princeton, NJ, U.S.A.
Nicholas Roosevelt Papers, Special Collections Research Center at Syracuse University Libraries, Syracuse, NY, U.S.A.
The National Archives, London, UK.

Primary Printed Sources
Congressional Record
Foreign Relations of the United States
Hoover, Herbert. *Containing the Public Messages Speeches and Statements of the President, January 1 to December 31, 1930, Public Papers of the Presidents of the United States*. Washington: United States Government Printing Office, 1976.

League of Nations. *The League of Nations Reconstruction Schemes in the Inter-War Period*, Geneva: Economic, Financial and Transit Department, 1944.

League of Nations Journal

League of Nations Treaty Series. Publication of Treaties and International Engagements Registered with the Secretariat of the League of Nations. Lausanne: Imprimeries Réunies S.A, 1934–35.

Link, Arthur S., ed. *The Papers of Woodrow Wilson.* vols. 1–69. Princeton, NJ: Princeton

University Press, 1987.

Department of State. *Peace and War: United States Foreign Policy 1931–1941.* Washington: United States, Government Printing Office, 1943.

Rosenman, Samuel I. ed. *The Public Papers and Addresses of Franklin D. Roosevelt.* Vol. 4. New York: Random House, 1938,

Secondary Sources

Adlgasser, Franz. "The Roots of Communist Containment: American Food Aid in Austria and Hungary after World War I." *Austria in the Nineteen Fifties, Contemporary Austrian Studies* 3 (1995): 171–88.

Aguado, Iago Gil. "The Creditanstalt Crisis of 1931 and the Failure of the Austro-German Customs Union Project." *The Historical Journal* 44, no. 1 (March 2001): 199–221.

Ahamed, Liaquat. *Lords of Finance: The Bankers Who Broke the World.* New York: Penguin Books, 2009.

Allen, Frederick Lewis. *Only Yesterday: An Informal History of the Nineteen-Twenties.* New York and Evanston: Harper & Row, Publishers, 1957 [1931].

Apponyi, Albert. *The Memoirs of Count Apponyi.* New York: The Macmillan Company, 1935.

Armarius. "Potpourri." *The North American Review*, 252, no. 4 (Jul. 1967): 41.

Axelrod, Alan. *Selling the Great War: The Making of American Propaganda.* New York: Palgrave Macmillan, 2009.

Baker, Leonard. *Back to Back: The Duel between FDR and the Supreme Court.* New York: The MacMillan Company, 1967.

Baker, Ray Stannard. *What Wilson Did at Paris.* New York: Doubleday, Page & Company, 1919.

Baldwin, Neil. *Henry Ford and the Jews: The Mass Production of Hate.* New York: Public Affairs, 2001.

Bandholtz, Harry Hill. *An Undiplomatic Diary*. New York: Columbia University Press, 1933.

Barber, William J. *Designs within Disorder: Franklin D. Roosevelt, the Economists, and the Shaping of American Economic Policy, 1933–1945*. Cambridge: Cambridge University Press, 2006.

Bartlett, Vernon. *Behind the Scenes at the Peace Conference*. London: G. Allen & Unwin Ltd., 1920.

Baruch, Bernard M. *The Making of the Reparation and Economic Sections of the Treaty*. New York and London: Harpers & Brothers, 1920.

Berdahl, Clarence A. "The United States and the League of Nations." *Michigan Law Review* 27, no. 6 (April 1929): 607–36.

Bischof, Günter, Anton Pelinka, and Alexander Lassner, eds. *The Dollfuss/Schuschnigg Era in Austria: A Reassessment*. Contemporary Austrian Studies 11. New Brunswick, NJ, and London: Transaction Publishers, 2003.

Blum, John M. "*A Front Row Seat* by Nicholas Roosevelt." *The Mississippi Valley Historical Review* 40, no. 3 (Dec. 1953): 554–55.

Braeman, John. "Theodore Roosevelt: The Man as I Knew Him. By Nicholas Roosevelt." *The Journal of American History* 54, no. 3 (Dec. 1967): 693–94.

Buchsbaum, Tamar. "A Note on Antisemitism in Admissions at Dartmouth." *Jewish Social Studies* 49, no. 1 (Winter 1987): 79–84.

Burgess, John W. *Political Science and Comparative Constitutional Law*. Boston: Ginn & Company, 1890.

Catledge, Turner. "War Veterans and Bonus Politics." *Current History* (1916–1940) 42, no. 4 (July 1935): 360–64.

Chace, James. *1912: Wilson, Roosevelt, Taft and Debs—The Election that Changed the Country*. New York: Simon & Schuster, 2004.

Chase, Theodore. "Charles Moorfield Storey." *Proceedings of the Massachusetts Historical Society*, Third Series 92 (1980): 151–56.

Churchill, Allen. *The Roosevelts: American Aristocrats*. New York: Harper & Row, 1965.

Clarke, Stephen V. O. *Central Bank Cooperation: 1924–1931*. New York: Federal Reserve Bank of New York, 1967.

Clavin, Patricia. *Securing the World Economy: The Reinvention of the League of Nations, 1920–1946*. Oxford: Oxford University Press, 2013.

Coolidge, Harold Jefferson, and Robert Howard Lord. *Archibald Cary Coolidge: Life and Letters*. Boston and New York: Houghton Mifflin, 1932.

Costigliola, Frank. *Awkward Dominion: American Political, Economic, and Cultural Relations with Europe, 1919–1933*. Ithaca, NY: Cornell University Press, 1984.

Creel, George. *How We Advertised America*. New York: Harper & Brothers Publishers, 1920.

Dallek, Robert. *Franklin D. Roosevelt and American Foreign Policy, 1932–1945: With a New Afterword*. Oxford: Oxford University Press, 1995.

Darwin, Charles. *The Descent of Man, and Selection in Relation to Sex*. London: John Murray, 1882.

Davis, Kenneth S. *FDR: The Beckoning of Destiny, 1882–1928*. New York: History Book Club, 1972.

———. *FDR: The New Deal Years, 1933–1937. A History*. New York: Random House, 1979.

Dinnerstein, Leonard. *Anti-Semitism in America*. New York, Oxford: Oxford University Press, 1994.

Dulles, Allen. "The Protection of American Foreign Bondholders." *Foreign Affairs* 10, no. 3 (April 1932): 474–84.

Dutcher, George Matthew. "*The Philippines, a Treasure and a Problem* by Nicholas Roosevelt." *Political Science Quarterly* 42, no. 4 (Dec. 1927): 624–26. Casey, Steven. *Cautious Crusade: Franklin D. Roosevelt, American Public Opinion, and the War against Nazi Germany*. New York: Oxford University Press, 2001.

Eichengreen, Barry. *Golden Fetters: The Gold Standard and the Great Depression, 1919–1939*. Oxford: Oxford University Press, 1996.

Elleman, Bruce A. *International Competition in China, 1899–1991: The Rise, Fall, and Restoration of the Open Door Policy*. London and New York: Routledge, 2015.

Ellis, James F. "*A New Birth of Freedom* by Nicholas Roosevelt." *The Journal of Politics* 1, no. 3 (Aug. 1939): 321–23.

Fanning, Richard W. *Peace and Disarmament: Naval Rivalry & Arms Control, 1922–1933*. Lexington, KY: The University Press of Kentucky, 1995.

Feller, A. H. "OWI on the Home Front." *The Public Opinion Quarterly* 7, no. 1 (Spring, 1943): 55–65.

Fischer, Conan. *The Ruhr Crisis, 1923–1924*. Oxford: Oxford University Press, 2003.

Flehinger, Brett. *The 1912 Election and the Power of Progressivism: A Brief History with Documents*. Boston: Bedford/St. Martin's, 2003.

Frank, Tibor, ed. *Discussing Hitler: Advisers of U.S. Diplomacy in Central Europe 1934–1941*. Budapest, New York: Central European University Press, 2003.

―――. *Double Exile: Migrations of Jewish-Hungarian Professionals through Germany to the United States, 1919–1945*. Oxford: Peter Lang, 2009.

―――. "Editing as Politics: József Balogh and *The Hungarian Quarterly*." *The Hungarian Quarterly* 34, no. 129 (Spring 1993): 5–13.

―――. "Literature Exported: Aspects of *The Hungarian Quarterly* (1936–1944)," *Studies in English and American*, 4 (Budapest: Eötvös Loránd University, 1978): 255–82.

―――. "Patronage and Networking: The Society of *The Hungarian Quarterly*, 1935–1944." *The Hungarian Quarterly* 50, no. 196 (Winter 2009): 3–12.

Freidel, Frank. *Franklin D. Roosevelt: A Rendezvous with History*. Boston: Little, Brown and Company, 1990.

Frome, Michael. "*Conservation: Now or Never;* By Nicholas Roosevelt." *Forest History Newsletter* 14, no. 3 (October 1970): 35.

Gaddis, John Lewis. *The United States and the Origins of the Cold War, 1941–1947*. New York: Columbia University Press, 2000.

Galloway, J. M. "The Public Life of Norman H. Davis." *Tennessee Historical Quarterly* 27, no. 2 (Summer 1968): 142–56.

Gelfand, Lawrence E. "Towards a Merit System for the American Diplomatic Service 1900–1930." *Irish Studies in International Affairs* 2, no. 4 (1988): 49–63.

Gerber, David A. *Anti-Semitism in American History*. Urbana, IL: University of Illinois Press, 1986.

Gergely, Jenő. *Gömbös Gyula: Vázlat egy politikai életrajzhoz* [Gyula Gömbös: Sketches for a political biography]. Budapest: Elektra Kiadóház, 1999.

Gibbs, Norman. "The Naval Conferences of the Interwar Years: A study in Anglo-American Relations." *Naval War College Review* 30, no. 1 (Special issue, Summer 1977): 50–63.

Glant, Tibor. "Herbert Hoover and Hungary, 1918–1923." *Hungarian Journal of English and American Studies* 8, no. 2 (2002): 95–109.

Goldstein, Erik. and John H. Maurer, eds. *The Washington Conference, 1921–22: Naval Rivalry, East Asian Stability and the Road to Pearl Harbor*. London and New York: Routledge, 1994.

Gould, Lewis L. *Four Hats in the Ring: The 1912 Election and the Birth of Modern American Politics*. Lawrence, KS: University Press of Kansas, 2008.

Grund, Francis J. *The Americans, in Their Moral, Social, and Political Relations*. Boston: Marsh, Capen & Lyon, 1837.

Gunst, Péter. *Magyarország gazdaságtörténete, 1914–1989* [The economic history of Hungary, 1914–1918]. Budapest: Nemzeti Tankönyvkiadó, 1996.

Gyáni, Gábor. "A napló mint társadalomtörténeti forrás" [The diary as sociological source]. In *Szabolcs-szatmár-beregi levéltári évkönyv*, vol. 12, 1997.

Hajdú, Tibor. *The Hungarian Soviet Republic*. Budapest: Akadémiai Kiadó, 1979.

Hamerli, Petra. *Magyar-olasz diplomáciai kapcsolatok és regionális hatásaik (1927–1934)* [Hungarian-Italian diplomatic relations and their regional effects]. Budapest: Fakultás Kiadó, 2018.

Harper, John Lamberton. *American Visions of Europe: Franklin D. Roosevelt, George F. Kennan, and Dean G. Acheson*. Cambridge: Cambridge University Press, 1994.

Harris, Henry Wilson. *Peace in the Making*. New York: E. P. Dutton, 1920.

Haskins, Charles Homer, and Robert Howard Lord. *Some Problems of the Peace Conference*. Cambridge, MA: Harvard University Press, 1920.

Havas, Eugene. *Hungary's Finance and Trade 1927*. London: General Press, 1928.

Hawkins, Lester G. and George S. Pettee. "OWI: Organization and Problems." *Public Opinion Quarterly* 7 no. 1 (Spring 1943): 15–33.

Heinrichs, Waldo H. *American Ambassador: Joseph C. Grew and the Development of the United States Diplomatic Tradition*. Boston and Toronto: Little Brown and Company, 1966.

Herring, George C. *From Colony to Superpower: U.S. Foreign Relations Since 1776*. Oxford: Oxford University Press, 2008.

Hess, Stephen. *America's Political Dynasties*. New Brunswick and London: Transaction Publishers, 1997.

Hodgson, Godfrey. *The Colonel: The Life and Wars of Henry Stimson, 1867–1950*. New York: Alfred A. Knopf, 1990.

Hoopes Townsend, and Douglas Brinkley. *FDR and the Creation of the U.N.* New Haven, CT: Yale University Press, 1997.

Hoover, Herbert Clark. *The Memoirs of Herbert Hoover*. vols. 1–3. New York: The Macmillan Company, 1951–1952.

Horthy, Nicholas. *Memoirs*. Safety Harbor, FL: Simon Publications, 2000.

Huddleston, Sisley. *Peace-making at Paris*. London: T Fisher Unwin Ltd., 1919.

Hunt, Michael H. *Ideology and U.S. Foreign Policy*. New Haven and London, Yale University Press, 1987.

Iglehart, Ferdinand Cowle. *Theodore Roosevelt: The Man as I Knew Him*. New York: The Christian Herald, 1919.

Johnson, Willis Fletcher. "The White Man's Burden." *The North American Review* 223, no. 833 (Dec. 1926–Feb. 1927): 712–16.

Karabel, Jerome. *The Chosen: The Hidden History of Admission and Exclusion at Harvard, Yale, and Princeton*. Boston: Houghton Mifflin Company, 2005.

Karolyi, Michael. *The Memoirs of Karolyi: Faith without Illusion*. London: Jonathan Cape, 1956.

Kennan, George F. *The Kennan Diaries*. Edited by Frank Costigliola. New York: W. W. Norton, 2014.

———. "The Sources of Soviet Conduct," *Foreign Affairs* 25, no. 4 (July 1947): 566–78, 580–82.

Keynes, John Maynard. *The Economic Consequences of the Peace*. New York: Harcourt, Brace, and Howe, 1919.

Kimball, Warren F. *The Juggler: Franklin Roosevelt as Wartime Statesman*. Princeton, NJ: Princeton University Press, 1991.

Kluger, Richard. *The Paper: The Life and Death of the New York Herald Tribune*. New York: Alfred A. Knopf, 1986.

Knickerbocker, Hubert Renfro. *Can Europe Recover?* London: John Lane, The Bodley Head Ltd., 1932.

Krasnoff, Lindsay Sarah. *Views From the Embassy: The Role of the U.S. Diplomatic Community in France, 1914*. Preview Edition, September 15, 2014, Washington, D. C.: U.S. Department of State: Office of the Historian.

Lamont, Edward M. *The Ambassador from Wall Street: The Story of Thomas W. Lamont, J. P. Morgan's Chief Executive*. Lanham, MD: Madison Books, 1994.

Langer, William L. "Some Recent Books on International Relations." *Foreign Affairs* 6, no. 4 (July 1928): 682–93.

Langford, Rachael, and Russell West, eds. *Marginal Voices, Marginal Forms: Diaries in European Literature and History*. Amsterdam: Rodopi, 1999.

Lansing, Robert. *The Peace Negotiations: A Personal Narrative*. New York: Houghton Mifflin, 1921.

Laurie, Clayton D. *The Propaganda Warriors: America's Crusade Against Nazi Germany*. Lawrence: University Press of Kansas, 1996.

Leuchtenburg, William E. *The Supreme Court Reborn: The Constitutional Revolution in the Age of Roosevelt*. New York, Oxford: Oxford University Press, 1995.

Little, Douglas. "His Finest Hour? Eisenhower, Lebanon, and the 1958 Middle East Crisis." *Diplomatic History* 20, no. 1, (Winter 1996): 27–54.

Louria, Margot. *Triumph and Downfall: America's Pursuit of Peace and Prosperity, 1921–1933*. Westport, CT, London: Greenwood Press, 2001.

Mabon, Mary Frost. "The Salad Master." *Sports Illustrated* 11, no. 4, (July 27, 1959): 40.

MacNair, Harley Farnsworth. "The Far East: A Political and Diplomatic History by Payson Jackson Treat; The Restless Pacific by Nicholas Roosevelt; Within the Walls of Nanking by Alice Tisdale Hobart." *The American Political Science Review* 23, no. 1 (Feb. 1929): 212–15.

Maderthaner, Wolfgang and Michaela Maier. *"Der Führer bin ich selbst": Engelbert Dollfuß – Bennito Mussolini Briefwechsel*. Vienna: Erhard Löcker Verlag, 2004.

Margolin, Leo J. *Paper Bullets: A Brief Story of Psychological Warfare in World War II*. New York: Froben Press, 1946.

Marks, Sally. "The Myths of Reparations." *Central European History* 11, no. 3 (Sep. 1978): 231–55.

Márkus, László. *A Károlyi Gyula kormány bel- és külpolitikája* [The domestic and foreign policy of the Károlyi government]. Budapest: Akadémiai Kiadó, 1968.

Martin, Rod A., and Thomas E. Ford. *The Psychology of Humor: An Integrative Approach*, 2nd edition. Cambridge, MA: Academic Press, 2018.

Mathey, Éva. "Nicholas Roosevelt in A Front Row Seat: Hungary in the 1930s as Reflected in the Memoirs of an American Diplomat." *Acta Neerlandica* 15 (2019): 149–62.

Mencken, H. L. *"America and England."* *Now and Then* (London), no 35 (Spring 1930): 11–12.

Messner, Johannes. *Dollfuss: An Austrian Patriot*. Norfolk, VA: Gates of Vienna Books, 2004 [1935].

Michael, Robert. *A Concise History of American Antisemitism*. Lanham, MD: Rowman and Littlefield Publishers, 2005.

Miller, Nathan. *The Roosevelt Chronicles*. New York: Doubleday & Company, 1979.

Montgomery, John Flournoy. *Hungary: The Unwilling Satellite*. New York: DevinAdair Company, 1947.

Morison, Elting E. *Turmoil and Tradition: A Study of the Life and Times of Henry L. Stimson*. Boston: Houghton Mifflin Company, 1960.

Morris, Edmund. *Colonel Roosevelt*. New York: Random House, 2010.

Morrison, Rodney J. "The London Monetary and Economic Conference of 1933: A Public Goods Analysis." *The American Journal of Economics and Sociology* 52, no. 3 (July 1993): 310–13.

Moulton, Harold G. *The Reparation Plan*. New York: McGraw-Hill Book Company, 1924.

O'Brien, Phillips Payson. *British and American Naval Power: Politics and Policy, 1900–1936*. Praeger Studies in Diplomacy and Strategic Thought. Westport, CT, London: Praeger, 1998.

Offner, Arnold A. *American Appeasement: United States Foreign Policy and Germany, 1933–1938*. Cambridge, MA: Belknap Press of Harvard University Press, 1969.

Ormos, Mária. *Magyarország a két világháború korában (1919–1945)* [Hungary in the age of the world wars]. Debrecen: Csokonai Kiadó, 1998.

Pastor, Peter. *Hungary between Wilson and Lenin: The Hungarian Revolution of 1918–1919 and the Big Three*. Boulder, CO: East European Quarterly Distributed by New York: Columbia University Press, 1976.

Peterecz, Zoltán. *Royall Tyler and Hungary: An American in Europe and the Crisis Years, 1918–1953*. Reno, NV: Helena History Press, 2021.

———. "The Visit of the Most Popular American of the Day: Theodore Roosevelt in Hungary." *Hungarian Studies* 28, no. 2, (2014): 235–54.

Peterson, Theodore. *Magazines in the Twentieth Century*. Urbana: The University of Illinois Press, 1956.

Pollak, Oliver B. "Antisemitism, the Harvard Plan, and the Roots of Reverse Discrimination." *Jewish Social Studies* 45, no. 2 (Spring, 1983): 113–22.

Pritz, Pál. *Magyarország külpolitikája Gömbös Gyula miniszterelnöksége idején, 1932–1936* [The foreign policy of Hungary during the premiership of Gyula Gömbös, 1932–1936]. Budapest: Akadémiai Kiadó, 1982.

———. "Napló és történelem" [Diary and history]. *Múltunk* 62, no. 1 (2017): 4–6.

Püski, Levente. *A Horthy-korszak szürke eminenciása Károlyi Gyula (1871–1947)* [Gyula Károlyi, the éminence grise of the Horthy era]. Pécs-Budapest: Kronosz Kiadó – Magyar Történelmi Társulat, 2016.

Ransel, David L. "The Diary of a Merchant: Insights into Eighteenth-Century Plebeian Life." *The Russian Review* 63, no. 4 (Oct. 2004): 594–608.

Réti, György. "Gömbös és a Római Hármas Egyezmény, 1934" [Gömbös and the Rome Three Power Pact]. *Történelmi Szemle* 36, nos. 1–2 (1994): 159–65.

Ribuffo, Leo P. "Henry Ford and 'The International Jew.'" *American Jewish History* 69, no. 4 (June 1980): 437–77.

Robertson, James Alexander. "The Philippines: A Treasure and a Problem." *The Hispanic American Historical Review* 7, no. 4 (Nov. 1927): 482–83.

Roosevelt, Nicholas. *Account of the Republican National Convention at Chicago, June 1912, compiled from notes taken on the spot by Nicholas Roosevelt*. Typescript, 1912. Houghton Library, Harvard University, Cambridge, MA, United States.

———. *A Front Row Seat*. Norman: University of Oklahoma Press, 1953.

———. *A History of a Few Weeks.* (unpublished manuscript) Syracuse University Libraries, United States, Box 18, Nicholas Roosevelt Papers.

———. *America and England?* London: Jonathan Cape, 1930.

———. *A New Birth of Freedom.* New York: Charles Scribner's Sons, 1938.

———. *Conservation: Now or Never.* New York: Dodd, Mead & Company, 1970.

———. *Creative Cooking.* New York: Harper and Brothers, 1956.

———. *Creative Dollars Abroad: An Address Delivered by Nicholas Roosevelt at the 27th National Foreign Trade Convention, the Americas' Session, at the Palace Hotel, San Francisco, California, July 30, 1940.* New York City, 1940.

———. "Franklin Delano Roosevelt." *The American Mercury* 39, no. 155 (Nov. 1936): 329–31.

———. *Good Cooking.* New York: Harper & Brothers, 1959.

———. "Laying Down the White Man's Burden." *Foreign Affairs* 13, no. 4 (Jul. 1935): 680–86.

———. "Russia and Great Britain in China." *Foreign Affairs* 5, no. 1 (Oct. 1926): 80–90.

———. "Salvaging the Debts of Eastern Europe." *Foreign Affairs* 12, no. 1 (Oct. 1933): 134–40.

———. *Theodore Roosevelt: The Man as I Knew Him.* New York: Dodd, Mead & Company, 1967.

———. "The New Governor-General of the Philippines." *The American Review of Reviews* 77, no. 2 (Feb. 1928): 144–46.

———. *The Philippines: A Treasure and a Problem.* New York: J. H. Sears & Company, Inc., 1926.

———. *The Restless Pacific.* New York, London: Charles Scribner's Sons, 1928.

———. "The Ruhr Occupation." *Foreign Affairs* 4, no. 1 (Oct. 1925): 112–22.

———. *The Townsend Plan: Taxing for Sixty.* Garden City, NY: Doubleday, Doran & Company, Inc., 1936.

———. *Two Amazing Years.* Washington, D.C.: American Liberty League, 1935.

———. *Venezuela's Place in the Sun: Modernizing a Pioneering Country.* New York: Round Table Press, Inc., 1940.

———. "Wanted: An Honest President." *The American Mercury* 38, no. 150 (June 1936): 196–200.

———. *Wanted: Good Neighbors.* New York, The National Foreign Trade Council Trade Council, Inc., 1939.

Roosevelt, Theodore. *An Autobiography.* New York: The Macmillan Company, 1913.

———. "A Cougar Hunt on the Rim of the Grand Canyon." *The Outlook* 105 (Oct. 4, 1913): 259–66.

———. "Across the Navajo Desert." *The Outlook* 105 (Oct. 11, 1913): 309–17.

———. "The Hopi Snake Dance." *The Outlook* 105 (Oct. 18, 1913): 365–73.

———. *The Winning of the West*. New York: The Review of Reviews Company, 1910.

S., F. C. "Roosevelt, Nicholas. *The Restless Pacific*." *Review of Current Military Writings*, no. 29, (April-June 1928): 448.

Sallai, Gergely. *Az első bécsi döntés* [The First Vienna Award]. Budapest: Osiris, 2002.

Saxon, Wolfgang. "Nicholas Roosevelt is Dead; Writer and Diplomat Was 88." *New York Times*, Feb. 17, 1982.

Schlesinger, Arthur M. Jr. *The Politics of Upheaval*. Boston: Houghton Mifflin Company, 1960.

Schmitz, David F. *Henry L. Stimson: The First Wise Man*. Wilmington, DE: SR Books, 2001.

Schubert, Aurel. *The Credit-Anstalt Crisis of 1931*. Cambridge: Cambridge University Press, 1991.

Schuker, Stephen A. *The End of French Predominance in Europe: The Financial Crisis of 1924 and the Adoption of the Dawes Plan*. Chapel Hill, NC: University of North Carolina Press, 1976.

Schulzinger, Robert D. *The Making of the Diplomatic Mind: The Training, Outlook and Style of United States Foreign Service Officers, 1908–1931*. Middletown, CT: Wesleyan University Press, 1975.

Simpson, Colin. *Lusitania*. London: Longman, 1972.

Singleton, M. K. *H. L. Mencken and the American Mercury Adventure*. Durham, NC: Duke University Press, 1962.

Smith, Jean Edward. *FDR*. New York: Random House, 2007.

Steel, Ronald. *Walter Lippmann and the American Century*. Boston and Toronto: Little, Brown and Company, 1980.

Steiner, Zara. *The Triumph of the Dark: European International History, 1933–1939*. Oxford: Oxford University Press, 2011.

Stimson, Henry L. *On Active Service in Peace and War*. New York: Harper & Brothers, 1948.

Storey, Charles Moorfield. *Journal, 1918–1919*. Massachusetts Historical Society, U.S.A.

Sweeney, Michael S. *Secrets of Victory: The Office of Censorship and the American Press and Radio in World War II*. Chapel Hill & London: The University of North Carolina Press, 2001.

Thayer, William R. "The Armed Truce of the Powers." *The Forum* 12 (Nov. 1891): 312–29.

Thompson, Charles T. *The Peace Conference Day by Day*. New York: Brentano's Publishers, 1920.

Thompson, John M. *Russia, Bolshevism, and the Versailles Peace*. Princeton, NJ: Princeton University Press, 1967.

Toniolo, Gianni, with the assistance of Piet Clement. *Central Bank Cooperation at the Bank for International Settlements, 1930–1973*. Cambridge: Cambridge University Press, 2005.

Townsend, Francis E., and Nicholas Roosevelt. "Townsend Pensions: Sense or Nonsense? A Debate." *Forum and Century* 95, no 5 (May 1936): 282–87.

Vonyó, József. *Gömbös Gyula* [Gyula Gömbös]. Budapest: Napvilág Kiadó, 2014.

W. L. H. *"America and England* by Nicholas Roosevelt; *America Conquers Britain* Ludwell Denny." *Pacific Affairs* 3, no. 8 (Aug., 1930): 786–788.

Walterskirchen, Gudula. *Engelbert Dollfuss: Arbeitermörder oder Heldenkanzler*. Vienna: Molden, 2004.

Wambaugh, Eugene. "Moorfield Storey (1845–1929)." *Proceedings of the American Academy of Arts and Sciences* 71, no. 10 (Mar. 1937): 552–56.

Weinberg, Sydney. "What to Tell America: The Writer's Quarrel in the OWI." *Journal of American History* 55 no. 1 (June 1968): 73–89.

Werking, Richard Hume. *The Master Architects Building the United States Foreign Service, 1890–1931*. Lexington, KY: University Press of Kentucky, 1977.

Wertheim, Stephen. "Reluctant Liberator: Theodore Roosevelt's Philosophy of Self-Government and Preparation for Philippine Independence." *Presidential Studies Quarterly* 39, no. 3 (Sept. 2009): 494–518.

Weyl, Nathaniel. *The Jew in American Politics*. New Rochelle, NY: Arlington House, 1968.

Wheeler-Bennett, J. W. "*The Restless Pacific* by Nicholas Roosevelt." *Journal of the Royal Institute of International Affairs* 7, no. 5, (Sept. 1928): 345.

Whittelsey, Charles B. *The Roosevelt Genealogy, 1649–1902*. Hartford, CT: J. B. Burr & Company, 1902.

Wilbur, Ray Lyman. "*The Restless Pacific* by Nicholas Roosevelt." *Annals of the American Academy of Political and Social Science* 138, Some Aspects of the Present International Situation (July 1928): 182.

Wilkins, H. Ford. "Dwight F. Davis: Governor General of the Philippines." *Current History* (1916–1940) 34, no. 3 (June 1931): 348–52.
Williams, Benjamin H. "*America and England by Nicholas Roosevelt.*" *Political Science Quarterly 46, no. 1 (Mar. 1931): 118–20.)*
Winkler, Allan M. *The Politics of Propaganda: The Office of War Information, 1942–1945*. New Haven: Yale University Press, 1978.
Woodward, C. Vann. *The Old World's New World*. New York: Oxford University Press, 1991.

Newspapers and Magazines
8 Órai Ujság
Amerikai Magyar Népszava
Az Est
Boston Transcript
Budapesti Hírlap
Detroit Michigan Free Press
Information Digest
Nemzeti Ujság
New York Herald Tribune
New York Times
New York Tribune
Pesti Hírlap
Pesti Napló
Philippines Free Press
Review of Reviews
Sporthírlap
Time
The Brooklyn Daily Eagle
The Christian Science Monitor
The Outlook
Ujság
Victory
Washington Star

Online Sources

"About WQXR," https://www.wqxr.org/about/

"Biographical History," Syracuse Library site: https://library.syr.edu/digital/guides/r/roosevelt_n.htm#d2e101

"Board of Overseers," https://www.harvard.edu/about/leadership-and-governance/board-of-overseers/

"Harvard Board of Overseers," https://en.wikipedia.org/wiki/Harvard_Board_of_Overseers

"Harvard University – Social Networks and Archival Context," https://snaccooperative.org/view/84889135

Hefner, Brooks E. and Edward Timke, eds. *Circulating American Magazines*. James Madison University, http://sites.jmu.edu/circulating/

File: American Hungarian Relief, Inc. United Nations Relief and Rehabilitation Administration (UNRRA), 1943–1946, https://search.archives.un.org/american-hungarian-relief-inc-2855

"Franklin D. Roosevelt. Day by Day." A Project of the Pare Lorentz Center at the FDR Presidential Library. http://www.fdrlibrary.marist.edu/daybyday/

Franklin D. Roosevelt, State of the Union, January 6, 1941, https://voicesofdemocracy.umd.edu/fdr-the-four-freedoms-speech-text/

"The Life Summary of Tirzah Maris," https://ancestors.familysearch.org/en/K1DP-W4D/tirzah-maris-gates-1906-1961

Report of the Special Committee on Investigation of the Munitions Industry (The Nye Report), U.S. Congress, Senate, 74th Congress, 2nd Session, February 24, 1936, 3–13. https://www.mtholyoke.edu/acad/intrel/nye.htm

"World War I military service abstract for Nicholas Roosevelt, Army Officer," https://digitalcollections.archives.nysed.gov/index.php/Detail/objects/40266

Index

Acheson, Dean, 149
Alexander, King of Yugoslavia, 101–2, 104, 124
American Mercury, The, 117, 118, 119, 214
Anschluss, 30, 44, 123, 124, 220
Apponyi, Albert, 32–33, 49, 79, 98–99, 180, 181, 182, 184

Bank of England, 105, 206
Benedikt, Ernst Martin, 30, 41, 44
Beneš, Edvard, 54, 101, 103–4
Berlin, 54, 174, 192, 217
Berthelot, Philippe, 35, 186
Bethlen, István, 73, 79, 82, 83, 84, 85, 96, 129, 205–6
Brentano, Theodore, 74, 75
Bruce, Henry James, 89
Bucharest, 26, 29, 35, 105, 178, 184–86, 188, 192
Budapest, 1, 26, 29, 30, 32, 35–38, 44, 45, 49, 70–71, 74–75, 77, 78–82, 84, 86, 92, 94–96, 101, 103, 106, 107, 109, 110–11, 112, 128, 149, 156, 177–79, 183, 191, 194, 205, 206

Chamberlain, Neville, 220, 231

Charron, René, 84, 205, 206–7, 208
Clemenceau, George, 21, 39
Committee on Public Information (CPI), 140–41
Coolidge, Archibald Cary, 21, 25, 26, 30, 32, 35, 36, 39, 48, 49, 53, 151, 172, 177, 178, 179, 188, 193, 194
  Coolidge Mission, 9, 25–26, 29–30, 34, 37n, 40, 44, 48, 77, 150
Coolidge, Calvin, 55, 65, 117
Constantinescu, Alexandru C., 41, 189–90
Cowles, Gardner, Jr., 142, 143

Davis, Dwight F., 66, 67
Davis, Elmer, 142, 143, 145, 146
Davis, Norman H., 105
Davis, Walter Goodwin, 29, 34, 44, 45, 177, 179
Dawes Plan, 55–57
Debs, Eugene V., 15
Dollfuss, Engelbert, 123–24
d'Oremieulx, Laura Henrietta (Nicholas Roosevelt's mother), 9
Dulles, Allen W., 39, 40, 48, 49, 87, 151, 157, 193, 211
Dulles, John Foster, 157

Eisenhower, Dwight D., 154, 157
Eisenhower, Milton S., 142
Feis, Herbert, 86, 88, 91, 99
Financial Committee of the League of Nations, 76, 89, 105
Fish Armstrong, Hamilton, 75, 129n
Foreign Affairs, 10, 55, 87, 122, 124, 129

Gates, Egbert James, 125
Gates, Tirzah Maris, 10, 86, 125, 126
Geneva, 52, 57, 77, 86, 100, 104, 105, 124
George, Lloyd, 39
Ghika, György, 77, 109
Gilbert, Printess, 100, 105
Gömbös, Gyula, 96–97, 107
Goodwin, Philip L., 36, 178, 179, 180, 182, 183, 184, 194, 195
Grant-Smith, Ulysses, 75

Havas, Eugene, 82
Hay, John, 52, 57
Hitler, Adolf, 102, 104, 123, 126–27, 137, 156, 215, 216, 218–19, 220, 221–23, 224, 231
Hoover, Herbert, 10, 31, 39, 42, 49, 53, 66, 67, 68, 70, 77, 93, 100–101, 112, 113, 116, 151, 227
Horthy, Miklós, 79, 96, 104, 107, 127, 128, 155–56

Imrédy, Béla, 97, 107, 127

Károlyi, Gyula, 85–86, 96
Károlyi, Mihály, 32, 33–34, 36–37, 49, 180
Kennan, George F., 63
Kennedy, John Fitzgerald, 157–58

Kent, Frank R., 145–46
King, Ernest Joseph, 145
King, Rufus, 217
Knickerbocker, Hubert Renfro, 94, 95
Krock, Arthur, 101, 153–54
Kun, Béla, 104

Lamont, Thomas, 88, 133
Landon, Alf, 118, 119
Lansing, Robert, 30, 38, 39, 43, 46, 193–94, 195
League of Nations, 25, 45, 53, 54, 55, 57, 73, 74, 76, 81, 82, 86, 89, 92, 104–5, 106, 123, 124, 137, 152, 195, 203, 207
Lippmann, Walter, 65, 67, 110, 118
Lodge, Henry Cabot, 53
London, 21, 22, 77, 82, 100, 129, 174, 228
London Naval Conference, 52, 67, 112

MacArthur, Douglas, 95
Mencken, Henry Louis, 65, 117
Montgomery, John Flourney, 107, 148, 149, 156
Mussolini, Benito, 96, 101, 102–3, 104, 124, 137, 215, 231

Office of War Information (OWI), 10, 140, 141–46, 147, 148, 151, 161
Outlook, The, 56, 160

Paris, 9, 21, 22, 24, 37, 39, 48, 77, 80, 177, 178, 191, 192, 193, 196
Paris Peace Conference, 24–26, 27, 29, 31–32, 34, 35, 38, 39, 45, 50, 67, 104, 123, 150, 154
Pelényi, János, 148

Roosevelt, Franklin Delano (FDR), 7–8, 10, 100, 101, 106, 107, 110–15, 117–21, 124, 126, 131, 134, 138, 139, 141, 413, 151, 155, 214–16

Roosevelt, James West, 9

Roosevelt, Nicholas
and *A Front Row Seat*, 10, 49, 151–53
and Austria, 30–32, 40, 44–45, 53, 85, 110, 123–24, 171–77, 219, 220, 231
and Hungary, 10, 26, 32–34, 36–39, 45, 49, 70–72, 73–107, 109, 124, 127–29, 148–49, 155–56, 179–84, 193, 205–8
and Jews, 17, 41, 42, 43, 44, 104, 152, 171, 179, 180, 185, 190
and the *New York Herald Tribune*, 10, 110, 114, 122
and the *New York Times*, 9, 53, 58, 68, 69, 71, 77, 80, 101, 110, 147, 150, 152, 153
and the Office of War Information (OWI), 140–16, 147
and the Philippines, 10, 58–62, 63, 66–70, 124–25, 197–204
and the Republican Party, 10, 15–16, 18–19, 33, 37, 65, 111, 112, 114, 115, 120, 129, 131, 158, 163–70
and World War I, 19, 21–24, 78, 158, 218, 229
and World War II, 10, 134–40, 142–48, 152, 156, 218, 221, 222–23, 229
relationship with Cary Coolidge, 21, 26, 32, 36, 48, 151, 177, 178
relationship with Franklin D. Roosevelt, 8, 110–15, 117, 118–21, 131, 134, 143, 161–62, 214–16
relationship with Theodore Roosevelt, 11–12, 15, 111, 158–60
views on Albert Apponyi, 32–33, 98–99, 171–82,184
views on Gyula Gömbös, 96–97
views on Gyula Károlyi, 85–86
views on Herbert Hoover, 39, 67, 100–101, 113
views on István Bethlen, 79–80
views on Mihály Károlyi, 33–34, 36–37
views on Miklós Horthy, 79, 127, 128, 155–56
views on Pál Teleki, 34, 97–98, 182, 184

Roosevelt, Theodore (TR), 7, 8, 9, 11–15, 17–18, 22, 23, 32, 60–61, 63, 69, 74, 98, 110, 111, 120, 131, 137, 138, 151, 154, 158–61, 165, 167, 169, 170, 204

Schoenfeld, Arthur, 78, 149
Smith, Jeremiah, Jr., 74, 76, 83, 107, 205, 206
Smith, Paul C., 143
Smith, Ulysses Grant, 75
Stimson, Henry Lewis, 65–67, 89, 110, 123, 143, 151, 208
Storey, Charles M., 29–30, 32, 33, 34, 45, 46, 178, 179, 180, 185, 187–89, 190
Sulzberger, Arthur Hays, 147–48, 150, 151, 152
Suvich, Fulvio, 101, 102
Széchenyi, László, 89

Teleki, Pál, 32, 43, 49, 79, 97–98, 180, 182, 184
Trianon Peace Treaty, 38, 74, 92, 98n
Truman, Harry, 138, 142, 148

Tuck, Somerville Pinkney, 71, 78
Tyler, Royall, 82, 83, 86, 88, 89, 104, 106, 209

United Nations Relief and Rehabilitation Administration (UNRRA), 148

Văitoianu, Artur, 190–91
Versailles Peace Treaty, 53, 56, 152, 219, 223, 224
Vienna, 25, 26, 29, 30, 31, 34, 36, 37, 40, 44, 47, 48, 49, 51, 54, 83, 94, 95, 123, 171, 172, 173, 174, 176, 192, 194, 218

Vix, Fernand, 37n, 191–92
Vix Note, 37, 195–96
Vopicka, Charles J., 185–87, 189, 192

Washington, George, 9, 92, 93, 137, 162, 229
Wilson, Woodrow, 14, 22, 23, 24–25, 26, 33, 38, 39, 46–47, 54, 140, 181, 184, 194, 195, 196
Wolf, István, 149–50
Wood, Leonard, 51, 58, 198, 201
WQXR, 147–49, 150
Wright, Joshua Butler, 70–71, 74, 196

www.ingramcontent.com/pod-product-compliance
Lightning Source LLC
Chambersburg PA
CBHW052128070526
44586CB00016B/2135